I0127560

Charles Pelham Villiers

The Free Trade Speeches of the Right Hon

Vol. 1

Charles Pelham Villiers

The Free Trade Speeches of the Right Hon
Vol. 1

ISBN/EAN: 9783744726580

Printed in Europe, USA, Canada, Australia, Japan

Cover: Foto ©Suzi / pixelio.de

More available books at **www.hansebooks.com**

THE

FREE TRADE SPEECHES

OF THE

RIGHT HON. CHARLES PELHAM VILLIERS, M.P.

WITH A POLITICAL MEMOIR

EDITED BY

A MEMBER OF THE COBDEN CLUB

Under circumstances of infinite difficulty, the cause of total and
immediate Repeal was first and solely upheld by the terse eloquence
and vivid perception of Charles Villiers — DISRAELI'S *Life of Lord
George Bentinck*

IN TWO VOLUMES — VOL. I.

LONDON
KEGAN PAUL, TRENCH, & CO., 1 PATERNOSTER SQUARE
1883

TO

THE CONSTITUENCY

OF

THE BOROUGH OF WOLVERHAMPTON.

YIELDING to the wish frequently conveyed to him, Mr. VILLIERS has consented that his Speeches on Free Trade, for the advocacy of which he first obtained your suffrages, should be collected together; and, with his permission, they are now devoted to your service anew, in remembrance of the unbroken trust that, for close upon half a century, has connected him with your Borough.

THE EDITOR.

February 1883.

CONTENTS

OF

THE FIRST VOLUME.

———•◦•———

Erratum.

Page 239, line 27, *for* ' presided at nearly ' *read* ' was present at.'

POLITICAL MEMOIR.

THE STATESMAN by whom the speeches contained in these volumes were delivered holds the unique position of having uninterruptedly represented the same constituency, the constituency of Wolverhampton, for nearly half a century. And during that long period he has enjoyed a triumph that no other statesman has ever before enjoyed. He has seen all the leading men of the empire become converts to the principles of a great commercial policy which, fulfilling to the utmost his reiterated predictions, has freed the people from the heaviest burden of injustice that ever pressed upon a nation, and completely changed the financial and economical intercourse of England with foreign nations ; but which at the beginning of his Parliamentary career, ' almost alone in the House of Commons, and without support in the country,' he advocated in the face of the scorn and ridicule of all parties, and afterwards continued to advocate and inculcate with unfaltering fidelity and

consistency through years of determined and oppro-
brious opposition until the cause of Free Trade was
gained, and the blessing of untaxed bread secured for
the people.

In 1815 the Corn Laws were passed at the
point of the bayonet, and their course was marked
by scenes of violence resulting, on more than one
occasion, in the execution of some of those who
had been driven to desperation by the sufferings they
endured from want of bread.

In 1846 the pressure of famine wrung from a
reluctant Legislature the repeal of the Corn Laws,
which the pleas of justice and expediency had been
equally powerless to win from successive Governments blinded by self-interest and the superstitions
of custom.

But famine itself would have availed little against
the combined strength of legislative power and landed
influence had the mass of the people remained in ignorance of the real cause of the misery that was crush-
ing them, and of the legitimate means within their
own reach to compel its removal. And, even knowing
the cause of their wretchedness, and aided by famine,
the people would have been a very long time in
making their power felt had their rulers been suffered
to follow untaught and unrebuked by men of their
own order the narrow lines of the selfish and destructive policy of Monopoly.

No one single cause effected the repeal of the Corn Laws, and with it the overthrow of Protection. It was not Mr. Villiers's eight years' vigorous advocacy, in and out of Parliament, of untaxed bread for the people that alone did this. Nor the influence of Sir Robert Peel ; nor the 'unadorned eloquence' of Richard Cobden ; nor the untiring energy of Mr. Bright ; nor the trenchant writings of Peronnet Thompson ; nor the thrilling lines of Ebenezer Elliot ; nor the gigantic wave of subscriptions ridden and ruled by the Member for Stockport ; nor 'famine itself, against which we had warred, which afterwards joined us '—not any one of these alone effected Repeal. The repeal of the Corn Laws—the Devil's Laws, as the ' Times ' boldly called them—was due, as all great measures are due, to the concurrence of numerous causes, to the united action of various agents, to the sagacity and firmness of many leaders. But Mr. Villiers will be known in history as the first leader of that band of earnest men who, with a singular grasp of fact and circumstance, clearly estimated the different forces of class interest, prejudice, and ignorance which, under the name of Protection, enthralled commerce, and kept the masses of the people constantly exposed to all the miseries of want and its consequences ; and undertook the laborious task of initiating the overthrow of the pernicious system of Monopoly in the only effectual way in which it

could be undertaken : namely, by fully exposing the
fallacies by which, with incalculable detriment to the
community at large, a crying injustice was being
maintained ; and, whilst rousing the people out of
the lethargy of ignorance, to guide and restrain them,
in the early hours of their waking, from an unwise or
unlawful use of their knowledge.

The pangs of hunger opened the eyes and ears of
those who toil for the necessities of the day, and
made them comparatively apt and docile pupils.   But
political economy is a dry study for the opulent and
leisured classes.   Steeped in the prejudices of 'special
interests' and the fallacies of Protection, the typical
landowner of the early part of this century, blind
himself, blinded the farmer and the labourer dependent on him, and treated the concrete arguments
of scarcity and distress which went home to the poor
as if they were the mere abstractions of the theorist.
' He made everything clear, and said naething but
what was perfectly true,' said the shrewd Scotchman
after his first lesson from the Free Trade lecturer,
' and proved that the Corn Laws did us nae guid, and
that their repeal would do us nae ill ; but it's of nae
use to convince us unless he convinces our landlords
too, for we maun just do as they bid us.' Now it was
precisely with this class—the great landed interest, as
it was called—that Mr. Villiers had to deal directly in
the first instance.   And most fortunate it was that

he could do so as the representative of Wolverhampton. Together with Manchester, Wolverhampton took the lead of all the other boroughs created under the Reform Bill of 1832 in opposing the Corn Laws. And it was his representation of that great manufacturing constituency, closely connected by commercial relations with America, that, in addition to his social rank, gave weight and significance to his advocacy of Free Trade in general and the repeal of the Corn Laws in particular when as a young man Mr. Villiers was first returned to Parliament.

Mr. Villiers, the third son of the late Hon. George Villiers and Theresa, the only daughter of the first Lord Boringdon, and brother of the late Earl of Clarendon, was born in London in 1802. After studying some time at Haileybury College, with a view to an Indian career, Mr. Villiers, his health not being found sufficiently strong for India, went to Cambridge, where he graduated in 1824. At Haileybury he was the pupil of Malthus and Sir James Mackintosh; and there he not only became a diligent student of economical science, but he also showed decided bias in favour of those distinctive principles that were the foundation of his public life. His course of studies in political economy was finally completed under Mr. M'Culloch, who was then esteemed the soundest exponent of the doctrines of Adam Smith.

At the General Election of 1826 Mr. Villiers was a candidate for the representation of Hull on Free Trade principles, and as a supporter of Huskisson and Canning, whose determined opposition to commercial monopolies naturally attracted his sympathy. He was defeated by a small majority, and from that time till 1834 abstained from seeking any other seat.

In 1827 he was called to the Bar, and afterwards became successively Secretary to the Master of the Rolls, and Examiner in the Court of Chancery.

Prior to the above appointments, he was, in 1832, selected as an Assistant Commissioner under the Royal Commission for inquiry into the administration and practical operation of the Poor Laws. This inquiry was of great advantage to one so capable of profiting by the experience to be derived from it as Mr. Villiers was. It brought him into direct contact with the labouring classes, and introduced him to one of the most instructive branches of political science. He ' actually touched the political facts that surrounded him.' And it was the real apprehension of the condition and needs of the people he then gained that constituted one of the sources of his strength during the prolonged opposition he afterwards met with when he came to deal with some of the gravest economical questions of our times.

Under the old Poor Laws, the greater part of the

whole nation was becoming pauperized and demoralized at an annual cost of over 7,000,000*l.* to the ratepayers. That wretched system, in truth, offered a premium to idleness and vice, and threatened the extinction of all honest, independent labour. Parliamentary Committees were appointed one after another to inquire into the evils, manifestly on the increase year by year, which were generated by it. But it was not until the Royal Commission of 1832 had thoroughly investigated the condition of every parish in England and Wales, and completed its Report disclosing the appalling nature of the mischief which had brought the country to the brink of ruin, that it was possible to devise and mature such a comprehensive measure of reform as the Poor Law Amendment Act of 1834.

This Act, by its stringent provisions designed for throwing the labourer on his own resources, supposed and necessitated the repeal of the Corn Laws upon which it depended for its successful operation. And this was impressed upon Lord John Russell and Lord Althorp, the Ministers who were responsible for the measure ; but the point was at the time disregarded.

When Mr. Villiers first came forward for Wolverhampton at the General Election of 1835 it was as the exponent of the same principles as those he had supported nine years previously at Hull, and he was returned avowedly in opposition to the Corn Laws.

On the hustings in 1837 he went further: he pledged himself to move in the House of Commons for the total repeal of the Corn Laws. This step, a very bold one in those days, when the bare idea of interference with the Corn Laws was looked upon as something far worse than quixotic, was the result of a meeting at Sir William Molesworth's, when the small party of remarkable men, including Grote, Hume, Warburton, James Mill, and Charles Buller already renowned as the Radical Reform party, and distinguished for their strong advocacy of the various measures of reform with which their names are now historically associated,[1] urged upon Mr. Villiers to take for his special subject in Parliament the opposition to the Corn Laws, and the question of Repeal, as affording the best field for the exercise of his

---

[1] 'There was no other party which, in 1837, was known to include such men as Grote, Molesworth, and Roebuck, and Colonel Thompson, and Joseph Hume, and William Ewart, and Charles Buller, and Ward, and Villiers, and Bulwer, and Strutt; such a phalanx of strength as these men— with their philosophy, their science, their reading, their experience; the acuteness of some, the doggedness of others, the seriousness of most, and the mirth of a few—might have become, if they could have become a phalanx at all. But nothing was more remarkable about these men than their individuality. . . . They were called upon, before the opening of the new Parliament, to prove that they were not single-subject men, as reformers are pretty sure to be considered before they are compacted into a party, but to show that the principles which animated their prosecution of single reforms were applicable to the whole of legislation. . . . They were never more regarded as a party during the period under our notice; and it may be observed now, though it was not then, that their failing to become a party in such a crisis as the last struggles of the Melbourne Ministry was a prophecy of the disintegration of parties which was at hand, and which is, in its turn, a prophecy of a new age in the political history of England.—Martineau, *A History of the Thirty Years' Peace.*

known mastery of economical science in its political and social bearings, and his singular gift of close and acute argumentative power.

In the speech that Mr. Villiers made the year following his return to Parliament, at a public dinner given by the constituency of Wolverhampton to him and his colleague Mr. Thornley, we have a complete sketch of the general line of liberal policy which he has never once departed from, and which has connected his name with all the great popular measures of the period. Any consideration of his political career, therefore, would be imperfect without a special notice of this speech.

After he had alluded to the approbation manifested by his constituents of the course he had pursued during the preceding long Session, and their cordial recognition of his services, he went on to express his satisfaction at his exceptional fortune in representing the borough of Wolverhampton :—

' Its interests,' he said, ' are completely identical with those of the nation at large. As you are interested in no monopoly, and holders of no privileges with which the mass of the nation do not heartily sympathize, I may conclude that when I have secured your approval of my public conduct, I have done something to deserve the praise of the country at large ; and animated by this reflection, believe me that I shall return with fresh heart to the

place where you sent me this time last year, there
cordially to labour with others in that reform of our
laws and institutions which alone can secure for
them the confidence and esteem of the people.'

And then, having dwelt upon the great measure
of reform in the representation of the people of five
years back, and the almost more important one that
closed the Session of 1835—the Municipal Reform
Bill, 'a noble work, passing power from the evil
doer to the rightful owner'—he forcibly insisted
upon the duty that devolved upon the representatives
of the people to devote their energies to the reforms
that were yet most urgently needed in the country,
and passed in rapid review the abuses in the civil
and ecclesiastical institutions of Ireland, the civil dis-
abilities that harassed the Dissenters, restrictions on
trade, the mal-administration of law, and the need of
education for the people.

His language relating to Ireland and the intolerable injustice it had sustained at our hands was distinguished by a largeness of mind so exceptional in
those days that it is difficult to realize its full significance now that we have grown accustomed to
generous acts of reparation which, under presently
existing circumstances, seem to the impatient to
have been made in vain to heal the wounds of that
unhappy country :—

'Let us also ask what we should feel if we belonged to four-fifths of a population honestly differing in religion from the remainder, bound to contribute the property bequeathed for the support of our own religion to that of the minority ; and with this wrong aggravated, as we should think, by the declaration of honest Protestants in England that the Irish Church, in all its superfluities, in all its inefficiency, in all the iniquity with which it has been maintained, has been a scandal to Christendom! Ireland is the only instance in Christendom where religion has been so administered as to bring Protestantism into discredit ; for Protestants cannot deny the evidence of their own witnesses that after the experiment of a hundred years under the influence of that vast and wealthy Establishment, Protestantism has diminished! . . .

'I am almost ashamed of thus dwelling upon this topic among men of generous feeling, as I know the unity of sentiment that must prevail among you ; but when we see the sophistry employed to mislead the public mind upon the matter, it is right that upon such occasions as the present we should raise our voice to proclaim the truth.'

He next denounced the late Ministers for their efforts to defeat the measure for devoting the surplus revenues of the Irish Church ' to the sacred purpose of extending moral and religious instruction among British subjects in Ireland without distinction of religion ;' and then defended O'Connell—afterwards one of his most steadfast allies in the long fight for the repeal of the Corn Laws—against his political assailants, and claimed municipal reform for the Irish on the same grounds that he had supported it for England and Scotland : namely, 'because it makes the people parties to their own government, trains them to the use of power, and trusts them with the duty as it teaches them the interest of upholding law and extending security to all.'

Coming to the subject of Free Trade, though on the whole he viewed the success of the question with more hope than after years proved there were grounds for, he showed that he foresaw the kind of opposition that was in store for him ; and impressed upon his audience the necessity for combination against the efforts that Monopolists were uniting to make for the promotion of their own ends :—

'I am now reminded by the emblem [1] before me to refer to a matter most important to your interest ; and one in which the rulers of this country have acted with much of the caprice that has been exhibited in the matter of religion. I refer to freedom in commerce, which, like freedom in thought, all say they approve, but to which, when asked to give practical effect to their approval, all are sure to find

[1] Referring to a transparency at the end of the room, upon which was inscribed 'Free Trade,' 'Justice to Ireland,' &c.

an o bstacle. The landowner, the shipowner, the West Indian merchant, all approve of Free Trade in what they consume ; but in the sources of their income and profit there are no more staunch supporters of prohibitive law ; they are always reasoning as if the country were made for them, and not they for the country, and in their ignorance they are ever blind to the fact that while they seek to profit by the losses of others, they are again injured by a like injustice. On this point, gentlemen, I begin to hope that successful experiment, and the prospect of danger that may arise from the opposite system, are beginning to open the eyes of the most dense in this town to the advantage of Free Trade. Observe, for instance, the outcry that was raised against opening trade with the East, and see the results which one year has shown in favour of that measure. It was repeatedly asserted by the friends of Monopoly that the people had as much and as cheap tea as could be consumed in this country ; that the people in China had no further demand for our manufactures ; and that Free Trade in tea was only the vision of a theorist. I need not tell you what increase of consumption nor what fall of price has occurred in that article ; nor need I say (which, indeed, I have been told in this borough) that the increase of our exports to the East is one cause of the present improvement in trade. See, then, the advantage of

Free Trade to the poor man : whatever he pays less for his tea, he has that more in his pocket to pay for what else he requires. And again, the more tea we bring into this country, the more goods we produce to send out to China, and the more employment is thus given to the industrious classes of this country.

' And now for one moment observe the effect of fettering our commerce. We impose high duties upon timber and corn, which articles we might get cheaper and better from countries in Europe than anywhere else. But by our high duties we have given to these countries a pretext for excluding our goods ; and within two years a union in Germany has been formed of twenty-five millions of souls to resist the import of our manufactures. And, let me remind you, these countries have not all the disadvantages with which England, notwithstanding all her advantages, is encumbered. Their habits are as peaceful and industrious as ours ; they have no debt in proportion to ours ; their living is cheaper than ours ; and their chief manufactures are those which your customers chiefly demand. Let not, then, I say, any present improvements in trade induce you to lose sight of that great principle of policy, Free Trade ; but rather, in these days when Monopolists are uniting to promote their own ends, let districts like these associate together to secure for the people the more benevolent system which will give them cheap food, good trade, and a friendly intercourse with all the nations of the globe. On this subject I am happy to think that the sentiments of the Ministry accord with your own ; and you have therefore additional reason to give them support.'

Further on he adverted to the changes which were then urgently needed in the law, and insisted particularly upon the necessity for rendering it more accessible to the people by providing local tribunals —such as the County Courts which have since been established :—

' There is another matter also in which public interest is deeply concerned, and in which the Government have lately shown honest purpose of attending to the long-sought demands of the people : I mean the reform of the law and the arrangements for its administration. It might well be asked by a foreigner in this country, how it could occur that the English, so prudent in many respects, should overlook so important a condition of their social wellbeing as a cheap and effective administration of justice. Such, however, is the case ; and it is the reproach of this country that our law is without those essentials which have from all time been named by every speaker, writer, or thinker upon the subject as belonging to any good system : namely, cheapness, certainty, and expedition. . . . What, then, is it that the representatives of the people should exert themselves to procure for the people ? That which it was said under the Commonwealth would above everything cause that Government to be loved : the law expressed in plain language, and not in a jargon which takes a life to understand. To let it mean what it expresses, and not a dozen other things, which are traps for the unwary. And to make it accessible to all—not, in the sense of the "London Tavern," to all who can pay to enter, but to the poorest man who can be wronged. . . . But above all, I should say, the establishment of local courts, presided over by responsible and competent men, is most indispensable to the wants and business of this country.'

To meet the distrust of the people manifested by his political opponents, especially in their resistance to the Municipal Corporation Reform Bill, and their reliance on military force to quell the disturbance and rioting common at election times, Mr. Villiers quoted Sir Robert Peel, and, in showing that it was as much the interest of the poor householder as of the rich to prevent confusion, said that with the late Prime Minister he particularly approved of one part of the Bill as specially calculated to prevent in all corporate towns the odious collisions of the military with the people that, previous to the passing of the Act, had been of frequent occurrence, though some partisans were thought to be building hopes of power on their more frequent occurrence, adding :—

' Peace and good order are the interest of the people. Despotism is the fruit of confusion, which those who are ever talking of fighting doubtless well know. I say, give the people instruction, and give them power; strike to the ground every obstacle to their information; then their interests will be obvious to them, and they will act upon their interests, which are those of the community at large.'

Two years after this speech, on the 15th of March, 1838, Mr. Villiers brought forward the question of the Corn Laws in the House of Commons. The wording of his first annual motion showed how accurately he had gauged the temper of the House, and how thoroughly he then realized the profound hostility that prevailed in Parliament to anything approaching Repeal.

The Corn Law question was called an open one because, on forming his second Administration, Lord Melbourne allowed Mr. Poulett Thomson, Sir Henry Parnell, and Lord Dalmeny—when they stipulated for it as the condition of their joining his Ministry—to vote as they pleased on it; knowing from the strength of the landed interest in the House of Commons that their support could avail little to the small minority for Repeal, whilst it would give him the advantage of colleagues who stood well with the Manchester, Dundee, and Dunfermline constituencies.

This speech exhibits at the very outset of his career in the cause of Free Trade the spirit of moderation that in later times Mr. Villiers exercised with a most salutary effect when, class being set against class, the people were in danger of being carried away by their feelings, and damaging a just cause. It, moreover, embraces most if not all of the leading points of the controversy that were again and again brought forward during the succeeding years, and again and again had to be treated from every point of view with greater or less amplification—often necessarily involving more or less repetition—to meet the exigencies of the moment, and conquer the stubbornness or stupidity as well as the fears of prejudiced and interested opponents.

Fully cognizant of all the circumstances of the steadily increasing distress in the country, and foreseeing its inevitable results if the main cause of it were not at once dealt with, Mr. Villiers predicted how in a moment of desperate excitement the nation would at a future day compel the concession of Repeal if it were not granted with deliberation in that moment of calm—a prediction that, to the dismay of both Lord John Russell and Sir R. Peel, was fulfilled only too literally in 1845. And his clear, concise charge against the Corn Laws as an embodiment of Protection, false in principle and evil in effect, is followed by a categorical exposure of the most prevalent fallacies involved in the Protectionist pleas of indemnity, special burdens on land, the revenue, general taxation, local taxation, the tithes, the malt-tax. The estimate—imperfect because too moderate—of the annual cost to the community at large of the Protection afforded by the Corn Laws to a mere class interest on the strength of these pleas is shown to have amounted to 15,600,000*l.*

Next, turning to our foreign trade, we find the pernicious influence of the Corn Laws traced in the paralysis of most of our manufactures, the complete loss of our market for others, and the blundering policy with other nations that our Ministers had been led into through their disregard of the great commercial interests of England. All of which were telling unmistakably on the condition of the people, including the agricultural population of both farmers and labourers, and bringing about the gravest distress. There was but one conclusion to be drawn from this indictment against the Corn Laws :—

'Commercial liberty is now as essential to the well-being of this country as civil and religious liberty have been considered to be in former times ; . . . and, therefore, it becomes every public man who seeks reform for public good to procure for his country the emancipation of its industry ; and to win for its hard-working people freedom to fulfil the designs of nature, by exchanging with their fellow-men in other countries the fruits of their respective labours.' [1]

[1] *Speeches*, vol. i. p. 44.

On the 9th of May following, Colonel Seale moved for the second reading of his Bill to permit the grinding of wheat in bond for foreign export. It was a measure that could not in the smallest degree affect the landed class ; it would simply have saved ship-owners the inconvenience and loss of provisioning their vessels at foreign ports, with the additional advantage to this country of creating employment at our seaport towns. But after the Bill had passed the first reading, there was a scare among the land-owners ; and so suspicious were they of the least change in the existing law that might affect their monopoly that they raised a cry of class legislation, declared the measure to be for the benefit of the commercial at the cost of the agricultural interest, and actually threw out the Bill lest the bran from the foreign wheat should be used to feed pigs and poultry.

Mr. Villiers's speech on the occasion told in the country, though his warning was received with derision in the House :—

‘ I am glad, however, to think,’ he said in conclusion, ‘ that whatever the result of the vote of to-night may be, it cannot be otherwise than serviceable. If the measure is carried, a new channel for employment and profit will be opened to our trade, and the commerce of the country will, in a slight degree, be benefited. But if it is rejected, advantages still more desirable will probably ensue. What is most wanted just now is some practical illustration of the working of the Corn Laws, and the spirit of those who maintain them ; something to strike the imagination ; something to rouse those who have too long kissed the rod that has scourged them. All great changes have been preceded by some wanton act of power that was resisted and assailed. I should regard the rejection of the measure now before the House as the East Retford of the Corn Laws. It would be like the preliminary folly that characterizes those whom Heaven has marked as its victims. It would, I believe, really awaken the feeling on the subject of the Corn Laws that has too long been dormant ; and therefore I shall go to the division perfectly at ease, fully satisfied that nothing but good can follow from it.'

In the debate of the 2nd of July of the same year, which followed Lord Fitzwilliam's presentation of a petition from Glasgow praying for the repeal of the Corn Laws, Lord Melbourne's declaration that the Government would not take a decided part in the question till it was certain that the majority of the people were in favour of a change, added to the prospect of a wet autumn and bad harvest, gave a decided impetus to the Free Traders ; and towards the end of the year the Manchester Anti-Corn Law Association was formed. This was quite independent of the one formed in London some years previously, of which Mr. Villiers was a member.

Early in 1839, Mr. Villiers was invited by the new Association to a public dinner at Manchester to meet all the Members of Parliament who had supported him and voted for his motion of the previous Session, and delegates from the other Anti-Corn Law Associations that had sprung up in various parts of the country. Already an object of their regard before he came in personal contact with them, Mr. Villiers, on his first arrival amongst the Manchester people, was received with enthusiasm : 'his appearance, . . . the tone of his address, the knowledge of his subject, the closeness of his argumentation, his obvious determination to persevere in the course he had undertaken, and the hopefulness of his expectation that the struggle would end in victory, confirmed his hearers in their belief that he possessed high qualifications to be the leader in the Parliamentary contest.'[1]

The day after this dinner, at a general meeting of the representatives of all the Associations then in Manchester, it was resolved that on account of the mischief that the Corn Laws were doing to the manufacturing and commercial interests, and thereby to the country generally, petitions should be forwarded from all parts of the kingdom, praying to be heard by counsel and evidence at the Bar of the House of Commons, in the approaching Session, on

---

[1] Prentice, *History of the League.*

the operation of the Corn Laws. And this resolution was the substance of the motion of which Mr. Villiers gave notice as soon as Parliament met.

Though the Queen's Speech omitted all allusion to the Corn Laws, Mr. G. W. Wood, President of the Manchester Chamber of Commerce, in seconding the Address, was induced, at the instance of his constituents, to dwell on the injury sustained by the manufacturers and operatives through the exclusion of foreign corn; but the next moment, with unaccountable perversity, he completely destroyed the effect his words were designed to produce, and gave Sir R. Peel an advantage of which he was not slow to avail himself in upholding the existing system by groundless assertions of the prosperity of the country. The delegates listening under the gallery were perfectly amazed at the turn thus given to affairs, whilst the delighted country gentlemen received it with great cheering. Mischievous consequences to the cause of Repeal seemed inevitable from this sudden blow at the hand of a faithless friend; but immediately after Sir R. Peel had acknowledged his obligations for the very able speech the House had heard in defence of the existing system, Mr. Villiers, with his characteristic promptitude in debate, at once exposed the worthlessness of the alleged proofs of an improvement in trade, and defeated Sir R. Peel's adroit use of them.

On the 19th of February Mr. Villiers made his

famous speech introducing his motion that J. B. Smith and others be heard at the Bar of the House. Abstaining from any consideration of the general effects of the Corn Laws, and limiting himself, according to the requirements of the occasion, entirely to the grave depression and loss of home and foreign trade caused by the Corn Laws, he argued with unanswerable force and point the necessity of an inquiry, at least, into the allegations of the delegates as to their injurious operation. The occasion and the result of the debate—when Sir F. Burdett declared that such an inquiry would be a waste of time, and Lord J. Russell, though he had told his constituents at Stroud that the laws were indefensible, went into the same lobby with Sir R. Peel, who, maintaining that repeal of the Corn Laws would be grossly unjust to the agriculturists labouring under heavy peculiar burdens, said that he should give a decided negative to the motion—are too well known to need more than a passing allusion here. Happily the people had a champion in the House who was courageous as well as sagacious in looking after their interests before they knew how to look after them themselves.[1]

Nothing daunted by his defeat in February, Mr. Villiers brought forward his second annual motion on the 12th of March. Apathy concerning the Corn Laws was perceptibly diminishing outside the House

[1] Cobden, *Speech at Manchester*, 1843.

as well as within. Mr. Villiers's speech and that of Mr. Poulett Thomson were printed and supplied in thousands to the Corn Law Associations throughout the country ; and whereas on the first motion in 1838 the question was dismissed with only one night's discussion, five nights' debate followed the motion of 1839, which was warmly supported by O'Connell.

From his exceptional position, the labours that devolved upon Mr. Villiers increased in the course of time with almost overwhelming rapidity, and brought with them corresponding anxieties. The Anti-Corn Law movement, from its being so eagerly taken up by the Manchester men, early incurred the disadvantage of being treated by the landed interest as a 'vulgar manufacturers' agitation ' ; and unquestionably there was at times considerable danger of the national character of the movement being injured by the angry retorts that were flung to and fro by the commercial and country parties. Indeed, quite lately it has been thought by his admirers no slur upon Cobden to attribute—most unjustly we should say— a retaliatory character to his action in the League. However, whether it be so or not, the imputation has been fastened upon by a clever adversary, and urged with no little effect as damaging in the highest degree both to Cobden and the other leaders of the agitation. But it is not without its use, since it brings into a fresh light one of the peculiar diffi-

culties Mr. Villiers had to contend with. His keen
perceptions made him acutely sensitive of the embarrassments to which the predominance of one body
of men in the movement exposed the cause of Repeal
in both Houses of Parliament ; whilst their comparative ignorance of Parliamentary procedure, and
the stubborn strength that was arrayed against them
in the Legislature, placed them in no little danger, in
their impatience of temporary defeat and the con-
sciousness of numerical superiority in the country, of
compromising the cause by such acts of indiscreet
zeal as could only retard the object they had in view.

Cobden himself would not believe that there could
be much difficulty in securing Repeal from the 'reformed Parliament,' as it was called, until, shortly after
the commencement of his friendship with Mr. Villiers,
he was present in the House of Commons during a
discussion on the Corn Laws. Then, utterly disgusted
at the whole scene—the demeanour of the Members,
the treatment to which his friend was exposed for
advocating Repeal—'Cobden suddenly left the House,
returned to Lancashire that night, and determined
that he would never cease to work until the public
should be apprised of the character of those laws,
and the difficulty of repealing them.'[1]

But incessant as were the calls of the movement
on the attention of Mr. Villiers, they were not

---

[1] 'The Times,' June 28, 1867, *Villiers upon Cobden.*

allowed to absorb it ; his assistance was constantly claimed to forward the popular cause in any branch of trade or commerce in which the people felt the paralyzing touch of Protection.

Scarcely had the angry sounds of the debate of 1839 on the Corn Duties died away, when he was required by his constituents to present a petition for the total repeal of the protective duties on timber ; and on the 9th of July he moved for a Committee of the whole House to consider the duties levied on foreign and colonial timber.

This speech shows the same mastery of detail, the same seriousness and absence of mere rhetorical display, the same care in selecting and testing evidence, and disposing the broad facts best calculated to arrest the attention of an indifferent audience, the same shrewd detection and unsparing disclosure of fallacies with which Monopolists veiled and preserved their unjust privileges, that had distinguished his previous statements to the House. It is a history in miniature of the question for those who under happier circumstances have remained ignorant of the enormous injury that was once inflicted on the shipping interest of England on the pretence of supporting it ; and of the demoralization that was caused in our Canadian colonies, where the wasteful, reckless, gambling business of *lumbering* was carried on under the shelter of Protection at an annual cost of 1,500,000*l.* to this country—in addition to the injury the poorest section of the community sustained in the wretched hovels that the high price of building materials entailed upon them, and the losses and inconvenience that, from the same cause, were sustained by their rich neighbours.

The President of the Board of Trade, Mr. Poulett Thomson, though he acknowledged the force of Mr. Villiers's statements, and dwelt upon the necessity of urging so important a subject upon public attention, and at the same time expressed his special satisfaction that Mr. Villiers had brought it under the consideration of the House, nevertheless declared that such was the apathy of Parliament upon all questions of the kind that it would be useless for himself to introduce any measure dealing with the matter before them, and that under such circumstances it would likewise be useless for Mr. Villiers to press his motion to a division.

By 1842, after he had objected to the Whig measures of 1841 for the alteration of the corn, sugar, and timber duties, Sir Robert Peel came— partly, as he admitted, through the influence of the great Committee on Import Duties—to appreciate the mischiefs caused to the varied industries of the country and the housing of the poor by the enormous inequalities in the existing differential duties shown by Mr. Villiers in 1839 ; though, still bound in the meshes of Protection, he refused to 'admit an unlimited competition with the colonies in an article of so much importance to them.' Colonial and Baltic timber were put upon an equal footing in 1866, during which year all timber duties were abolished.

When the League summoned the meeting of delegates at Manchester at the beginning of 1840, it was above everything else as an experiment to test the popularity of the subject of Free Trade for agitation ; and they were consequently most anxious to secure the presence of the leading advocates of Repeal. From first to last the meeting was an unprecedented success. The demand for tickets to the banquet given on the occasion could not be supplied when it was known that both O'Connell and the Parliamentary leader of Free Trade were to speak at it.

Now if anything could have excused a man for momentarily losing sight of the general good of the community in urging the grave needs of an important section of it, or for pressing the special interests of one class to the disregard of another that had been made antagonistic to it, it would have been the sight of that vast assembly in the very centre of commerce and manufacture, crippled by the restrictions imposed upon them for the Protection of what was termed the agricultural interest. But Mr. Villiers never once forgot his statesmanship and allowed his audience to think that they were met to consider the separate interests of even so considerable a class as they repre-

sented ; but whilst he dwelt upon the mischief that
the Corn Laws were inflicting on trade and commerce, he also impressed upon them in clear and
unmistakable language that they were equally fatal
to agriculture, a deception and a fraud upon the farmer, and opposed to the real and permanent interests
of the landlord himself; and then, insisting that
trade existed for the benefit of the community and not
the community for the benefit of trade, he showed,
as he had already shown in the House, that the real
ground for opposing the Corn Laws was that they
were ruinous to the country at large, destructive of
the general good of the community, and the curse
of the people.

On this memorable occasion, Mr. Cobden delivered a speech of only ten minutes, and Mr. Bright,
still little known out of his native town, found a
place amongst the rest of the delegates in the body
of the hall.

The following day Mr. Villiers addressed 5,000
working men at a second banquet. He had special
cause for satisfaction at the support they were giving
him in his laborious work in the House ; for, as he
told them, after such a meeting he could no longer
be taunted with the indifference of the working classes
to the question : their presence that day had silenced
the cry, ' The working-men are not with you, and
therefore your plea for repeal is vain.'

Before the delegates separated, Mr. Villiers had promised to bring forward a motion on the Corn Laws on the 26th of March. By that time they had reassembled in London, and arranged deputations to Lord Melbourne, Sir R. Peel, Sir J. Graham, and other leading members of Parliament, to urge upon them the deplorable state of the country through the operation of the Corn Laws, and the consequent necessity of supporting Mr. Villiers's motion.

Lord J. Russell, in conjunction with the Chancellor of the Exchequer and the President of the Board of Trade, had appointed to receive the largest deputation, including Cobden and most of the leading Manchester men ; but when the deputation arrived in Downing Street, Mr. Baring and Mr. Labouchere only were ready to receive them—Lord J. Russell, it was alleged, was prevented by indisposition from being present. The accounts of the depression in trade given by members of the deputation were of the gravest character ; but they were stated with the utmost moderation and calmness, and their advocacy of Repeal was rested solely on the grounds of justice and humanity—the pretence that it was a manufacturers' question being explicitly disclaimed. When, however, the worthy Boroughreeve of Manchester, Mr. John Brooks, ' came to give a detail of the distresses of the working classes, and to describe one particular family, the members of which, after a life of economy and industry, had been compelled to pawn articles of furniture and clothes one after another, till nothing was left but the bare walls and empty cupboards, his feelings completely overpowered him ; ' according to an eye-witness, ' convulsive sobs choked his utterance, and he was obliged to pause till he recovered from his deep emotion. The tears rolled down the cheeks of Joseph Sturge ; J. B. Smith strove in vain to conceal his feelings ; there was scarcely a tearless eye in the multitude ; and the Ministers looked with perfect astonishment at a scene so unusual to statesmen and courtiers.'[1]

Notwithstanding all this evidence of increasing distress, and the evident determination of both the people and manufacturers and their Parliamentary leader not to take a refusal of their most just demands, Mr. Villiers received no support from the Ministers, or indeed the House, when he brought forward his motion in April ; and had it not been for the adroitness of Mr. Warburton in defeating the unfair tactics of the opponents of Repeal, a vote would not even have been obtained on the question that year.

Mr. Warburton moved the adjournment of the debate after many of those who were prepared to vote for Mr. Villiers had gone away, in the belief that there would not be a division that night. The

[1] Prentice, *History of the League.*

House then went to a division and defeated the motion for the adjournment of the debate by a large majority. Mr. Warburton thereupon at once moved the adjournment of the House, which, having been agreed to, prevented a division on the main question; and so, the original motion having become a dropped order, Mr. Villiers was able to bring forward the question of the Corn Laws in the May following.

But in May the conduct of the House—vividly reminding us of scenes recently enacted there—was worse than it had been in April, and would have disheartened any man who failed to apprehend that there are occasions when the most offensive and violent opposition is to be preferred to the dead weight of lukewarmness and indifference. Clearly perceiving the relation of cause and effect between the daily increasing misery of the people throughout the country and the Corn Laws, anticipating the violence that would ensue—and that immediately did ensue in Ireland, when the starving populace of Listowel boarded a vessel loaded with oats, part of which they secured, and the people of Limerick broke into the flour and provision shops of the city—Mr. Villiers could not even obtain a hearing until the Speaker, losing all patience, commanded the Bar to be cleared and Members to take their seats. But the lull was only a temporary one ; the authority of the Speaker was again set at naught by a renewal of the disgraceful interruptions, which continued until the most riotous went to dinner. Their return was marked by fresh uproar, and when Mr. Mark Philips, the Member for Manchester, whose constituency was numerically equal to the aggregate of fifty boroughs then returning seventy-two members, rose to enforce the claims of the most important manufacturing community of the United Kingdom, the House became so unmanageable that it was found necessary to bring the debate to an abrupt close—no less than six members on the side of Repeal having been obliged to give up all idea of even attempting to gain a hearing.

The assertions of the landowners that the farm labourers were enjoying the benefits of protection to agriculture whatever might be the distress amongst the manufacturing population—distress which they were ready to attribute to over-production, or any other cause than the right one—were disproved by a public examination as to the condition of a number of agricultural labourers, who were brought to London for the purpose by the League early in this Session. The evidence of these men showed incontrovertibly that the wages of the agricultural labourer, even in the summer, were scarcely sufficient to procure the bare necessaries of life, that there was no foundation for the notion that high prices gave him high wages, that he could not live without charity or parish relief—in a word, that his condition, so far from being benefited by the Corn Laws, was seriously impaired by them.

But what excited far deeper interest, and ultimately effected much greater, almost incalculable, good, was the Committee of 1840 on Import Duties. In his speech at Manchester,[1] Mr. Villiers briefly alluded to it as a Committee that made some noise, and gave greater offence to the Bread-taxers than any other ever gave. But the Committee itself, as well as its success, was almost entirely due to Mr. Villiers, whose thorough mastery of the subject enabled him to lead up to and to elicit all the most important evidence involving the question of the monopoly of food, and thereby to establish the advantage of the principles of Free Trade generally.

Never before or since did any Blue-book so completely rivet public attention as the Report of this Committee. It was, as Sir R. Peel afterwards acknowledged, a body of evidence that took the world by surprise. Twenty thousand copies of it were struck off by the Carlisle Anti-Corn Law Association ; and the Council of the League republished all the evidence bearing directly on the food monopoly. The leading portions of the evidence were given in all the chief newspapers of the country, and formed the topic of their leading articles ; and the ' Spectator ' reproduced it in an abridged form. It was, moreover, the subject

---

[1] *Speeches*, vol. i. p. 239.

of discussion at lectures and public meetings in all parts of the empire. And it was reprinted in America. In fact, it formed an epoch in the history of the Free Trade question ; and, after passing through the phases of disregard, ridicule, and angry denunciation, was generally accepted as an authority by both parties in the State, and was the foundation of the commercial legislation that freed our statute-book from the disgrace of the Corn Laws and the pernicious principles of Monopoly and Protection. After its publication there could no longer be any confusion in the public mind about the two distinct kinds of taxation that, to the detriment of the revenue and the misery of the people, were confounded in the existing tariff : namely, taxes for Protection and taxes for revenue. It was shown too clearly to be misunderstood that whilst the latter were levied for the general weal of the State, the former were imposed for the sole purpose of benefiting private individuals ; and that taxation so levied for Protection exceeded the total of the public taxation of the country.

The Whig Budget of 1841 was the first legislative act that showed the influence of the Report, which later on was practically felt throughout the country in each of the successive revisions of the tariff commenced by Sir R. Peel in 1842 ; and on the 30th of April, 1841, Mr. Villiers had the satisfaction of hearing Lord J. Russell move for a Committee of the whole

House to consider the laws affecting the importation of foreign corn in terms identical with those that in the preceding years had brought down upon him showers of ridicule and abuse. Lord Palmerston at that time had joined the Free Trade ranks. All the Parliamentary disturbance that followed this Budget was entirely due to the Bread-tax question. It was the Corn Laws that obliged the Ministers to appeal to the country after Peel carried his vote of want of confidence in the Government by a majority of one on the 4th of June, 1841. It was the Corn Laws that formed the theme of the Queen's Speech on the return of the Melbourne Ministry, and made the debate on the address a Free Trade debate ; when Lord Melbourne, mindful, perhaps, of his unlucky speech about the mental state of those who differed from him on the question of repeal, began with euphemistic candour to acknowledge that he had on former occasions been for putting off agitation and discussion of the question, but went on boldly to state that he had always known that it must come ; that it was a matter of time ; that the laws had been introduced and supported by those who had a direct interest in maintaining them ; that they were sanctioned by the two Houses of Legislature, one of which was entirely, and the other mainly, composed of landowners ; that it was *not safe* for the governing powers to be open to an imputation of so popular, so plausible, so specious a nature as that they had passed the Corn Laws from interested motives ; and that a change in the Corn Laws was necessary.

In this last conflict of the popular and landed interests the Whig Ministry were defeated and the Tories came into power, with Sir R. Peel at their head, pledged to maintain Protection. Possessed with the notion of the surpassing 'importance of laying the foundations of a great Conservative party,' the new Minister, admitting the awful distress in the country, denied that the Corn Laws were the cause of it, in spite of all the arguments and all the evidence to the contrary lying straight before him, and celebrated his advent to power with the promulgation of a new sliding scale—sliding from everything honest, as O'Connell said—to 'meet the special burdens on land,' and to 'make ourselves, as far as we can consistently with the maintenance of a moderate price, independent of a foreign supply.' [1]

This threw upon Mr. Villiers the arduous task of again attacking the old question, and the wearisome duty of reiterating arguments not old only because they had been so completely ignored ; which must have been specially trying to a man of his keenness of vision. But, nevertheless, his speech of the 18th of February, 1842, is singularly restrained and conciliatory. The roars of laughter that greeted Mr. Monckton Milnes's

[1] Sir R. Peel, *Speech at Tamworth*, June 28, 1841.

description of him as 'the solitary Robinson Crusoe, standing on the barren rock of Corn Law repeal,' the levity with which the allusions to the distress of the people by the Free Traders were received, and the applause that Mr. Ferrand won for every allegation of the cruelty of the manufacturers, showed far better than the division-list the composition of the new Parliament, and the obstacles that yet stood in the way of untaxed bread for the people. No wonder that the people began to ponder Fox's sovereign remedy for all evils, and to think that representative reform must precede every other.

Sir R. Peel introduced his financial scheme in April, and the struggle between the three parties into which the political world was now divided became closer. But the Whigs with their fixed duty, and the Free Traders, adverse to fixed duties and sliding scales alike, were both outnumbered by the supporters of Sir Robert Peel and the sliding scale ; and with the new tariff the Income-tax became law.[1]

---

[1] During the Committee on the Customs Act of 1842 Sir R. Peel's proposal to remove the prohibition on foreign cattle by substituting a ' moderate duty ' of 1*l.* per head met with strong opposition. Moreover, the Government, though this part of the new tariff was calculated to greatly benefit the people, did not urge it as a means to meet the prevailing distress. Mr. Villiers, therefore, moved that a nominal duty of 1*s.* should be substituted for the proposed duty of 1*l.* In a powerful but brief speech he insisted on the right of the people to have their trade in food free ; and adduced statistical and medical evidence showing that the famished condition of the working classes was due to an inadequate supply of proper nourishment.

The incongruity of the Income-tax under the existing circumstances Mr. Villiers was prompt to point out. In throwing a fresh burden of 4,000,000*l.* on an already impoverished people, this tax could but be calculated to deepen still further the distress in the country by causing a diminution in the rate of wages, and adding to the already enormous number of unemployed workmen. In one district alone of Wolverhampton, out of 134 blast furnaces, each employing 160 persons, 62 were idle in the month of July, thus leaving 10,000 men without work. The majority of the iron mills of the neighbourhood, employing from 200 or 300 hands each, had stopped. The japanned trade was so depressed that one master was then working for 50 per cent. less than he had done for three years previously. Honest capable workmen, driven by sheer lack of employment to the workhouse, were spending their days in breaking stones ; and a jeweller of the town deposed to the fact that mothers of families were forced *to sell*—they did not attempt *to pawn*, for they had no hope of ever being able to redeem them—their wedding-rings to get food for their children. The state of distress at Wolverhampton was but an instance of what was to be found all over the country. There was no exaggeration in the lines of Ebenezer Elliott, the 'Corn Law Rhymer.' He only described what he saw, and hence his great influence in the movement, especially amongst the poor. He stirred multitudes with a picture like this:—

Child, is thy father dead ?
Father is gone !
Why did they tax his bread ?
God's will be done !
Mother has sold her bed ;
Better to die than wed !
Where shall she lay her head ?
Home we have none.

Father clamm'd thrice a week—
God's will be done !
Long for work did he seek;
Work he found none.
Tears on his hollow cheek
Told what no tongue could speak
Why did his master break ?
God's will be done !

Doctor said air was best—
Food we had none ;
Father, with panting breast,
Groaned to be gone ;
Now he is with the blest—
Mother says death is best !
We have no place of rest—
Yes, ye have one !

But with their prolonged sufferings the people began to lose faith in God as well as trust in man. 'Talk to us no more about thy Goddle Mighty,' was the wild outburst of the Leicester artisan recorded by Thomas Cooper [1] as typical of the new spirit that was

---

[1] *Life of Thomas Cooper. Written by Himself.*

spreading amongst the starving people, ' there isn't one ! If there was one he wouldn't let us suffer as we do.' And indeed it was small wonder that the people did grow fierce and desperate under the pressure of hunger, with no sign of relief to comfort them.

But unfortunately the disturbances, and in some cases violence, that arose, all encouraged and increased by the Chartists, were laid to the charge of the Anti-Corn Law Leaguers ; and in consequence they became the objects of increased abuse and denunciation on the part of the Protectionists, who, both at their meetings and in their publications, gave full rein to the perverseness of prejudice. Mr. Villiers was unable to comply with the wish of the League to be present at their meetings at the end of the Session, when Mr. Cobden repelled the gross calumnies uttered against them ; but at the very beginning of the new year, true to the Association that had done so much to assist outside the House in the tough battle he was fighting within, he went down to Manchester, cordially defended the course they were pursuing, and encouraged them never to relax their efforts until the Corn Laws were abolished and Free Trade was established. And, again, when the League transferred its centre of operations to London, and hired Drury Lane Theatre, he was ready, amidst the constant calls on his time by his Parliamentary and other duties, to give his assistance whenever it was required, and addressed the great meeting of March 22, when the theatre was filled to overflowing.

It is curious, and indeed almost inconceivable, that after his tariffs of 1842, and all that he had said in commendation of the Committee of 1840, Sir R. Peel in 1843 should still venture to assert that the land did bear special burdens which justified the Corn Laws ; that even the Malt-tax was of the nature of a peculiar incumbrance on the agricultural interest; that he did not think the Corn Laws bad laws ; and that he had no concealed or lurking intention of repealing them, and did not contemplate any immediate alteration of them. Mr. Gladstone supported him, and said that any further change would be a breach of faith on the part of the Government and the House, and after the Act of the previous year a proof of the grossest imbecility ; and at the same time he fell back upon the export of bullion fallacy.

But perhaps the most remarkable feature of the debate on Mr. Villiers's motion in 1843 was the passage in his own speech drawing attention to the fact of the changed attitude of the farmers to the question, and the prediction—fulfilled only two months afterwards at Colchester—of their open avowal of the utter delusion under which they laboured in supposing that the profit arising from the Corn Laws, which gave artificial value to land, could belong to any but the owner of the land.

There can be no doubt that the Colchester meet-

ing of 1843 was of very great importance to the
cause of Repeal and Free Trade generally. From
information that reached him, Mr. Cobden did not
anticipate it without apprehension, though all pre-
cautions had been taken to guard against a breach of
the peace. He was most anxious to be supported by
the Parliamentary leader of Free Trade in attacking
this stronghold of Conservatism, where everything
that the cream of Protection, represented by the
landed, agricultural, and clerical interests of the
neighbourhood, could effect to defeat the object of
the League had been effected. And it was well that
he was so supported. The agitation which had been
carried on by the Tories previously throughout the
surrounding country in anticipation of the meeting
had excited and irritated the agricultural population
to such a degree that at first the farmers were appealed
to by the popular orator with as little avail as their
representatives in another place had been two months
previously, when Mr. Cobden was obliged, by the
cock-crowing, the hissing, and the general clamour,
to defer addressing the House of Commons till the
fifth night of the debate on Mr. Villiers's motion. Mr.
Villiers had a very different reception. He was as
popular at Colchester as he had been at Penenden
Heath on the 29th of June. And his raillery and
satire told as much amongst the farmers against Sir
J. Tyrell, as they had with the assembly at Penen-

den against Mr. Osborn. From the first his audience were with him ; he completely carried them along with him, and finally won their vote. And from that day to this the Colchester meeting has been ranked as one of the greatest triumphs of Free Trade principles with the agricultural class.

The Session of 1844 has been treated recently, as it was in some quarters at the time, as one fruitless to the cause of Repeal ; and the debate on Mr. Villiers's motion as 'a very hollow performance.' Those in the thick of the struggle viewed it otherwise. Better weather, and consequently better harvests and improved trade, had somewhat relieved the public mind from the pressing fear of want ; and the landed interest, reassured by Ministerial utterances, took comfort in the thought that there would be no interference with their monopoly that year at least. Nevertheless Repeal gained ground, and the debate was not a barren one because the leading Whigs ostentatiously absented themselves from the House on the second night. The conviction of the Prime Minister that the existing legislation was merely empirical, or rather provisional, and depended for its continuance on the accidents of our climate, was in no way concealed, though it may have been somewhat confused by the Ministerial declaration that the Government had no intention of altering the Corn Laws of 1842, and that it was a matter of duty to oppose the motion for Repeal. Onlookers who knew how to read between the lines were not deceived by these 'voces in vulgum ambiguas'; and the organ of the League, reviewing the Parliamentary labours of Mr. Villiers for the year, justly estimated the real state of affairs :—' Since Mr. Villiers first began to raise Anti-Corn Law debates in the House of Commons, he has entered on the third cycle in the history of the question. He commenced when counteracted by the effects of abundant harvests and the influence of abundant ignorance—when agriculturists were contemptuously indifferent, commercialists sufficiently supine, and, consequently, the House of Commons utterly apathetic. He continued when winter had descended on our national affairs ; when the wolf howled at the national door ; when country gentlemen became alarmed, and the entire community interested. He perseveres now that spring appears again, and there is the proba-bility of a short-lived summer of prosperity ; but he continues it with the knowledge that there is not a man within the compass of Great Britain capable of putting two ideas together, be he Cabinet Minister, landed proprietor, merchant, manufacturer, or hand-worker, who does not feel that the Corn Laws but wait the next " fall of the leaf," in order to be blown into the gulf of oblivion, there to rot with the things that were.' [1]

[1] 'The League,' August 10, 1844,

Trusting as the Ministers did for the prevalence of fair weather and good harvests to enable them to retain their influence with the landed interest by the continuance of the Corn Laws, there seemed every prospect of their enjoying that advantage in the summer of 1845 ; and some thought it a bad augury for Mr. Villiers that he would have to contend against a false sense of security amongst the people, as well as the active opposition of the Whig and Tory landed interest, when he sought Repeal in June. But the end of his long struggle with Monopoly was nearer than it seemed. Slowly and steadily a change had come over the leaders of the two great parties since he first undertook to lead the apparently forlorn hope of Free Trade in the House of Commons in 1838. Step by step Protection with its fallacies had retreated before the advance of Free Trade principles, never regaining an inch of ground it had once been compelled to concede to the steady progress of its antagonist. Parliamentary Protectionist majorities diminished, while Free Trade minorities increased. The people, from a dull, apathetic ignorance as to their true interests, had been awakened to a keen, intelligent appreciation of the necessary means to secure them. Even Hodge himself was alive to the situation, and could indulge in grim humour when the importunity of the Monopolist became too much for him. ' I be protected and I be starving,'[1] was an argument the most specious fallacy could not withstand. Each change in the tariff that marked the financial policy of 1842 was a blow to the Corn Laws and a gain to the cause of Repeal. And when, on the 10th of June, 1845, Mr. Villiers brought forward his eighth and last motion for Repeal, on every side he found reason for encouragement. He could cite the statements of Sir J. Graham and Colonel Wood during the Session as so many declarations in favour of the principles he upheld ; he saw Lord J. Russell by his side ; and heard Sir Robert Peel say that the sound policy he and his colleagues had pursued and meant to pursue was no other than the establishment of principles embodying the gradual abatement of purely Protective duties ; whilst Sir J. Graham could discover little to advance against the motion than that it was too precipitate. And whereas in 1842 a majority of 303 had been against his motion for total and immediate Repeal, and the proportion of Monopolists to Free Traders was seventeen to four, he now found that the majority was only 132, the proportion of Monopolists to Free Traders having been reduced by one half.

And this was in the face of sunshine, with every prospect of a fine harvest ! It was not the rain that rained away the Corn Laws in 1846. It hastened the great change that had long been pre-

---

[1] Mr. Bright, *Speech in the House of Commons,* Feb. 1846.

paring, because it brought famine in its train at a time when no living statesman could be found who would attempt to grapple with it if his hands were bound with the fetters of Monopoly. But the near doom of the Corn Laws was felt under the brilliant sunshine of June, with no one dreaming of potato-disease or famine ; and was due pre-eminently to the unanswerable arguments and irresistible eloquence with which Session after Session a great economical principle had been enforced on the Legislature by men deeply convinced of its truth from the outset of their political career, as Lord Palmerston reminded Sir R. Peel when, in the first moment of his professed conversion to Repeal, the Prime Minister with strange persistency still pretended that the leaders of Free Trade had rested their advocacy of Repeal on mere abstract principles and *à priori* arguments, whereas the change in his conduct was justified by the *experience* of the three previous years and his observation of the working of the tariff of 1842.

Inveterate Protectionists talked of the ' children of panic,' and ' sudden conversions,' and ' apostacy,' and ' outraged public opinion,' when the ' powerful Minister ' went openly against them, and ranged himself on the popular side. But of sudden conversions there were none in high places. The measure that in 1846, from January to June, agitated the whole country ought not to have taken any politician by surprise. It belongs to the irony of politics that powerful Ministers should often run counter to the traditions of party, and give effect to the policy of the far-seeing statesmen they have conspicuously opposed. Disraeli carried Household Suffrage, and the Duke of Wellington Catholic Emancipation; it was really no more strange that Peel should overthrow Protection—he had certainly previously helped to undermine it, though all his followers were not, perhaps, wide awake during the process.

Like three great landmarks in the Free Trade movement stand out the Committee of 1840, the tariff of 1842, and the Act of 1846, which effectually blotted the Corn Laws out of the statute-book—the one leading to the other; and all are found to follow from and to be linked together by the years of patient exposition and consistent advocacy of the principles they finally established by a handful of sagacious, earnest men in Parliament, led by Mr. Villiers, and supported from without by the greatest combination of a law-abiding people against unjust legislation that this century or any preceding had witnessed, under the guidance of Richard Cobden.

The historian of the League has pointed out that in the close argument and general arrangement of his speech announcing his conviction of the necessity for a new commercial policy, Sir R. Peel adopted the speeches of Mr. Villiers as his model. Three days after the virtual repeal of the Corn Laws had received the royal assent, and the policy that Sir R. Peel had been returned in 1841 to oppose had through his instrumentality become an established fact, the Government was defeated on the Coercion Bill for Ireland. When he announced his resignation the Prime Minister disclaimed for himself and his party the sole merit of the great Free Trade measure. It seems something more than a coincidence that, on this occasion, after he had made the often-quoted allusion to Cobden, with his last words he should enforce the *justice* of Repeal above all other considerations ; and so—echoing the plea that from 1838 onwards Mr. Villiers had never allowed his hearers to forget amidst all the different phases of the discussion and all the various contentions of party prejudice and class interests—should on the break-up of his party expressly derive comfort from the thought that he would be remembered with good-will by ' those whose lot it is to labour, and to earn their daily bread by the sweat of their brow, when they shall recruit their exhausted strength with abundant and untaxed food, the sweeter because it is no longer leavened by a sense of *injustice.*'

In the first blush of surprise and gladness at Sir R. Peel's open renunciation of Protection, public gratitude was not all absorbed by the Minister whose strong hand was forcing the last ward of the lock that kept

their bread from the people.   When Mr. Villiers—his
Amendment for immediate Repeal having been defeated
—gave the weight of his cordial support to Sir R. Peel
in his speech of the 27th of February, the press, rejoic-
ing over the ' great and glorious alteration of our commercial code ' in the course ' of achievement through
the intervention of the Premier and the indomitable
struggles of the public will,' was not forgetful of the
recognition that was due to Mr. Villiers.   And later,
when the ' victory of reason and the triumph of
justice' was finally achieved, the same spirit, free
from the acrimony or adulation of partisanship, was
manifested in the tribute simultaneously rendered in
the following words to the five men then in the full
enjoyment of general attention and esteem :—

' Nor can our prominent and distinguished legislators escape the most enviable fame which can be
acquired by public servants, by public benefactors.
Sir R. Peel, as having possessed the moral heroism
to sacrifice personal ties, party power, and the most
fostered policy of a career, because he recognized the
benefits which would thereby result to the nation ;
Lord J. Russell, as having, irrespective of all other
considerations, first shown that opinions might be
changed with consistency ; Mr. Cobden and his
Siamese colleague, as the most untiring and earnest
orators for the dissemination of Free Trade principles
without the House; and Mr. Villiers, as the most

persevering and undaunted supporter of those principles within the House—have individually and
collectively obtained a most enviable renown.'

Severe things have been said about the substantial rewards that fell to the share of the leading members of the Anti-Corn Law League when, its object
having been attained, the Association was dissolved.
As regards the recognition of the labours of the
Executive Council, including the 10,000l. voted to
Mr. George Wilson, there could be no question of
their infringing any rule of Parliamentary etiquette in
accepting it, because none of them were in Parliament.
With regard to the two chiefs of the League, Mr.
Bright as well as Mr. Cobden may be said to have
been exceptionally situated. · The gift of 75,000l.—
which ultimately reached a very much larger sum—
was certainly a royal acknowledgment of the splendid
services of Mr. Cobden, and unparalleled in the history of national gratitude. But, as we have said,
Cobden's position was exceptional, and when his
losses came upon him, the people for whom he had
toiled in the best years of his life were generous in
their gratitude. And with respect to Mr. Bright,
the greatest stickler for Parliamentary proprieties
could hardly venture to assert that the valuable
library presented to him was more than a suitable
recognition of his distinguished labours in the cause
prior to his entry into the House of Commons.

But what was strange with regard to the final proceedings of the League was their omission of all public recognition of their Parliamentary leader. There was praise for the Premier, who 'in losing office had gained a country,' for Lord J. Russell, for Mr. Deacon Hume, Mr. McGregor and Mr. Porter—the three important witnesses on the famous Committee of 1840—but nothing was said about Mr. Villiers. And this was resented by Free Traders generally. A committee was consequently organized in London to repair what was looked upon as a grave neglect. But immediately Mr. Villiers saw it announced in the papers he wrote to Mr. Ricardo, the chairman of the committee, and begged him to dissolve it without delay, since, much as he was touched by such a mark of their appreciation of what he had done, he could never accept a pecuniary acknowledgment of it. He had given his time, and taxed his health, and encroached upon his moderate means, to secure the one object that had dominated him from the commencement of his career ; but he so shrank from the least semblance of anything approaching a mercenary motive that—it is an open secret, so we are free to allude to it here—he never could be prevailed upon to accept any sum offered to him by the League to meet the personal expenditure he incurred in connection with the movement. 'The reward of public services is public confidence, and I will accept nothing else,' was his characteristic reply to Mr. Ricardo ; and all that he looked for was a post in which he could better serve his country than in the one he then filled.

It was the knowledge of this probably that, apart from other and political considerations, made Cobden anxious that Ministerial recognition should be secured for his friend. 'But why do I write to you ?' he asked Mr. Parkes in a letter dated from Llangollen, July 1846 ; 'why, to call to mind the midnight conversation we had together on the Carlton Terrace, when we talked of Villiers. You said you knew I need not trouble myself about him—that he would be well cared for whether Peel or Lord John was in power. Is it so ? He has been offered a post which, I suppose, it was known he could not with propriety take.[1] But is there nothing that he could with advantage to himself and credit to your party accept ? Where there is a will there is a way. I think now, as we both thought then, that an embassy, from which he would not be likely to be removed by any *probable* change of Government, would suit him, and be most gratifying to the Free Traders. . . . If I were Lord John, I would not sleep without first having found an appointment for Villiers, the higher

[1] Lord John Russell had offered Mr. Villiers the Vice-Presidentship of the Board of Trade—Lord Clarendon, Mr. Villiers's brother, having accepted the Presidentship. When he made the offer, Lord John Russell was in a considerable minority in the House of Commons.

d

the better. The Free Traders have felt confident that he would be rewarded at the hands of the next Government for his services to the cause. To pass him over under any plea will give a colouring to the rumours that the Whigs are more disposed to conciliate the Protectionists than to satisfy the Free Traders. If there be any truth in the report, which I don't believe, the party will drive to their doom in one Session. To return to the embassy. If Villiers were appointed to any court where Protectionist principles are in the ascendant (and where are they not so, excepting Switzerland and Tuscany?) it would be most useful in influencing the Government, it would be a graceful way of promoting an honest man and pronouncing on the part of our rulers to a foreign nation. Now, be a good fellow for once, and tell me confidentially if you think I can in any way put a spoke in the wheel for Villiers. I would not ask a favour of any Government to the extent of an exciseman's place to serve my own brother, but I should be glad to put on the screw for Villiers in any way possible. He is not a party man, and therefore not likely to promote his own interests. But, as a man of the people myself, I do feel nettled that the only man of his class who from the first has been true to our cause should be neglected by the Government which has come into power upon the wreck of parties occasioned by our popular movement.'

Cobden and the Free Traders evidently did not realize the odium Mr. Villiers had incurred by his 'disloyalty' to the traditions of his party, and the independent course he had from the first assumed. The above extract was forwarded to Lord John Russell by Mr. Parkes, who wrote very frankly to the Prime Minister on the occasion, and said à *propos* of the enclosure :—

'Now Cobden's feelings are shared by many excellent members of the House of Commons, and by all the leading Free Traders of the English and Scotch towns. It is a common honesty and generosity which originate this interest in Villiers, and it does honour to Cobden especially. I have only shown his letter (within extracted) to Warburton, who concurs with me that I should make it known to you. Villiers, I have reason to know from himself, was well satisfied with his recent communication with you, but plainly he considers himself unfortunately situated in his present miserable office,[1] and also in a degree a sacrifice to the League, and without that reward which his services in the Free Trade question and his position as a public man entitle him to expect. . . . Receiving Cobden's letter, I rather write to you in justice more than friendship towards Villiers, though I have a great friendship for him. Also, I apprehend that if Villiers, the (and disinterested) leader of the

---

[1] That of Examiner in the Court of Chancery.

Free Trade question in Parliament, is left where he is, it will be a scandal to your Administration, and I think it is of great importance that no impression against the Government should exist on Villiers's account, when it is not difficult to avoid such an evil.'

Lord J. Russell wrote back to the effect that he agreed that anything that could be done for Mr. Villiers ought to be done, and that he would try if anything could be found abroad. Cobden, on being informed of this correspondence, wrote to Mr. Parkes on the subject again :—

' One point occurs to me in reading your narrative. Contrive to let Lord John know that you staved off some leading Lancashire men from going on a deputation to press Villiers's claim upon him, and that they were for acting quite unconnected with *me*. *That* would show him the strong interest felt about him in the North. . . . Now for our friend Villiers, I agree with you that he will never make an administrator, if by that we mean a House of Commons partisan. He is too honest, too sensitive, too much like an unbroken high-spirited steed. . . . The more I think of it, the more do I lean to the idea of a foreign embassy for him. . . . I know him well, have watched and probed him for eight years, and am ready to swear by him as a true man. I love and venerate him more than he is aware of. I have felt for him what I could not express, because my esteem has grown out of his noble self-denial under trials to which I could not allude without touching a too secret chord. I have trod upon his heels, nay, almost trampled him down, in a race where he was once the sole man on the course. When I came into the House, I got the public ear and the press (which he never had as he deserved). I took THE position of the Free Trader. I watched him then ; there was no rivalry, no jealousy, no repining ; his sole object was to see his principles triumph. He was willing to stand aside and cheer me on to the winning goal ; his conduct was not merely noble, it was godlike. . . . I verily believe that I have suffered more on account of the slights and mortifications he has experienced than he has done. The purity of his motives has prevented him from seeing or feeling it himself. I wish he knew how long and anxiously the leading Leaguers discussed the subject of a testimonial to him and Bright jointly with myself, and how anxious they were not to expose him to the invidious neglect of singling me out personally for all the honours. I was as anxious as any of them that he should not be overlooked, and therefore I heard what passed. They talked of including three in a joint subscription. Well, it was then discussed how should the money be divided. *Nobody could say.* Next it was discussed whether as much money could be collected for the three as for me individually. And it was agreed that it could not, for I need not tell *you* that *I* unite all parties, and that our excellent, thorough-going friend Bright has a host of opponents amongst the thin-skinned moneyed people. Then it was proposed to put forth a sheet, ruled with three columns, for subscriptions to each separately ; a few minutes' discussion made every man shrink from such a dangerous test of public feeling.   Every discussion ended in the unanimous opinion that only one *incarnation* of the Free Trade principle could be adopted.   I felt most keenly how much this must annoy Villiers.   Since I have been here, I have written to him, to explain fully what my sacrifices had been.   Now the leading men in Manchester knew of my position ; that I had called together half a score of them last August and resolved to abandon my public position ; that nothing but the potato-rot prevented my resigning my post ; that the moneyed men in Manchester knew all this, and hence their zeal to serve me in a pecuniary way.   I told him everything, for I thought it would at least mitigate the sting. He has returned me a noble answer just like himself. I could cry over it, and kiss the hand that penned it. But now between ourselves we will have a substantial and durable memorial for him yet—ay, as durable, if possible, as the good he has done for mankind, and as bright and pure and beautiful, if possible, as his motives; and my name shall stand at the head of the list.'[1]

Events proved that Cobden under-estimated the place Mr. Villiers held in the regard of the general body of Free Traders, whatever may have been the case with the League, as Mr. Parkes over-estimated the generosity of Governments.

At the General Election of 1847, South Lancashire, showing him the highest proof of their esteem, chose Mr. Villiers, still at his old post of Examiner in the Court of Chancery, for their representative, and sought to win him from his allegiance to Wolverhampton by the rare honour their unsolicited confidence would confer upon him. From a Parliamentary point of view, above all, the temptation in the face of official neglect[2] was a dazzling one ; but Mr. Villiers, deeply as he felt the generous recognition of his labours by the South Lancashire constituency, gave a fresh proof of his disinterestedness, and remained faithful to the borough that had trusted him when his singular gifts and devotion to the popular cause were little known beyond a small circle of discerning men, and had not been proved by the severe test of political life.

[1] This is the letter that was alluded to by Lord Granville, at the unveiling of the statue of Mr. Villiers in Wolverhampton in 1879.

[2] Lord J. Russell, it is true, had offered Mr. Villiers the Governorship of Bombay in 1846, after his unfortunate proposal of the Vice-Presidentship of the Board of Trade, but the East India Company refused to confirm the appointment because Mr. Villiers had been a prominent member of the League.

From 1846 to 1850 the policy of Free Trade was working and developing so successfully that there was no need for the Free Traders to take any action with regard to the principles established on the repeal of the Corn Laws. Repeated attempts were made by the Protectionists to disturb it on the ground of agricultural distress as the necessary effect of Free Trade, and to establish the claims of agriculturists to compensation; but so satisfied were the leaders of Free Trade of the hold their principles had taken on the country and of the firmness of Sir R. Peel—who boldly met Mr. Disraeli's axiomatic contention that hostile tariffs can only be encountered by countervailing duties with the declaration that the best way to compete with hostile tariffs is to encourage free imports—that they took little part in the debates raised by the Protectionists under the leadership of Mr. Disraeli.

By 1850, however, the pertinacity of Mr. Disraeli's party in their claims for the agriculturists threatened to become so inconvenient and unsettling to the country that in January of that year Lord J. Russell asked Mr. Villiers to move the Address in the House of Commons, and set the country and foreign Governments at ease by showing the entire agreement between the Whig Government and the Free Traders, and their acceptance of Free Trade policy as an irrevocable act. And so much importance did Lord J. Russell attach to Mr. Villiers's co-operation in this matter, that when Mr. Villiers excused himself from the task on the ground of being only a borough member, and therefore disqualified according to precedent from moving the Address, Lord J. Russell told him that by the choice of South Lancashire in 1847 he was virtually a county member, and pressed the matter with such importunity that Mr. Villiers yielded to his wish. With the unanswerable argument of fact he demonstrated that there was no cause for anything but satisfaction with the results of Free Trade, and that it would be most injurious to the welfare of the country to take one backward step or to allow any halt in the commercial policy we were then pursuing.

In 1852, Lord Derby, on assuming office, with Mr. Disraeli as Chancellor of the Exchequer, caused fresh uneasiness among Free Traders by his openly avowed intention to reconsider the whole question of Protection, and desire for a fixed duty on corn. And Mr. Disraeli's mystifying allusions to 'remedial measures' to redress the grievances of the agricultural interest only tended to increase the anxiety produced by the Prime Minister's candid declaration.

On the motion for Supply, therefore, Mr. Villiers —the stormy petrel of Protection, as Mr. Disraeli called him—closely watching the current of affairs, pressed the Government for a distinct statement of the policy they meant to pursue with regard to foreign commerce, especially that branch of it engaged in the supply of food for the people. The question really was evaded; though the design of the Government to gain time and delay an appeal to the country as long as they could, with a view ultimately to reverse the policy of 1846, was clearly manifested. Mr. Disraeli in his reply repeatedly asserted that it was the intention of the Government to consider the grievances of the agricultural interest. He even went so far as to say that it would be *their duty* to redress the grievances of that 'great productive interest,' as he termed it, and to propose those measures which in *their opinion* were best calculated to attain that object. But after the dissolution in July, when the new Parliament met in November, the final blow was dealt to Protection. For then it was that Mr. Villiers, consistent to the end, brought forward his famous Resolutions pledging the Legislature to accept explicitly the Act of 1846 as a 'wise, just, and beneficial measure.' With logical force he supported the well-balanced Resolutions, carefully framed not only to bind the Government to a Free Trade policy, but also to put an end once for all to the perpetual fidgeting and claim for 'compensation to the agricultural interest' with which the country was harassed by the Monopolists; who, whilst they could not, in the face of facts patent to all, deny the unparalleled prosperity traceable in a great measure to

Free Trade, endeavoured to maintain that it was at the cost of the agriculturists, and that therefore compensation was due to them on the part of the Government.

The intense aversion of the Protectionists to the Resolution was shown more than anything else by Mr. Disraeli's bitter denunciation of ' the three odious epithets.'   But, prompted by his genuine regard, manifested more than once in the heat of Repeal debates, for Mr. Villiers, whose consistent adherence to his early principles had a special attraction for him, Mr. Disraeli made his Amendment the occasion of one of the warmest tributes of admiration he ever paid to a political adversary :—

' There is one person in this House who has been constant from the beginning, and has a right to make the speech he made to-night, and that is the hon. Member for Wolverhampton.   I have sat in this House many years with the hon. and learned gentleman, and I had the honour and gratification of his acquaintance for some years before either of us, I dare say, thought of having a seat in this House. There are two qualities which I have ever observed in him—precision of thought and concinnity of expression ; and that is the reason why I do not believe he is the author of the Resolutions which he has brought forward.   Whatever may be the fault of those Resolutions, I find no fault with his speech.

His speech is the same he has always made. I make the observation without any feeling that approaches to a sneer. I may say that he may look back with proud self-complacency to the time when I remember him sitting on almost the last bench on this side of the House, and bringing forward, with the command of a master of the subject, never omitting a single point, and against all the prejudices of his audience, the question of the Corn Laws. There were no cheers then from the followers of Sir Robert Peel. There were no enthusiastic adherents then in a defunct Whig Ministry. On the contrary, the right hon. Baronet the Member for Carlisle[1] came forward and threw his broad shield over the territorial interest of England ; and anybody but the hon. and learned Member for Wolverhampton would have sunk in the unequal fray. I honour, respect, and admire him ; but I cannot agree to his Resolutions.'

If so much could be allowed by an opponent, it would have been more than surprising if Mr. Villiers's own party had been wanting in loyalty to their chief at such a moment. Before Lord Palmerston, in his anxiety to avoid an immediate defeat of the Ministry, had (to the surprise and regret of Whigs and Liberals alike) moved his Amendment which called forth Mr. Milner Gibson and Cobden in warm support of their leader, Mr. Bright rose up and forcibly

---

[1] Sir James Graham.

pointed out the striking inconsistency the House would be guilty of, when giving its final sanction to the great principles of a national Free Trade policy, if it turned from the advice of the statesman who at great personal sacrifices had for fifteen years led the question in Parliament, to submit to the dictation of its most vehement antagonist :—

'My hon. friend[1] could with perfect honesty say that he could not be actuated by factious motives in bringing this subject forward, for he brought it forward fifteen years ago, and probably no public man suffered more in his political associations than my hon. friend suffered by his undeviating advocacy of what to him, at least, seemed a great and sacred question. My hon. friend is, therefore, precisely the man to bring this question forward ; and every person must admit that he is harmonious in the position he occupies to-night, when measured by the position he always occupied on this question. . . . Now, when Parliament is going to pronounce its final verdict on the question of Free Trade, I should have thought that my hon. friend, who for fifteen years had been the consistent leader of the Free Trade question in Parliament, should be the person to draw up the terms of that verdict, and not one like the right hon. gentleman, who has been a Protectionist during the whole period of his career. . . . If claims

[1] Mr. Villiers.

are to be considered and advice to be taken, surely the advice and recommendation of the long-devoted friend of the question should be taken in preference to those of the right hon. gentleman the Chancellor of the Exchequer.'

At the close of the debate, and after much unreal talk about the impolicy of humiliating 'recent converts' and such like, the country was pledged to maintain and develop for the future a Free Trade policy ; but by the unfortunate intervention of Lord Palmerston the verdict of the Legislature on the question that, ever since 1815, had kept the country in a chronic state of discontent and distress, whilst gaining nothing for its prospective utility, was robbed of its retrospective force ; and the completeness of a great national decision was sacrificed to the sensitive feelings of a minority whose defeat would lose its sting if their own cherished principles were not superseded by others that were *wise*, *just*, and *beneficial*.

Almost immediately after the conclusion of the debate Lord Derby resigned. Mr. Villiers then joined Lord Aberdeen's Coalition Ministry as Judge Advocate-General, and was re-elected without opposition for Wolverhampton.

In considering Mr. Villiers's political career in connection with the great commercial revolution with which his name is most widely associated, it is impossible not to be struck with the penetration and sagacity

that made him seem before his time in the almost
intuitive clearness with which he anticipated other
legislators both in perceiving the cause of a gigantic
evil and prescribing the sole remedy that could be
efficaciously applied to it. This same far-seeing
appreciation of popular necessities was manifest in
his action with regard to the licensing system, after
his labours for Free Trade were over ; as it had been
before they may be said to have begun, when he
forwarded another great measure for the welfare of
the people, and in compliance with Rowland Hill's
wish, brought the scheme of postal reform before the
Government ; and when, after repeated rebuffs, a
Committee of the House of Commons on the question
was finally secured by the persevering author of the
measure, he, at his request, represented Mr. Hill, and
took charge of the scheme in the Committee. This
was in 1837.

On the licensing question, as on the Corn Laws,
he ran counter to the prejudices of great vested
interests. This was in 1853–54. He was elected
chairman of the Select Committee of the House of
Commons on Public-houses, appointed at the insti-
gation of the late Mr. William Brown, Member for
Liverpool, the duties of which post he discharged
without interruption during two Sessions, and then
himself drew up the Report and indicated the means
for coping with the evils disclosed by the evidence

taken before the Committee ; [1] but though more than
a quarter of a century has passed since he did so,
little has as yet been done to profit by his recommendations.

With the exception of an intimation in 1851 on
the part of Lord Grey that the Governorship of the
Mauritius was open to him, and an equally unsuitable
post at the Ionian Isles, Mr. Villiers received no
Ministerial recognition of his public services between
1846 and 1853.

On the formation of the Palmerston-Russell
Administration in 1859, Lord Palmerston at last
showed Mr. Villiers the consideration that was due
to him, and rendered him the act of justice that
ever since 1846 the country had looked for in vain,
by asking him to join the Government in a way that
would be more in accordance with the position he
held in public esteem than the office he had been per -
suaded to accept under Lord Aberdeen.

The 'Times,' in announcing this event, was so
happy in its summary of the circumstances of the
occasion, and so sensible of the forgetfulness of the

---

[1] 'There were two Reports of the Committee of the House of Common s
on Public-houses in the year 1853–54, of which Mr. Charles Villiers in
his old age has the consolation of remembering that he was the chairman
and chief promoter. Till I read these two Blue-books I had no con-
ception of the state of the country, and I am confident that you who hear
me, if you will only buy and read them, will have your eyes opened to
that which hitherto you have never imagined.'—Cardinal Manning,
Address at Newcastle-on-Tyne, Sept. 1882.

events of the Free Trade movement, which even at that early day was in some quarters narrowing men's memories, that, far from needing excuse for referring to it, we should rather be to blame if we failed to quote from it the grounds of the public satisfaction which, at the time, this tardy recognition of national services called forth :—

' Few people who remember the origin of the Free Trade movement will refuse their hearty sanction to this tardy acknowledgment of high desert. It was Mr. Charles Villiers who practically originated the Free Trade movement. For years before Messrs. Cobden and Bright were heard of as politicians, Mr. Villiers annually brought the subject before Parliament. He it was who had to contend with all the odium and all the ridicule of urging a proposition which in those days was looked upon much in the same light as a serious motion for realizing the ideas of St. Simon or Proudhon would be regarded in our time. Young politicians who are just entering upon the arena of public life have no idea of the fierce animosities of twenty years ago. In those days a Radical was still looked upon as a kind of monster, and a Free Trader was to a Radical what a Radical was to a truly respectable man. Still, even so, there were differences. Mr. Cobbett, or even the late Mr. Hume, might make proposals " subversive of the throne and the altar," and it was taken that he

was merely acting as a low vulgar fellow naturally
would act.   It was otherwise when a man connected
by birth, education, and family with the territorial
classes dared to raise the standard of rebellion against
their views, and what they supposed to be their
interests.   Such a man was instantly " Anathema "—
a traitor to his order, as well as a disturber of the public
peace.   Now Mr. Villiers did this.   As a youth he
began the contest which he only saw ended when he
had already attained middle life ; he dissociated himself from the traditions of his class ; he incurred
their animosity ; he sacrificed the ease and comfort of
his own days, and all to fight a battle in which, as it
turned out, he lost half the merit of success in the
opinion of the vulgar.   Charles Villiers stood half-
way between Adam Smith and Richard Cobden.   He
therefore never got the credit of the philosopher who
for practical purposes may be said to have originated
the idea, or of the popular leader who manipulated
the masses, and finally forced the Minister's hand.
Mr. Villiers's share in the transaction was, however,
quite as important.   To him it was mainly due that
the settlement of the question was carried on in an
orderly and Parliamentary way.   One of the most un-
generous acts of the great Minister who at last suffered himself to be convinced was that at the moment
of surrender he did not give his fair share of praise to
Mr. Villiers, who had so long brought the question

before the House. His compliments were reserved for the "unadorned eloquence" of the popular leader to whom he succumbed. The Free Trade party were more just,[1] as well as more generous. In the hour of victory they at least did not forget to acknowledge the claims of the gentleman who had been the first to advocate their cause. . . . Mr. Villiers has not sought the position which has been offered to him. If the addition of Mr. Cobden could have strengthened the Liberal Administration, Mr. Villiers was perfectly content to stand aside. . . . We are glad to hear that he has accepted the office, . . . and to think that he has at last an opportunity for displaying those administrative talents which found no scope in the formal duties of Judge Advocate.'

The office which Mr. Villiers accepted on joining the Ministry of Lord Palmerston was that of President of the Poor Law Board, and he may be considered to have been the first chief of that department who was honoured with a seat in the Cabinet.[2]

There could be no question that he had special qualifications for this office. As already stated, he had been one of the Assistant Commissioners in the searching inquiry which led to the Poor Law Amendment Act of 1834, and although his sympathies were

---

[1] Probably an allusion to the Lancashire return and Mr. Ricardo's committee.

[2] We do not take into account the previous appointment of Mr. Milner Gibson, who held the office for a few days only.

largely with the working classes, as shown by his public career, his well-known economic views were a sufficient guarantee that he was not likely to encourage a lax administration of the law.

But it was not only as an administrator that much was expected from Mr. Villiers in his new sphere. Legislation was still needed to give full effect to many of the principles laid down by the Poor Law reformers of 1834, and the following reference to the chief measures which were introduced and carried by him show that the public had no reason to be disappointed.

Almost immediately after his accession to office he moved for the re-appointment of a Select Committee to inquire into the laws relating to the irremovable poor, and early in 1861 he introduced his first measure for dealing with that subject.

At that time it was necessary, in order to protect a poor person from the hardship of removal to the parish of his settlement, even when he had spent his best years in increasing the wealth of one of our large centres of industry, that he should have resided continuously in some particular parish for a period of five years without receiving relief. By his Bill Mr. Villiers reduced the period of residence from five to three years,[1] and extended the area of residence from

---

[1] Reduced still further to one year, by a Bill brought in by Mr. Villiers in 1866.

the restricted limit of a single parish to the whole union.

This was of itself a great boon to the poor, especially in those large towns where the parishes were very numerous, as it often happened that by shifting from one house to another, even in the same street, a poor person became deprived of his *status* of irremovability, and could be sent back to his place of settlement, no matter how distant, or how long he had ceased to be connected with it. The security thus afforded against removal was not limited to the English poor, but extended to the Scotch and Irish of the same class also.

Another important change was that which provided that the parochial contributions to the common fund of the union should cease to be based upon the expenditure of each parish in the relief of its own poor (a system which exacted the largest proportionate contributions from the most pauperized parishes), and be computed upon the rateable value of the entire union.

A further noteworthy and humane improvement was that which cast the maintenance of all lunatics in asylums upon the common fund of the union, and thus encouraged the sending of this unfortunate class to establishments where they would be properly treated, with a view to their ultimate cure. Prior to this date the maintenance of pauper lunatics was

a parochial charge, and parishes shrank from incurring the heavy cost of sending them to an asylum.

The next measure of importance carried by Mr.
Villiers was the Union Assessment Committee Act of
1862, which transferred from the overseers, who were
often extremely illiterate men,[1] the duty of valuing
the rateable property within their parishes for the
purpose of assessment to the local rates.   Under
this statute fairness and uniformity of assessment was
secured throughout the entire union, whereas under
the former defective and capricious system almost
every parish adopted a different basis of value.

In the previous and following years we are indebted to Mr. Villiers for two Acts which greatly
mitigated the hardships to which the Irish poor had
been previously subjected when removed to their
native country, and conferred upon boards of guardians in Ireland the right of appealing against wrong-
ful removals.

In the winter of 1860–61 a long continuance of
intensely severe weather set in and occasioned a
great outbreak of distress in the metropolis.   Nearly
the whole of the labourers in the London Docks and
on the banks of the Thames were thrown out of

---

[1] Mr. Villiers, in his Report to the Poor Law Commission in 1833,
stated that when acting as Revising Barrister in North Devon, not less
than a fourth of the overseers were unable to read; and he mentions
one of these who was entrusted with the expenditure of rates amounting
to 7,000*l*. per annum.

employment, and their numbers were largely increased by the necessary cessation of market-gardening operations in the suburbs. It was then alleged that the Poor Law had broken down, and for the purpose of investigating this allegation a Select Committee was appointed by the House of Commons to inquire into the whole system of Poor Law relief. The Committee, of which Mr. Villiers was appointed chairman, sat during the three Sessions of 1861, 1862, and 1863, and in 1864 Mr. Villiers submitted to the Committee the Report prepared by him for their approval.

The Report, which was substantially adopted by the Committee, dealt comprehensively with the various matters referred to them, and whilst strenuously upholding the distinctive principles of the Act of 1834, and the main regulations under which it had been administered, recommended several important amendments in the law.

To most of these recommendations effect was soon given by the Legislature.

Almost immediately after the Committee made their Report, Mr. Villiers succeeded in carrying a Bill enabling Boards of Guardians to pension their old and meritorious officers ; and by another measure introduced by him in the same Session the cost of the maintenance of the casual poor in the metropolis was made a charge upon the whole metropolitan area. Previously the charge had to be borne by the union where the casual pauper happened to apply for relief, and the result was that the unfortunate wayfarer was often bandied about from union to union late at night, and sometimes left to die in the streets. It will be seen that this statute contains the germ of the Metropolis Poor Act, passed in 1867, under which various other items in connection with relief have been made a metropolitan common charge.

A measure of greater public interest was the Union Chargeability Act, introduced by Mr. Villiers in 1865, and passed in the same year. The effect of this measure was to distribute the cost of the maintenance of the settled poor, which up to that time had been a parochial charge, over all the parishes of the union in proportion to their rateable value. The Bill was violently opposed by the owners of those close parishes, who having no settled poor of their own, resisted to the utmost the proposal that they should be brought into contribution; but apart from other considerations it was shown that they were not entitled to claim any indulgence, as they derived their supply of labour from the neighbouring parishes, and in numerous instances had cleared their property of cottages in order that there should not be on their estates any resident poor who might become chargeable to the rates. Labouring men were thus driven to seek a dwelling in some neighbouring town or open parish, and it often happened that they were compelled to walk many miles to and from their daily work.   In his interesting speech on the second reading of this measure, Mr. Villiers referred to the fact that in some instances labourers were compelled to walk from forty to fifty miles a week, and he quoted from the work of a well-known authority [1] on agricultural matters, who stated that 'in one county the farmers actually provide donkeys, which their labourers ride out and home to prevent their tiring themselves with walking, so that they may be more vigorous at their work.'

After the Act passed there was no longer any inducement for clearances of the kind referred to, and landowners were encouraged, as the sequel proved, to provide suitable dwellings for their labourers where they would be near their employment.

By another Bill Mr. Villiers proposed to give effect to further recommendations of the Committee, especially those for securing the religious liberty of the inmates of workhouses, by allowing them to attend their own places of worship, for providing a creed register, and for enforcing the education of pauper children in the religion to which they belong. Owing, however, to the lateness of the Session the greater portion of this Bill had to be abandoned, although the whole of its provisions shortly afterwards became law.

The circumstances, however, which were best

[1] Mr, now Sir James, Caird.

calculated to test the administrative abilities of Mr. Villiers were those in connection with the event known as the 'Cotton Famine.' In consequence of the war between the Northern and Southern States in North America, the main supply of cotton had been cut off from this country, and the result was that during the years 1862 and 1863 intense distress prevailed in Lancashire and parts of the adjoining counties. Thousands of operatives were thrown out of work by the closing of the mills, and the Poor Law was subjected to a trial to which it had never been exposed before. Yet from the judgment and humanity with which, under the direction of Mr. Villiers, the relief was administered, the people became reconciled to the law, and the local authorities were enabled to carry out its provisions without incurring the odium or resentment of their distressed neighbours.

At the same time, it is obvious that Poor Laws unaided and alone were not designed to meet extraordinary and exceptional calamities like this.

Those laws are based upon the supposition that in each Poor Law area there will be occupiers of property capable of paying the rates required for the relief of the destitute poor. But when the great body of ratepayers are transformed into paupers, the very fountain from which relief is derived becomes dried up. And such was the case, to a considerable éxtent, in this unfortunate district. In Oldham alone 4,000 persons were on one day excused from the payment of their rates ; and throughout the entire district large numbers of ratepayers were weekly added to the pauper-roll, whilst the rates were so rapidly increasing as to become intolerable to those who were still able to pay them.

In order to meet this emergency, Mr. Villiers, adopting a principle shadowed forth in the Statute of Elizabeth, introduced the Union Relief Aid Acts, enabling the distressed unions to raise, by rates in aid levied on all the unions in the county, the means necessary to meet the expenditure when exceeding a given amount. By the same Acts, the guardians were enabled to borrow, within certain limits, to meet the extraordinary claims upon them.

But a still more important measure was proposed and carried by Mr. Villiers, known as the Public Works (Manufacturing Districts) Act. By this and other Acts the Public Works Loan Commissioners were enabled to advance sums amounting in the aggregate to 1,850,000*l.* for the employment of the distressed operatives on works of acknowledged sanitary utility.

A system of public works was thereupon organized which, by affording useful employment, effectually checked the demoralization which was beginning to pervade the operative classes, whilst, at the same time, it effected a large extent of sanitary improvement in localities where it had been long and urgently needed. To give some idea of the extent of these works, it may be stated that upwards of 300 miles of sewers were constructed, and 270 miles of streets were made or improved; extensive works of water supply were executed; parks and pleasure grounds were laid out for the people; cemeteries were provided; and extensive works of land drainage were undertaken. It was estimated that the number of the industrious classes who, directly and indirectly, received benefit by the employment thus afforded was nearly 40,000, whilst the works themselves were attended with the additional advantage of checking pauperism by enabling the guardians to offer work to all able-bodied applicants for relief.

In connection with this matter of the Lancashire distress it is right to add that during the whole of that trying period, and whilst large sums were raised by subscription for the relief of the operatives out of employment, Mr. Villiers succeeded in establishing the most cordial co-operation between the voluntary Relief Committees and the guardians in administering the funds that each had at their disposal.

It will thus be seen that during the seven years that Mr. Villiers presided over the Poor Law Board, he not only introduced numerous amendments of great importance in the law, but administered with remarkable success the affairs of his department under circumstances of unexampled pressure and difficulty.

It is no slight testimony to his prudence and tact, that whereas the House of Commons in 1861 refused, on an occasion when it was represented that the Poor Law Board exercised a very vexatious interference throughout the country, to renew the Board for more than three years, the feeling had become so completely changed in 1867, that an Act was passed making the Board one of the permanent departments of the State.

As regards the Cotton Famine, it was a most fortunate circumstance that the arduous task of dealing with it should have devolved upon one who had not only taken a leading part in raising the condition of the operative classes, by freeing the manufacturing industries of the country from all Protective duties on the first necessaries of life, and by opening up the markets of the world to their productions, but who was also able to grapple with their difficulties during a period of the gravest distress.

Much, therefore, as the Lancashire operatives owe to Mr. Villiers for his long and persistent conflict with Monopoly, in which, as time went on, he was joined by so many eminent men, they will doubtless not forget that the measures passed for their relief during the Cotton Famine must be regarded as mainly his own.

It was in the department over which Mr. Villiers

presided that the well-known electoral statistics in
connection with the Reform Bill of 1866 were prepared; and the last speech delivered by him whilst
in office was one almost at the close of the debate on
the motion of Lord Dunkellin to substitute in the
Bill 'rateable value' for 'clear yearly value' or
'gross rental,' as the basis of the proposed new
franchise.   The question was one upon which the
author of the Union Assessment Committee Act had
a special claim to be heard; and, in a speech delivered
with his accustomed vigour whilst the House was
extremely impatient for a division, Mr. Villiers con-
clusively showed that the effect of the motion, if
carried, would be to reduce the number of the enfran-
chised to such an extent as to render the measure
worthless, and at the same time to destroy all uniformity in the franchise itself, owing to the diverse
modes adopted by different unions in arriving at the
rateable value.   It was evident, however, that he
was arguing against a foregone conclusion, and the
Government, being defeated by a majority of 11,
immediately afterwards resigned.

Some time before ceasing to hold office the attention of Mr. Villiers was directed to the state of the
metropolitan workhouses, many of which were old
and ill-arranged buildings, without adequate accommodation for the sick or means for the isolation of
cases of infectious disease, and much too small for

the demands of a rapidly increasing population; and by his direction special inquiries were instituted in order to determine the steps which should be taken to remedy the serious evils to which these defects had given rise. Of the information then collected he was prevented availing himself in consequence of the resignation of the Government; but it was largely used by the succeeding President of the Poor Law Board, Mr. Gathorne Hardy, now Lord Cranbrook, in framing his Metropolitan Poor Act of the following year; a measure which, although criticized by Mr. Villiers in some of its details, was supported in its main principles in a generous speech made by him on its second reading.

The June of 1867 was marked by an event peculiarly gratifying to Mr. Villiers. He was asked to go to Salford to unveil the statue that had there been erected to the memory of Cobden. He went; and after a graceful allusion to Mr. Bright, and thanking the people of Salford for the pleasure their request had given him, he told them the story of his first acquaintance with the man whose memory they were met together to honour, and with whom he had been long and intimately associated in a great struggle for the public good.

He told them how thirty years before he had gone down to Lancashire for the sole purpose of making the acquaintance of Cobden, and taking counsel with him—prompted thereto by the wisdom and enlightenment that he had observed in his early writings.   And he told them how the impression of that early intercourse had never been effaced ; for he found in Cobden, though comparatively young, a man who had reflected deeply upon public affairs, who by travel and study had become well informed on all matters passing around him, and whose views regarding the improvement of the people of this country were as bold as they were benevolent.[1]

A little more than a decade after this Mr. Villiers's own statue was unveiled at Wolverhampton.   It had been erected by public subscription, supported equally by the Liberals and Conservatives of the borough, and set up in the open air where all could see it, in deference to the wish of the working classes, who ex - pressed themselves strongly against its being ' walled up ' in the Town Hall, when it was proposed to place it there in order to preserve it from the grimy atmo- sphere of the Black Country.   An honour of this kind had up to that time been most rarely, if ever, accorded to a living English statesman.   And Lord Granville, who presided at the ceremony, in his address, since most aptly described as a masterpiece of political etching, adapting Pliny's praise of Titinius Capito, happily emphasized the significance of the occasion by showing the honour done to their devoted repre-

[1] 'The Times,' June 28, 1867, *Villiers upon Cobden.*

sentative reflected on the loyal constituents who rendered it. 'Neque enim,' he said, 'magis decorum et insigne est statuam in foro populi Romani habere quam ponere.'

The period selected for paying this tribute to the public labours of Mr. Villiers was certainly not inopportune, as more than thirty years had elapsed since the inauguration of the policy for which he had striven under the most discouraging circumstances, and he could then triumphantly refer to its well-established results.

The foreign trade of the country had expanded to such an extent that the increase in our exports and imports was no longer counted by millions but by hundreds of millions. The tonnage of our shipping had doubled. The annual value of land as returned for the Income-tax showed, in spite of the prediction of the Protectionists that land would become almost worthless, an augmentation of fully one-fifth. Agricultural wages had risen one-third, those of the artisan class had improved at least in an equal degree, and the ratio of pauperism on the population had diminished quite one-half. In addition to all this a general spirit of contentment and of order had been induced amongst the working classes, who, being better fed, better clothed, and better housed, no longer showed a disposition to resort to those lawless acts to which they had previously been tempted by a sense of injustice and the privation of the first necessaries of life.

With the efforts to procure Commercial Treaties Mr. Villiers has shown little sympathy. Together with Ricardo, the late Sir R. Peel, the late Mr. Newmarch, and the present Lord Grey, he regards them as a deviation from the independent fiscal policy established in 1846. It must, therefore, be a satisfaction to him to see that further attempts to obtain them by sacrifice on our part have been abandoned, whilst, like a mighty stream ever widening and deepening in its course, English Free Trade advances with irresistible strength. What though its broad, calm current is occasionally disturbed by the breeze of some Reciprocity or Fair Trade sophism, or ruffled by the bubbles of a Corn-tax fallacy! The breeze dies down [1] and the bubbles burst, leaving the people to labour for their daily bread, 'liberas fruges et Cererem,' unfettered by the bonds of Protection, 'because we have long ago learnt, through a painful experience of a ruinous and disastrous policy, that such protection is the greatest injury we could inflict on the bodies whose interests we professed to have in view.' [2]

And now, taking a general survey of his political

---

[1] 'The fact is, practically speaking, Reciprocity, whatever its merits, is dead. You cannot, if you would, build up a reciprocal system of Commercial Treaties.'—Lord Beaconsfield, *Speech in the House of Lords on Lord Bateman's Motion, April* 29, 1879.

[2] Mr. Gladstone, *Speech during the debate on the Address, February* 8, 1882.

life, we find that Mr. Villiers has had the good fortune to witness the realization of all those great measures which formed the distinctive features of the programme with which he commenced his public career. For not only has its chief feature, commercial freedom, been accomplished, but municipal reform has been achieved, the law simplified and, by the institution of County Courts, justice brought home to every man's door, the franchise extended, the protection of the ballot given to the voter, a system of national education provided, and complete religious equality secured in Ireland by the disestablishment of the Protestant Church.

The great political events of the early part of our century are fast receding into that distance whence they assume to the eyes of all men their due relative proportions, and whence those who have taken the lead in them are estimated with a judgment that cannot be biassed by the prejudices of party, nor distorted by the glamour of self-interest. When in the fulness of time history shall be so revealed to posterity, the figure of Charles Pelham Villiers will stand out from amongst his contemporaries with a clearness greater even than it does now, as that of the far-seeing statesman who, with rare singleness of purpose, forgot himself in his zeal for the welfare of the people.

February 1883.

FREE TRADE SPEECHES.

I.

HOUSE OF COMMONS, March 15, 1838.

Mr. Villiers was first returned to Parliament for the borough of Wolver-hampton on Free Trade principles, especially in opposition to the Corn Laws, at the general election of 1835. In the fourth year of Lord Melbourne's second Administration he, at the request of the most earnest members of the Reform party, first brought forward the question of the Repeal of the Corn Laws in the House of Commons, March 15, 1838, in his Motion, ' That the House resolve itself into a Committee of the whole House for the purpose of taking into consideration the Act 9 Geo. IV., c. 60, relating to the importation of corn.' The Motion was rejected by 300 to 95. The House would not inquire, it would scarcely even listen to the proposal for inquiry, though the prospects of distress and consequent discontent of the people, manifest in Chartism and Trades Unions, were increasing on account of the successive bad harvests that in 1836 began to set in after the great period of plenty lasting from 1832 to 1835 inclusively.

I RISE to bring under the consideration of the House the Question of which I have given notice, with very great anxiety, proceeding from my knowledge of the interest that belongs to it, of its importance to the community at large, and of my utter incompetence to do it justice. Indeed, I fear that it may be asked how it comes that a person of such humble pretensions as myself could bring a Question of so much importance before the House. But without stopping to inquire whether it is one in which the ability of

the advocate is likely to affect its success, I will at
once say that if my coming forward could be taken
as any criterion of my own sense of fitness for the
purpose, my name would not have been seen in
connection with it.

The real matter, however, is not what business
I have to bring the Question forward, but why the
intelligent portion of the manufacturing and commercial community deem it essential that it should be
brought forward ; why it is that our fellow-subjects,
to whom the Legislature has lately extended the
Elective Franchise, should expect that those whom
they depute to this House should take the earliest
occasion, and every occasion, to bring under the consideration of the House those wrongs that were inflicted
upon them before they were represented—wrongs for
the redress of which indeed they sought the Franchise,
and by the redress obtained for which they purpose
to test the character of the reform that has been
effected.   It is in accordance with these reasonable
expectations, and not from any personal pretensions of my own, that I have consented to be the
humble instrument of the expression of their wishes
and feelings upon this occasion.   But, at the same
time, I shall not shrink from avowing my entire
accordance with their opinion, that of all the wrongs
inflicted upon the people by the unreformed Parliament, and of all the errors that sprang either from
the ignorance or the injustice of that body, there are
none that stand so conspicuously forth as those
foolish and unrighteous laws that. have for their

object to limit the amount and raise the price of human subsistence.

I am told that it is of little use to raise the question of the Corn Laws in this House, and that I have no chance of success. I have not been blind to this consideration myself; but I have not on that account been discouraged; and I have recommended those whom I represent to persevere in seeking justice from the House as at present constituted, because I am one who shares in the opinion that to be ever changing the constitution of authority in a country like this, is a great evil, and one only to be recommended by an obvious necessity. And as long as I see a chance of influencing the conduct of the Legislature by other means, I prefer to avail myself of them.

I hope, moreover, that there is beginning to be intelligence enough out of the House to render discussion serviceable within it; for I know that whenever this is the case, justice cannot long be withheld by the utterance of fallacy and the exercise of privilege. Still I cannot shut my eyes to the fact that thousands are now withdrawing their confidence from the Legislature in consequence of the manner in which they observe that it deals with the general interests of the country. And with respect to this question in particular, there is a tone assumed and a temper shown that no wise man can view without alarm; for they proceed not from those from whom violence is to be apprehended, but from those on whom we must depend to suppress violence whenever it may occur—men whose intelligence gives strength

to their feelings, and who now openly avow their
despair of justice from this House because they observe that the power of those who passed these Laws
and who still insist upon maintaining them, has been
strengthened by the Reform Bill ; and that they have
still to wait for the event of some circumstance when
that may be extorted from fear which is denied to
justice.   The working people, on the other hand, are
putting forward their claim to be included in the
political system in a manner hitherto unknown ;
and alleging distinctly, as their ground for doing so,
that their interests are postponed or neglected to
favour those that already greatly preponderate in the
Legislature.

I trust, then, that the House will proceed to
consider seriously a subject to which such importance is attached, and to encourage that patience
which would yet wait for its decision rather than to
confirm the opinion that our interest precludes the
fair discussion of it.   I make this observation somewhat in anticipation of the stale and unworthy
reproof usually offered to those who incur the odium
of meddling with this matter : namely, that it is
introduced at an unseasonable time ; that there is
no excitement on the subject ; that the country is in
a healthy state ; and that it is mischievous to moot
the matter at all—reasoning that, if I comprehend it,
I cannot admit.   I do not understand the morality or
the wisdom that would postpone the consideration of
a difficult question till we are precluded from entering upon it with calmness and caution.   And, with

regard to the want of excitement that appears necessary to procure interest and attention for this subject,
I cannot help surmising that the day is not far distant when there may be more excitement attaching
to it than may be convenient to those who now complain of its absence. Nor can I admit the exceeding healthiness of the country that is urged by
some as conclusive against the discussion of this
matter. When I look around and observe the numbers that are now dependent on public relief for
existence ; when I see a Commission now commencing its inquiry into the cause of the distress pervading
six or seven hundred thousand of our fellow-subjects ;
when I see that funds are being raised to assist our
fellow-subjects to emigrate from their country ; when
I see all this, I cannot help thinking that there is some
great fault in our social and political arrangements.
And when I see the questions that are now being
urged with so much importunity upon our attention ;
questions such as the combination of workmen, the
attempt by law to maintain the price and limit the
duration of labour ; when I see these, together with
all the nervousness that is manifested respecting the
administration of public relief, I am forced to conclude that there is a large portion of the people
pressing upon the means of subsistence. And what
is the Question that I now submit to the notice of
the House, but that of the price and the amount of
the means of subsistence that the Legislature will
allow to exist in this country ?

I trust, also, that this discussion will not be

deemed unseasonable by those who have stepped out
of the ordinary walks of their rank to profess unusual
sympathy with the poor, and who lately have been
denouncing in no measured language the law for the
relief of the poor, and the authorities appointed to
administer it.   And here I am not alluding to those
faithful friends of the poor who are ever at their side,
aiding them consistently to improve their condition,
and who if they complain of the strictness of the Poor
Law call the more for the abolition of the Corn Laws ;
but to those men of rank and influence who, supporters of the Corn Laws, are now heard lamenting
in taverns and at public meetings the severities of the
poor man's condition, and deploring his exposure to
the rigours of the workhouse and the hardships of the
factory.   This Question, I say, will enable them to
show that they are consistent in their kindness, and
that they are not mere quacks and impostors who will
prescribe for the symptom, but who will not eradicate
the disease.   But should it be found that such persons
(some of whom, perhaps, are indebted for their seats to
their recent professions) upon this occasion deem that
to be their duty which they know to be their interest,
and, therefore, oppose this Motion, then I trust that they
will explain in terms to be understood by the objects
of their sympathy upon what grounds they maintain
and justify Laws that limit the demand for the industry
of the poor and bar them from the abundance in the
world which God has provided.   If they can do this
with any consistency, they will give to the discussion
what I am unable to bring to it : namely, something

of novelty. Desirous of hearing what they have to allege, as well as what is to be alleged generally, in defence of the Corn Laws, I will proceed with all the brevity and precision of which I am capable to state the grounds on which I consider them indefensible in principle and injurious in operation.

And here I will first ask what is the principle of the Corn Laws? I believe that I adopt the phrase which is current in reply when I say that it is Protection—Protection of the landed interest. If it is deemed necessary to say more in its defence, it is alleged, that, heavily burdened as we are and living under our present artificial system, the British farmer cannot compete with the foreign grower without the Corn Laws. Now admitting this last position to be true, I dispute the justice of such a principle as that of Protection. I care not whether it applies to land or to trade. I object to it as unjust unless universally applied, and I say that it is incapable of such an application. It is very necessary to make this clear, for there is not a word in the English language more important in the review of our commercial and financial polity than that of Protection. If people believe that it means only a security extended by the State to a portion of the community whose interests are by any circumstance endangered, they will readily assent to its policy; but if, on the other hand, there is shown to be involved in it the perpetual privation of the community at large of some advantage within their reach, its expediency will doubtless be questioned.

Now whence is it that this claim for Protection arises ? Clothe it with all the plausibility of language, and what does it amount to ? Why, that when some persons have embarked their property, invested their capital, or become expert in the production of some object of human desire, and when the community in which they live have ceased to desire that object, or are able to procure it elsewhere, the employment of that property and skill is no longer demanded ; and then the question of Protection arises between the community at large and a portion of it. And the community are called upon to forego an advantage which is at hand, in order to continue for ever a comparatively few persons in a particular employment.

I contend that mankind have never sanctioned such a course upon principle ; but the contrary. And I say, that to do otherwise would be to bar all human improvement which is ever attended with some evil on its introduction. Temporary drawbacks have universally accompanied all those inventions for the economy of human labour that we have turned to such precious account in this country. Upon their first introduction they have all occasioned loss, if not ruin, to those whose employments they have superseded. But yet we have encouraged the use of machinery and carried it to an extent unknown in any other country, for the simple purpose of cheapening productions and benefiting the community. And what is urged upon the unfortunate persons who are rendered destitute by the introduction of machinery, does not make any the less true their complaint that by the improvement they are ruined. For when it is said that machinery occasions more employment and adds to the abundance of the thing produced, by both of which labourers or mechanics will benefit, this, though it be true as to the class generally, does not prevent inconvenience and loss being occasioned to the original producers by the transition from one system to another; but to prevent it, nobody has ever said that the community shall be injured for ever.

It has, indeed, never been contemplated to allow even time to the unfortunate persons displaced by machinery to pass from the employment in which they are skilled to any other in which they need to acquire experience. Nor, indeed, is any trouble ever taken to encourage people to change their employment, though all hope of its being continued with advantage has passed away ; and yet it is by the tenacity to old employments which is usually manifested that the greatest distress is occasioned. This is strongly illustrated by the case of the hand-loom weavers, who ever since Dr. Cartwright's invention of the power-loom have been suffering the severest privations, and who, partly from the expectation that their trade will revive and partly deluded by a hope of assistance from the Legislature, are themselves still adhering to the same employment and training up their families in it. Now this, doubtless, is a case where Protection would be demanded and exacted by the sufferers if they had the power to enforce their

claims. But what would the community think of
the reasonableness of Protection that would preclude
them from all the advantages that follow from this
economy in production ? What would they think
of a total prohibition of all cloths produced by the
power-loom ? Or, if any relaxation of such a law were
granted, what would they think if it went no further
than to tolerate articles woven by the power-loom
only when those produced by the hand-loom had
reached a certain price ? And yet might not such a
policy be expected if this class of producers were in
the proportion of three-fourths of this House, and
entirely occupied the Upper House of the Legislature ? Might not most of the arguments or things
said in defence of the Corn Laws then be urged in
defence of such objectionable regulations ? With
respect to the better machinery of the power-loom,
might not the Revenue with equal justice be pleaded ;
might not the present artificial system of the country
be equally urged as a reason against any change ?
And if the weaver were told that he was injuring
himself no less than the community, and that he
would risk the loss of his customers abroad by other
producers resorting to the better machinery ; why
might it not in that case be urged, as it probably
will be to-night, that all this is abstract; that it
might do for France, but that it would never do for
England ; and that the Revenue could not be collected
without protection to the British weaver ? I ask if
there is any difference in principle between the case
of a manufacturer who is injured by the use of better

machinery than his own, and that of the owner of
a bad soil who is affected by resort being had to a
better ?

And is there any doubt how we should act in
other cases where considerable disturbances of capital
and loss would be occasioned by changes in which
the community would benefit? I will suppose, for
instance, a case of which we have heard something
this year : namely, a discovery by which heat could
be distributed in chambers at a trifling cost, and
without the means of coal fuel. Can anything be
imagined that would occasion a greater disturbance of
vested or settled interests than such a blessing as
this ; and is there a single argument urged against
cheap food that might not equally be used against
cheap fuel? Should we not hear of the engagement
of the coal-owners, of settlements charged on the col-
lieries, of the coasting trade essential to our commercial marine on which the British Navy is said to
depend, of all the capital invested in wharves and
waggons in this town, and the contributions to the
Excise occasioned by the labourers employed in the
trade? And yet if we should chance to discuss a
claim to Protection by the coal-owners against the
community enjoying this enormous benefit in the
winter season, would any one escape derision who
advanced a word in its favour? And if this is admitted, what is it but the admission of that very
principle and policy which persons are so apt to
deride and so unwilling to discuss—freedom in
trade? For what is this freedom, but liberty for

persons to provide, and the community to enjoy, that which is needful and desired at the lowest cost and at the greatest advantage? This is at once the purpose of all Foreign Trade and the policy of Free Trade; and it is the very ground on which we now contend, in the name of justice and consistency, to be allowed to procure food by a better and cheaper machinery than we can at present, condemned as we are by law to adhere to bad and expensive soils which under extraordinary circumstances were forced into use in this country. If we could produce heat at a cheaper rate, we should not protect those who now depend for profit and employment upon our consumption of coal fuel: we *could* procure food at a cheaper rate, but we are not allowed to do so because of the Protection required and enforced by the landowners. Is there any difference between the two cases? And if not, how can we be acting justly, wisely, or consistently?

I own that I have often considered whether it might not be advisable when the community derives some great advantage from any change of system or any new invention, to give to the persons whose occupations may be thereby destroyed, some indemnity, or at least to allow the advantage to be introduced by degrees. But then, if this would be just to any, it would be due to all placed under similar circumstances; and my difficulty in proposing such a consideration to the land-owners would be that the same regard would not be shown to other persons if they were not equally powerful. My desire would be to save as much misery and inconvenience as possible ; but I desire also that no favour should be shown to one class more than to another.

In arguing against the principle of Protection for the purpose of maintaining persons in particular employments opposed to the interests of the community, I am not overlooking the cases in which Protection is wisely given : I allude to cases where a direct tax for the purpose of revenue is put upon any article manufactured at home ; because if the article were not protected by an import duty in that case, it would cease to be manufactured at home ; and therefore in order to preserve the means of raising the tax it is necessary to impose a corresponding duty upon the same article when imported. But the analogy of this case with that of land would be far from complete, supposing that there was any direct tax on the produce of land for the purpose of revenue ; for we know that the same produce is raised from lands of very different fertility : some lands, at a given cost of production, yielding eight bushels an acre, while others may yield twenty-five bushels or more ; and therefore any fixed duty for the purpose of retaining some lands in cultivation, might operate as a bounty upon others that could, from their fertility, bear competition with the soils of any other country.

By some, however, it is alleged that it is the heavy general taxation of the country that justifies the Corn Laws, inasmuch as the landed proprietors contribute to it in a far greater proportion than any other class. I wish that this could be alleged with truth, if it were only to satisfy the community that they are not injured without a pretext of justice. But, unfortunately, it is not easy to mystify the sources of our Revenue; and if the land-owners were taxed in greater proportion than the rest of the community, it would be as easy to prove it as it is now easy to show that such is not the case. For what is to be thought of such a defence of the Corn Laws, when we consider the chief sources of revenue, and it is shown that the Customs and Excise duties alone account for nearly 75 per cent. of the Revenue, and that both are reduced and limited in amount by the Corn Laws? The amount of Customs duties must vary with the amount of our imports, and they must, of course, vary with the extent of our trade with foreign countries. Now, it is clear that, as we do not export the produce of the soil, this trade must depend upon the export of our manufactures, which must be regulated by their cost of production here as compared with their price in other countries. Whatever, therefore, tends to raise the price of production must limit our foreign trade, which in turn must limit the Revenue now made dependent upon it for twenty millions and upwards; and as the high price of food necessarily raises the cost of production, and as this high price is the effect of the Corn Laws, it is not difficult to perceive how false a pretext the Revenue is for their existence.

Not less obvious is it, indeed, that they must operate in limiting the revenue derived from the Excise; for let any person consider on what articles of consumption these duties are imposed, and who

are the principal consumers, and then doubt, if he
can, that the consumption of those articles is limited
by the necessity of paying a high price for the first
necessary of life.

That in 'this country consumption generally is
dependent upon the state of trade—injured as I have
shown it to be by the Corn Laws, may be well inferred
from the simple fact, that in the Cotton Trade alone
upwards of thirty-seven millions of capital are employed and that in six departments of the labour
engaged in manufacture more than seventeen millions
sterling are annually paid in wages. And when to
this amount is added what we may surmise to be paid
in wages in the other departments of labour exclusive
of agriculture, and what proportion of such wages are
and would be spent in exciseable articles, we have some
measure of the assurance of those who tell us that
a high price of bread is essential to the maintenance
of the Revenue.

It has, moreover, been suggested to me, even by
Members of this House, that the assessed taxes would
hardly be paid without Protection to the landed
interest ; and this is stated and believed in face of
the notorious fact that what is termed the landed
interest has been more exempted from these taxes
than any other interest. For instance, farmhouses
never paid the house tax, they do not now pay the
window tax; the farmers pay no tax for their servants, their horses, their dogs, their carts ; they pay
no duty on insurance ; and landed property passes
by descent without legacy or probate duty, a duty

that has pressed heavily upon personal property and yielded an enormous sum since it was first imposed : added to which Ireland, which is chiefly an agricultural country, has never been made liable to the assessed taxes at all. The assessed taxes, then, are surely a strange ground on which to rest the plea for Protection to the landed interest, as making greater contribution to the Revenue.

But it would not be less manifestly absurd were we to test such pretence by any other branch of our public income. Take, for example, that which is usually considered as the next most important : namely, the Stamp Duty. I do not doubt that this, depending as it does upon the multiplied dealings between persons engaged in the active business of life, might be shown to be limited by whatever curtails the commercial transactions of the country, which of necessity is the effect of adding to the cost of living.

Then again, while some men allege general taxation, others adduce local taxation as an excuse for the Corn Laws. In this case, as in the preceding, the ground, when sifted and examined, will be found to be equally untenable. I deny, in the first place, that we have any proof that the particular property protected by the Corn Laws is assessed for local purposes in any greater proportion on the whole than other property. The legal liability for several of these charges attaches to local and visible property ; and though in some parishes the arable land may bear a greater proportion of them than other property so charged, yet, in many places, such other property is the more heavily burthened.

As regards individual properties nothing can be more unjust and capricious than the whole system of this taxation. This, however, does not show that tillage land is more burthened than houses or pasture land, or other property ; nor does it show in what proportion land-owners are unequally taxed ; and 1 believe that if individuals were allowed to prove each their own case, it would be shown that there are small householders who have much more reason to complain than the landholder.

I must here observe that if these local charges which have been so often alleged as an excuse for the Corn Laws, do afford any ground in truth or justice for them, we ought upon these charges being reduced or removed, to hear of some reduction of the duty upon foreign grain. But though we now hear of the poor rates being reduced some millions a year, of half of the county rate being fixed upon the Consolidated Fund, and of the value of land being raised by the Act for the Commutation of Tithes, the very slightest modification of the Corn Laws is resisted with greater fierceness and tenacity than at any time before. And yet if the landed interest have the Corn Laws to indemnify them for these charges, why are they to be indemnified at the expense of the community, without any mitigation of the national evil occasioned by the Corn Laws? Is that equitable? is it right? and if it is endured, what greater injury may not next be expected!

It is urged that the Tithe is in the nature of a direct and permanent tax upon the land for which the land-owner has a right to indemnity, and that this is an excuse for the Corn Laws. I should like to test this by the case and claim of any individual proprietor ; and for this purpose I should be willing to erect a tribunal before which he might appear and receive compensation wherever he could show himself entitled to it. I am much mistaken if any proprietor would not be put out of such a court by, at most, three questions which might be proposed to him. The first should be, whether he did not own the Tithe himself, as many do ; the second, whether his land were not Tithe free, which half the land of this kingdom is ; and the third, whether he did not take his land subject to the charge, and, if he were the purchaser, whether he did not pay less on that account. Thus the number entitled to compensation would be reduced to the comparatively few who after having improved or cultivated their land, would become subject to the Tithe upon the improved value of that land.

But it has again and again been asserted by those who condemn the Corn Laws, that they are not desirous of inflicting upon others the injustice of which they complain, and that they do not wish to see the owners of the soil taxed in unequal proportion with any other class of the community ; but that, on the contrary, they would gladly see every pretext for the enormous injustice of the Corn Laws removed by a more regular system of local taxation.

There is one tax to which I have not referred, and

which some of the more intelligent land-owners have admitted to be the only ground on which the defence of the Corn Laws can be rested: namely, the Malt Tax. Now, of all the forced and fantastical notions that are brought forward in defence of these Laws this appears to me to be one of the most striking. It rests upon the ground that more barley would be consumed if the tax on malt were taken off, and that the more barley consumed the better it would be for the barley-growers. This doubtless is true, because it is true that any tax upon an article of consumption limits the amount of the article consumed ; but then it is just as good a ground for Monopoly for any other producer who supplies the material for any other manufactured article. The manufacturers of glass, for instance, might with equal reason complain of the Window Tax as the barley-growers of the Malt Tax, and their complaint on such grounds would certainly equally. well illustrate the fancy that monkeys are said to have for feeding from their neighbour's pans, to which our whole commercial system has been not inappropriately likened. For if the Malt Tax diminishes the consumption of barley, how must the tax on bread —an article that cannot be dispensed with, diminish the consumption of all other articles? And even on the supposition that the Malt Tax falls upon the land-owners alone, how can the people be said to benefit by it if, in consequence of it, they are obliged to pay a heavy tax on bread? But the greater number of land-owners desire to repeal the Malt Tax, and yet to leave the tax on bread. Constant efforts are being

made for this purpose, which if successful would
have the effect of changing the use of much of the
land from the growth of wheat to the growth of barley ; and thus by limiting the amount of wheat produced they would add to its price ; and by raising
the price of bread they would add to the evil of the
Corn Laws.

When all these pretexts for Monopoly resting on
unequal contribution to the Revenue are shown to be
without ground, it is contended that Protection is
part of a system, and that the landed interest ought
to be protected as well as the interest connected with
manufacture.   The motto of these logicians is, ' Live
and let live,' which is strangely like, ' Take and let
us take ; ' for if examined it will be found to be the
defence of one injustice to the community at the cost
of another.   But, in the first place, it is no defence of
the policy arraigned to show that taxing the consumer for the benefit of the producer is done in more
cases than one.   Again, there is a convenient fallacy
in this mode of arguing, for it implies an equal application of the principle of Protection to every interest
that is protected ; whereas in this case, while the
land-owner has a protection of from eighty to one hundred per cent. and upwards, the manufacturers in no
instance are protected to a greater amount than thirty
per cent., and in most cases less.

In many cases manufacturers export the articles
on which the duty is imposed, thus showing that it is
not needed, and that it is wholly inoperative ; and in
all cases it is contended by them that the Protection

they seek is not against the superior skill and capital of the foreigner, but against the effect of the Corn Laws, which places them under a disadvantage with respect to every foreign producer. The truth is, that neither merchant nor manufacturer calls for Protection : both have for many years repudiated the principle altogether. And the merchants of London, when presenting their petition to this House, most distinctly denounced it as not affording them any advantage ; and declared that it was against every restrictive regulation of trade, and against all duties merely protective from foreign competition, that the prayer of their petition was presented to Parliament.

If it be said that some of those who signed that petition have changed their opinion, I would refer to the petition addressed to the House but a few weeks ago from the largest manufacturing district in the world, which was presented by my honourable friend the Member for Manchester from the Chamber of Commerce of that town ; and in which, in the most unequivocal terms, all Protection is repudiated as disadvantageous to manufacture.

There are other grounds, I am aware, on which Protection to the landed interest has been defended ; but it is the advantage of repeated discussion that certain fallacies, after being frequently exposed, become ridiculous and cannot be repeated. I hardly expect to hear some familiar to me mentioned this evening ; such, for instance, as that the Corn Laws are of the nature of a political institution in this country, and are as necessary to the maintenance of the aristocracy as any part of the Constitution. Upon this fallacy an able and humorous writer in the 'Examiner' has most justly observed that if the aristocracy of this country can be maintained only at the expense of the people, the fact should at once be avowed and provision made for them in the Estimates ; that an annual vote for esquires and magistrates should follow that for the army and navy ; and that thus a method less costly than that of the Corn Laws would be provided for their maintenance. But this pretext for the Corn Laws, like others equally preposterous, will not I expect be urged again.

And now having, I think, sufficiently examined the claim that the landed interest have to Protection at the expense of the community, it is important to show what the expense of that Protection is. For I cannot suppose that the public at large are yet aware of the extent of their loss ; and when it is known and understood, I cannot suppose that it will be much longer endured.

I have made my calculation of this loss by simple arithmetic, and if there is any error in it, the error can be easily detected. I take the admitted estimate of some years since of the amount of grain produced in this country, which was 52,000,000 quarters. At first it appears only reasonable to multiply that number by the amount of the present duty, which is nearly 32s. a quarter. This, however, might be deemed fallacious ; for if the corn were imported into this country free of duty, the price on the Continent would rise ; and it is not perhaps right to include in a calculation of public loss what the cultivators consume themselves. For fear, therefore, of any question arising on this ground, I will understate the loss in every respect. I will suppose that the price of grain will, on an average, fall only 12s. a quarter ; and that only one half of what is produced is brought into the market for public consumption, which would be 26,000,000 quarters. This at 12s. a quarter gives a sum equal to 15,600,000l., which must consequently be taken to be the very least that the community loses by the Corn Laws ; but which is greatly under the land-owners' own calculation of what their own loss would be if the ports were open ; and which is, therefore, according to them, greatly understating the loss to the community at present.

But what a sum to be annually lost to the country, 15,600,000l.! and not one 6d. of it carried to the public account or applied to alleviate the public burdens, but actually causing the aggravation of many of them ; for wherever the public expenditure has reference to the cost of provisions, everything that enhances that cost adds to the public taxation. For instance, the expense of the Victualling Department must be precisely increased by the difference in the price occasioned by laws that prohibit the importation of cheap provisions. Lord Fitzwilliam has calculated this loss within a certain period, upon the most moderate estimate, at not less than 600,000l. or 700,000l.

Again, the pay given to many persons employed

in the public service must have distinct reference to the cost of living; and the expense of maintaining the army—especially the cavalry—the navy, the police, is thus increased by these Laws. And it is increased without contributing anything to their comforts or condition, but the contrary; because, suffering as the people do from the pressure of taxation, they grudge every penny that is added to the public expenditure, and public servants therefore are pinched, and reduced to the very lowest scale on which they will consent to render service to the State. This, while we endure the enormous burden of the Corn Laws for the profit and satisfaction of a class who render no service in return, must, I maintain, be regarded as a hardship upon public servants rather than as an advantage to the State.

Indeed, I feel it so strongly that I can hardly take an interest in the labours of those who are ever toiling to reduce our public establishments—praiseworthy as those labours are—when I consider how little can be effected for the people by any reduction, compared to the advantage they would derive from the abolition of the odious Monopoly of food. I do not like to reflect upon the scanty pittance we award to our fellow-countrymen who hazard life and health in distant parts of the world in the public service, and for whom we dare not make an adequate provision after their best days have been so exhausted. I cannot bear to see that we are compelled to impose such harsh conditions upon employing other public servants, as almost to turn from our service men of liberal education. And I cannot suppress indignation when I remember that this is chiefly rendered necessary to enable us to bear a Monopoly grievous to the country at large, as well as operating with peculiar mischief upon many particular interests which have to struggle against active competition in their trade. The ship-owners, for example, see their rivals within a few hours of this coast, provisioning their ships at half the cost at which they themselves can provision theirs, and they are compelled on that account to reduce their freights to a rate that barely admits of a profit upon their capital. On the other hand, in order that the ship-owners may prosper, the community is visited with another most oppressive Monopoly which would not be required but for the mischievous operation of the laws that in the first instance crippled the ship-owners.

Again, observe the loss that is daily being sustained by those whose capital has been embarked in maintaining the intercourse of the country by means of public conveyances, and who are now brought into competition with railroads and locomotive engines. Why is the coach proprietor to be placed under the disadvantage of maintaining his horses at double the expense that is necessary? And why is he, if not protected against the steam engine, to be injured by Protection afforded to the producers of corn?

After showing that so enormous a loss is each year positively occasioned to the country without a semblance of justice or policy, it might well be thought that I had concluded the argument against the con-

tinuance of the Corn Laws. I cannot with truth
say that the case against the Corn Laws has as yet
been nearly stated. Everything that I have hitherto
advanced sinks into comparative insignificance when
we come to regard the Corn Laws in their operation
upon the sources of this country's greatness—its
wealth and credit. The greatness I ascribe to the
superiority of our manufactures and the extent of
our commerce. This it is that, in my judgment, has
given to England her present position, and made us
the envy of our neighbours. That my opinion is
sound could, I think, be proved to demonstration.
But to argue from it with the friends of the Corn
Laws, it is important to know how far they dispute
or deny it. And hence I am now desirous to learn
the agricultural creed upon the subject.

If the farmers' friends think that the vastness of
our power and the attitude that we have been able to
assume towards the rest of mankind for the last fifty
or sixty years, are to be ascribed to the high price of
food occasioned by the cultivation of poor soils, and
can prove this to be the case, I will admit at once
that we must pause before we suffer such soil to lie
waste. But if, on the contrary, I am right in my
conclusion that we owe the achievements accomplished during the late war, as well as the means of
now maintaining the debt we then incurred and of
supporting our present expenditure, to our manufactures and commerce—the result of all that science,
skill, capital and labour could accomplish, then, I
say, let us be careful that we do not by selfish and

foolish legislation impair these great mainsprings of our power.

My position briefly is this : our Foreign Trade depending upon our superiority in manufacture is essential to the maintenance of our Revenue and of millions of our people, and thereby of our credit and of our safety. My charge against the Corn Laws is that they limit and endanger our Foreign Trade, and that all such laws proceed upon a policy directly the reverse of that which is recommended by the present circumstances and condition of the country. And my charge against the Legislature is that this policy has been pursued in this country since the close of the last war, now twenty-three years ago, though each year has proved the folly of it by the injury that it has entailed and is now inflicting upon the country.

If more were not to be imputed to utter ignorance of the interests of the country than to deliberate injustice or indifference, it would be impossible for any man to rise from the contemplation of our present circumstances compared with our position at the close of the war, without anger and indignation at the manner in which all the interests of this great commercial community have been abandoned and neglected. At the close of the war we had exclusive possession of all the markets in the world. We had the means of maintaining that possession. We had the right to stipulate by treaty for its maintenance. And it was not against the interest of any country that we should so stipulate : we could no longer add to our wealth by agriculture, and other countries had not begun to acquire wealth by manufacture. To whatever part of the world we turned, there was an increasing desire and demand for our manufactures, in the production of which we had obtained a start of all other people which promised us lasting pre-eminence. It was, moreover, our interest above everything at that time to obtain customers in all parts of the world to supply and to compensate us for the prodigious void created in this country by the cessation of the vast expenditure that had been carried on by means of borrowed money. A great occasion was also offered for acquiring by means of commercial engagement, that which was then sincerely desired throughout Europe: namely, permanent security for the maintenance of peace ; and the condition of this country, the north of Europe, and the United States respectively, never . perhaps offered another opportunity so favourable for a permanent and peaceful union, based on mutual commercial interests.

It is difficult therefore to ascribe to anything but the grossest ignorance of all the real interests of this country, the manner in which that important moment was neglected and overlooked. How else can we account for the conduct of a Minister who, sent to represent this country at a Congress of Sovereigns indebted each one to England for the means so to assemble, failed to stipulate for a single advantage for our commerce ; neglected to demand indemnity of any sort for the vast expenditure that we had made in a cause in which every country was more interested than ourselves ; and in the division of the spoil only claimed for this country further engagements of difficulty and expense in which we had no kind of interest? And after all our sacrifices, for which to this day we are smarting dearly, we found ourselves bound to erect fortresses in one kingdom, to guarantee the integrity of another, and to occupy with an army a third.

Nor indeed could we complain that we were misrepresented abroad, when we observe the conduct of the Legislature at home. After deliberating upon the altered circumstances of the country, this House resolved itself into a Committee to consider by what means it could best raise and maintain the price of food—the first element in the cost of that very production by which we had so wonderfully extended our resources. So that, proceeding at home upon the monstrous fallacy that agriculture was the source of all our greatness, and abroad stipulating nothing for our foreign commerce, we were doing everything in our power to cripple our manufactures.

Now if all this had been the error of a particular Government or the folly of a party that had ceased to exist, it would, I know, be idle to refer to it, the time to remedy the evil being now past ; but it is our misfortune that it is the policy of the present hour. The policy of that day—that the home trade is the best trade and that we ought to create customers by Act of Parliament for that trade and be as little dependent as possible upon Foreign Trade, is the ground on which the Corn Laws are defended to-day.

By many, high rents were then thought to be identical with a large revenue, and whatever raised the rent of land was deemed a national advantage. But the objection now urged against the Corn Laws as a means of raising rent is, as it was then, that by raising the price of food we add to the difficulty of maintaining our Foreign Trade which the circumstances of the country do not admit of our either losing or lessening. And if, after an ample period for judging of its effect, appeal is now made to the result of this policy, I would ask whether the objection is not justified. Have we not entirely lost some markets? Have not others become less profitable? And are not our manufacturers daily threatened with further loss? I would ask those who maintain the Corn Laws, and who in fact rule this country, whether after such an experience they still deem it for the interest of England to continue a system by which our Foreign Trade is thus seriously injured.

It will not be denied, I presume, that in many respects we have lost the market of Germany; that with the Continent our commercial prospects are each day becoming worse; that with America our trade has been greatly limited; that we are also in danger from the competition of the United States in neutral markets; and that had we retained and extended our trade, as we might have done, we should have been in a better condition to have borne our public burdens, and have been spared much of the distress that has been experienced in this country. Nor will it, I conclude, be denied that this has all followed from our perverse adherence to the Corn Laws and the other restraints to the freedom of commerce.

If any person should doubt this, let him turn to the records of our diplomacy and observe the repeated remonstrances against our restrictive system from various nations who sought our market for the products of their several countries. There we have the distinct complaint of Prussia that we excluded her corn and her timber which she was ready to exchange for our manufactures. From our own Minister at Washington we learn that the American Government justified its tariff by the exclusion of her corn from our market. And we know that the tariff was opposed by those States whose products we did suffer to be imported. In fact we were warned and threatened in every way by other countries with the consequences of our Corn Laws before their tariffs were imposed ; and experience has sufficiently shown that whatever may be the disposition of particular Governments in adopting an unwise policy, if the interests of the influential classes are practically enlisted against it, it is impossible to carry it into effect.

And what has followed from the Corn Laws that was not distinctly predicted by those who opposed them? It was said that we should turn our customers into rivals ; that by raising the price of food at home we should give those rivals a great advantage in competition with us ; that we should lower the rate of profit here and drive capital to seek hazardous investments in the hope of higher profit ; that we

should tempt our capitalists and mechanics to leave
our shores with a view to the same object; and
that as the profits of Agriculture were made to depend
upon Monopoly, this interest would share in much
of the distress that it would occasion to others.
Which of these results, I ask, has been wanting to
prove the truth of their prediction? In what respect
has Mr. Huskisson been shown to be in error in that
most able speech which he delivered in this House
eight years since, and in which he taught us what
to expect from the undue pressure of Monopoly and
Taxation upon the productive classes? And what
may we not expect to follow if we continue to restrict
our capital and industry in its profitable employment?

I do not know what country gentlemen think of
the loss of any branch of our Foreign Trade; but of
this they may be sure, that whenever it does occur in
this country, it is immediately followed by the misery
and destitution of a portion of our people. At this
very moment there are thousands of persons suffering
the greatest privations from no other circumstance
than from their trade having passed into the hands of
foreigners; though it is unknown, perhaps, even to
the Members of the counties in which these persons
are that such is the case. In Nottingham, for instance,
how many are now enduring the greatest distress
from the loss of the Hosiery Trade of which they
have been successfully deprived by the Germans?
Indeed it is a fact which ought to startle those who
really understand in what the interest of this country

consists, that the Germans not only have ceased to demand the hosiery of this country—formerly an article of extensive import with them—and that they undersell us in every part of the world in this article, but that they undersell us in Nottingham itself, after paying 20 per cent. duty. Moreover, the only chance that we could have of recovering the trade would be the application of steam power to the stocking frame. This is now in contemplation ; but if it is accomplished it will add still more to the present misery and distress of a large number of inhabitants of the district. Is it possible to view such a state of things with indifference? Only five years ago the value of our Hosiery Trade was estimated at 900,000*l.* a year, and the people to whom it gave employment in the two counties of Nottingham and Derby alone, amounted to 40,000, most of whom are now suffering the direst distress. And yet the probability is that the landed proprietors whose estates have been enhanced in value by the consumption of this manufacture, will all direct the Members for those counties to vote against the consideration even of the operation of the Corn Laws to which the present distress is to be traced.

And why is not that which has happened in the Stocking Trade to occur also in any other trade? There is hardly a branch of our trade that has not been affected by foreign competition. We find from authenticated returns that all the countries that we have compelled by our restrictive system to engage in the cotton manufacture are, after several years' experience, not only able to maintain their ground but are also making progress. This is the case in France, Austria, Switzerland, Prussia, and the United States ; in each of which there is some peculiar advantage that enables them to enter successfully into competition with us either in the coarser fabrics or in manufactured goods.

And where is it that we have suffered most? Precisely where the cost of living has entered most into the cost of production. And this loss is at present completely indicated by the character of our exports to the Continent. A change in this respect has been gradually taking place in cotton goods. We now chiefly export such articles as we produce by means of our machinery at a lower cost than foreigners are yet able to do. They now demand from us a greater quantity of yarn and fewer manufactured goods because they are able by manual labour to manufacture the yarn spun in this country and to undersell us in such goods in the markets that we used to command. In the United States, on the other hand, we find that by means of the greater cheapness of water power and from proximity to the raw material, they are supplying themselves, and underselling us abroad, in the coarser fabrics.

Nor is this change confined to our cotton manufactures: it is still more the case in hardware, in many articles of which we have completely lost the trade. Whole branches of the Hardware Trade have left Sheffield, and are now carried on in the provinces of Rhenish Prussia, where it will be found that the best white bread is $1\frac{1}{2}d$. per lb. and meat $3d$. per lb.

In short, it is impossible for any candid person
to examine the evidence that we now possess on the
subject and not to conclude that as this competition
with foreigners will not be stationary, as it arises
from the exclusion of their surplus products of which
we are in need and from the cheapness in their mode
of living, we are now arrived at the period when we
must elect between the Corn Laws and our Foreign
Trade. I have come to this conclusion after careful
inquiry and due consideration of the evidence that
is put forth by credible authority. I do hope that
upon the present occasion Members of this House who
are connected with Manufacture will speak out ; that if
I am in error they will declare it ; that if I am not
they will confirm me in the views I have stated.
Their practical knowledge on these subjects must
give weight to their opinion; and as I collect from
them in private that the repeal of the Corn Laws is
of vital importance to the great interests they represent, I trust that they who were not used to fear
the frowns of the landed aristocracy, will not now
shrink from publicly avowing their opinions. I wish
the subject to be fairly considered, and for the public
to decide on which side evil preponderates : whether
in maintaining a permanent superiority in manufactures without the Corn Laws, or in adhering to our
present system.

And now having gone through the catalogue
of evils that I conceive to follow from these Laws,
where, I ask, are we to turn for their redeeming
results? To what cheering spot do the land-owners

point in order to reconcile us to their continued
endurance? Is it to the thriving and prosperous
condition of the landed interest? They have now a
period of twenty-four years of their policy to review.
Where is the evidence of its success? Is it the occupier of their land, or the labourer of their tenant that
they invite for this proof? Are these the witnesses
that they offer of a happy, prospering, and contented
class, dependent for their condition on partial legislation? Would the farmers or the labourers describe
themselves as a prospering, contented class? Or
have they ever so described themselves? Is this the
account that they would give of themselves, or that
they have ever given? Have the land-owners even
so described them? What is it that our shelves
are groaning with upstairs but allegations, debates,
inquiries, and reports on the distress, always described as unparalleled, of the very class whose well-
being is pleaded in excuse for the Corn Laws? It was
not more than five years after the first Corn Law came
into operation that a Committee of the House was
sitting to inquire into the cause of the excessive distress of the agricultural interest. And what was it
that was more than implied by the Report of that
Committee of the then unreformed House, but that
the distress was owing to the Corn Law itself—a
measure mischievous and delusive in its character, and
calculated to mislead and ruin all who had to do with
the trade in corn?

If it be said that this had reference to the Act
of 1815, I would ask what was alleged against it

which may not be proved to have followed, or may not be expected to follow from the present Corn Laws? If it was alleged against the measure of 1815 that it deluded the farmer into making engagements that he could not realize; to promise rent for his land that he was unable to pay while depending on the price for his produce which the law assured him, how has his position in this respect been improved by the modification of that measure in the Corn Laws now in operation? What were the promises of the Fluctuating Scale which was substituted for the Act of 1815? Mr. Canning introduced it. What were his hopes and even his promises with regard to it? Why, that the markets would assume stability and that the vibrations of price would be limited within the small range of 55s. to 65s. Let us then see how far these vibrations have been confined within their intended limits.

In 1828 the price of wheat was 75s. In 1830 this House was four nights occupied in discussing the distress of the nation, and the distresses of agriculturists were then chiefly dwelt upon. In 1831 three millions of quarters of wheat were imported, owing to the rise of price. In 1833 Committees sat in both Houses of Parliament to inquire into the distress of the agricultural classes; and they resulted in further advantages extended to these classes at the expense of the community. In 1835 Committees were again appointed with the same object. In 1836 the price of wheat was 36s.; which, to say the least of it, is 4s. below what the most gloomy prophets against Free Trade have ever expected as the conse-

quence of opening our ports to foreign competition.
The price now is 55s. per quarter, and the duty pay-
able upon every quarter in bond is 30s. ; and if the
crops are short this year, we shall once more have
importations, and a year after, the unparalleled distress of the farmers will be once more the subject of
inquiry.

And this is the Act which it is pretended exists
for the good of the farmer! What is to be thought
of the morality of any man who knowing that steadiness of prices is more than any other circumstance
essential to the well-being of the farmer, will stand
up to-night and plead the farmer's interest as the
pretext for the Corn Laws? The farmer, forsooth!
who is deluded into giving a high rent for land
upon the faith of a promise that is not fulfilled,
nor ever attempted to be. The law professes to
assure him of what is termed a remunerating price ;
that price is assumed by the landlord with reference
to rent ; and upon the faith of obtaining it, the
farmer engages to pay what is demanded for the land.
But all that the law does in fulfilment of its promise
to the farmer is to adopt one means of maintaining
the price of the produce of this country: namely, to
exclude the produce of foreign countries coming into
competition with our own. It does nothing effectually
to secure to the farmer a remunerating price, which
could be done only by limiting the quantity brought
into the market. It takes no precaution against
abundant harvests ; nor does it dare allow the farmer
the full benefit of a bad harvest. It makes no calcu-

lation of the difference between the soils of England
and the soils of Ireland, which latter are less exhausted
than those of this country. It does not prevent the
influence of quantity on price increased by importation
from the colonies with a low fixed duty ; nor the effect
of agricultural improvements. Yet all these things
tend to disappoint the farmer of the expectation
created by the law, and upon the faith of which he
has made his contract with the owners of the land.
What matters it, then, to him by what he is ruined,
if ruin is to be his fate ? And his fate it must be so long
as he calculates upon fixed or steady prices, and agrees
for his land upon that expectation raised under the
present law.

I have no hesitation in saying that the result to
be expected from the existing regulations with respect to the trade in grain is uncertainty in quantity
and unsteadiness of price, and that it would be difficult to devise a scheme more exactly calculated for
effecting that result than the present Corn Laws.
From the nature of his capital, no class of capitalist
has more reason to complain of them than the
farmer. It cannot be pretended that his interests
are not identical with those of other capitalists who
depend for their profit upon the proportion which
their returns bear to their outgoing. He will not
be allowed to obtain more than the average rate of
profits ; and the certainty of obtaining what he
expects is all that he desires. If he obtains more,
the landlord instantly demands of him a higher rent ;
if he obtains less, he falls in arrear with his landlord

and becomes distressed. All, therefore, that he cares for, is to obtain the same return for his capital that he might expect in any other employment of it ; but on this, at present, he never can prudently reckon. And what could a landlord reply to an intelligent farmer who should tell him this, and aver that he, as a farmer, had no interest in high prices ; that he was neither richer nor more secure because he kept his servants, fed his horses, and sowed his land with grain obtained at great cost ; and that if Monopoly tended to raise the price of produce, this increased value was given to land which would benefit the owner of that land alone ? I trust that every land-owner who pleads this evening for these Laws on behalf of the farmer will show explicitly in what way he considers they advantage him. The farmer certainly has an interest in a high rate of profit ; but this is an interest which he shares with every other capitalist in the country, and an interest that every capitalist in the country is deprived of by means of the Corn Laws, which increase the cost of all production and limit the field for the employment of all capital.

But do the Corn Laws find an excuse in any advantage afforded to the agricultural labourers ? Has their condition been raised by them, or have they been rendered happy and contented by their operation ? If so, when ? Not, surely, in 1830 when the great body of the peasantry were dependent for support on parochial relief, though the Corn Laws of that day had already existed for fifteen years ; and when Special Commissions were trying the labourers for riot and disorder and urging the destruction of machinery, and the labourers were alleging in their excuse the worst that could befall them from the repeal of the Corn Laws—the want of employment, which they ascribed to the use of machinery?

But who ever heard of this solicitude for the labourer, which we are told is the motive of the Corn Laws, when labour could be saved by the use of machines? How little should we heed the ploughman's remonstrance could we to-morrow apply steam power to the tillage of the soil! What lectures, indeed, would not be read to the labourers upon the ignorance of their interest should they wish us to forego its use!

Or, again, what is to be thought of the alleged care for the labouring man manifested by the Corn Laws, when we entirely prohibit the importation of animal food, which is unconnected with the employment of agricultural labour, but which, from its price at home, now places meat beyond the labourer's reach?

If the landed interest, then, be fairly analyzed, what do we find? That two-thirds of its parts have no permanent or positive interest in the continuance of the Corn Laws, and that it is the land-owner alone who profits by their existence.

To the land-owners, then, we must now turn to relieve the country from a serious evil and themselves from a serious imputation. And here I will neither pretend that they would not suffer by the change, nor undertake to show (though it might easily be shown) that they greatly overrate the loss they would incur, and that they would still receive a great price for their land if it were devoted to other uses than much of it is at present. I claim the repeal of the Corn Laws upon far higher grounds : I regard the Corn Laws as an enormous wrong, and I demand their repeal as the people's right.

And I really advise the great proprietors of this country to reflect upon the course they are pursuing in resisting this demand. Let them, after reviewing the history of this country and regarding its prospects, consider their present position in it. Let them as politicians judge of the wisdom of adhering to laws passed for the advancement of their own interest, and opposed to the interest, and by the intelligence, of all other people. It may not be a flattering reflection to them that their position in the country grew up at a period and out of circumstances when the country was far less civilized than it is at present; but it is true. In proportion as intelligence has increased, and information of all kinds has been diffused, and the intercourse between men facilitated, their influence derived from territorial possession has declined. And as the sources of public improvement cannot now be checked ; as the press must be free; as education must even be supported by them; as the different parts of the community must become more identified in feeling—it will be well for them to consider whether they can now depend upon other than moral means for preserving their influence in the country ; whether they are not more likely themselves to be brought further within the control of public opinion than to guide the judgment of the people by the mere exercise of political power ; whether, in a word, they can hope any longer to suppress popular feeling upon any question merely by majorities of this House in favour of their own interest on one side with argument and common good on the other.

For purposes of delusion, this question of the Corn Laws has been confounded with other questions on which men have differed much : with questions regarding changes in the Constitution for example. But surely there is a difference between a question of laws unsound in principle, discredited by experience and denounced by authority, and a question of measures that depend on speculation for the advantages that they promise ! The only connection between such questions is that an unjust resistance to the one is the strongest recommendation for an experiment of the other.

Indeed, I am satisfied that if it were our misfortune that the peace and security of this country should now be disturbed by any popular commotion, and that such commotion were connected with the present Corn Laws, posterity regarding calmly the object and effect of these Laws, would ascribe all the blame of such disaster to those who have passed and maintained them.

We know how in this day we judge of those conflicts between power and justice recorded in our history how ready we are to side with the popular party of the period, whether in the struggle against Privilege of 1641, or that against superstition of 1688; and how we regard the monstrous privileges of the French nobility as having justified as well as caused the Revolution in France.   And yet I will venture to say that none of the oppressions in those times were more acutely felt by intelligent and patriotic men than the Corn Laws are felt by the corresponding class at present.   Nor can it be expected that such feelings can be widely entertained for any length of time without the occurrence of some circumstance that will lead to their disclosure.

Commercial liberty is now as essential to the well-being of this country as civil and religious liberty have been considered to be in former times. Victories have been fought for and won in the course of each of these, and no one now dares to deny the right of the community to either.   It therefore becomes every public man who seeks reform for public good, to devote all his energies to procure for his country the emancipation of its industry ; and to win for its hard-working people freedom to fulfil the design of nature, by exchanging with their fellow-men in other countries the fruits of their respective labours.   Thus he will afford to them individually the best prospect of adequate reward for their toil, and to the nation generally that of peace and permanent prosperity.

I now move : That the House resolve itself into a Committee of the whole House for the purpose of taking into consideration the Act 9 Geo. IV. c. 60, relating to the importation of corn. And I beg to add that though I am friendly to a repeal of the Corn Laws, I have thus shaped my Motion in order that no person, unless he be a friend to these Laws, may find a pretext to abstain from supporting it.

II.[1]

HOUSE OF COMMONS, February 19, 1839.

At the close of 1838 the Manchester Anti-Corn-Law Association was formed. At the commencement of 1839, the distress in the country being on the increase, meetings attended by delegates from Manchester, Birmingham, Glasgow and other great manufacturing towns, were held in London to consider what steps should be taken in the matter. Discontent was publicly expressed on the opening of Parliament at the omission of all reference to the Corn Laws in the Queen's Speech; and on Feb. 7 Mr. Villiers gave notice in the House of Commons of a Motion that evidence on the operation of the Corn Laws should be heard at the Bar. Lord J. Russell created a sensation by declaring that it would be his duty to oppose the Motion. On Feb. 18 Lord Brougham presented in the House of Lords several petitions against the Corn Laws, and moved that they be referred to a Committee of the whole House for the purpose of taking evidence on the matter thereof. The Motion was negatived without a division. On the following day, Feb. 19, Mr. Villiers, after presenting a number of petitions for the repeal of the Corn Laws, brought forward his Motion, ' That J. B. Smith, Robert Hyde Greg, and others, be heard at the Bar of this House . . . . in support of the allegations of their petition presented to the House on the 15th inst. complaining of the operation of the Corn Laws.' One night only was given to the discussion, and after Sir Robert Peel had stated his belief that the repeal of the Corn Laws would be grossly unjust to the agriculturists and that he should give a decided negative to it, the Motion was rejected by 361 to 172.

IF in rising to move the Question of which I have given notice I do not apologise to the House for my incompetence for the task that has devolved upon me, I hope the House will consider that it is rather from a regard for their time than from any confidence

---

[1] ' . . . Mr. Villiers's speech that night was not lost. It was a statement of singular force and clearness; and the occasion was destined to great celebrity. . . . On that night he assumed his post undisputed as the head authority in the Legislature on the subject of the Corn Laws.'
Martineau, *History of the Peace.*

in myself or want of respect to them ; for I can un-
affectedly assure the House that nothing would have
induced me to have engaged in this task had I not
been convinced by those whose interests are involved
in the Question that its success depends simply on a
statement of its merits, and not upon the ability or
talent of any advocate.

These men have approached the House in the
spirit of men of business, and I trust that the present
discussion may be conducted in the spirit in which the
petitioners come before it.   Certainly nothing that I
shall say, nothing that I shall address to the House,
shall afford any one an example of a deviation from
this course.

In accordance with the Notice that I have given,
I have now to move that certain persons who have
petitioned this House be allowed to prove the allegations of their petition at the Bar of the House.   Who
these persons are, what it is that they allege and are
prepared to prove, and on what ground it is that they
have been induced to make this application, I will
as briefly and concisely as I am able now proceed to
state.

Deeply interested in the subject-matter of the
petition themselves, the petitioners have been selected
by their fellow-citizens and fellow-sufferers assembled
at great public meetings for the purpose, to make
known to this House by all legitimate means in their
power the specific grievance of which they complain ;
and they bring their complaint chiefly from those vast
districts of industry in this country where the mass

of the inhabitants depending for existence upon the employment of their labour, expect that employment as much from the people of other countries as from their countrymen around them.   The names of some places whence these petitions proceed will make their interests known to the House.   They are as follows: Glasgow, Leeds, Liverpool, Manchester, Nottingham, Derby, Birmingham, Wolverhampton, the Tower Hamlets, Kendal, &c.—which will be at once recognized as the seats of the great staple manufactures of the country, and the sum of whose population is above 2,000,000.

And here the House will not, I trust, object to my referring for one moment with particularity to the importance of some of these interests to the country: I will refer only to the special interests of those who have the most reason to apprehend danger to themselves from the grievance of which they complain: namely, the Cotton Trade, the Linen Trade, the Woollen Trade, and the Hardware Trade.

According to the most authentic estimates I find that on the Cotton Manufacture of this country not fewer than 1,500,000 persons depend for their support; that the amount of capital employed in it amounts to 20,000,000*l.* ; that the annual value of the manufacture is about 34,000,000*l.*; and that our export of this manufacture to other countries is about two-sevenths in value and three-fourths in quantity.

In the Woollen Trade, the annual value is about 27,000,000*l.*, of which about one quarter is exported ; the number of persons employed is nearly 400,000, receiving in wages about 8,750,000*l*. ; and consuming 108,000,000 lbs. of English wool. ‚

The product of the Linen Manufacture is about 8,000,000*l*., and wages about 3,500,000*l*.

Hardware and Cutlery, value about 17,000,000*l*.; and the people employed number 300,000. The prosperity of the latter trade depends upon the foreign demand.

In all the principal districts where these manufactures are carried on, large and open meetings have been held for the purpose of affirming the allegations of this petition ; and in nearly all the strongest wish has been manifested and expressed that more attention should be devoted to them by this House than is usually given by it. I have thought it right to describe the importance of the great interests specified in order to convince Hon. Members that it is no insignificant party that is at present asking attention of the Legislature.

And now I come to what the petitioners allege and what they pray you to be allowed to prove at your Bar. And here let me ask the House to distinguish between what they do allege and what they may be said to allege. They say that of late years they have had to observe a striking change in the character of their dealings with nations on whose custom they used to depend ; and that once valuable friends have now become alarming rivals. And they say something more : they say that you are to blame for this. In plain terms they say that the Legislature having denied to them the liberty of exchanging their

manufactures with other countries for the articles
those countries have in excess and are anxious to
offer in exchange—namely, human food, has compelled those other countries to divert their resources
from the production of food in order to satisfy their
own demand for manufactures. And this you have
done through the Corn Laws, which have not only
turned away our customers but having converted
those customers into competitors there is reason to
apprehend that they will ultimately render us unequal
to the struggle.

The points, therefore, which the petitioners on
behalf of the great manufacturing interests of this
country have to prove are : that there is a most active
competition going on in other countries of the world ;
that this has been chiefly occasioned and is now
greatly favoured by the Corn Laws ; and that should
it extend in a ratio proportionate to that which it has
reached already, the results will be prejudicial to the
country at large and peculiarly so to the productive
or working classes whose condition will be either that
of a serious deterioration or destitution.

They do not in their petition ask you to repeal
these Laws ; nor do they ask you to say why you will
not repeal them ; but, because consequences important
to them which follow from the Corn Laws, and because the facts that prove these to be true do not
necessarily fall within the notice of a majority of this
House, nor are admitted by many of you to be true,
they ask you to be allowed to place the facts beyond
doubt.

There is nothing, as they say, that takes their case out of the range of distinct and specific proof, and there is nothing to preclude them from completing their case within a very limited period. They have only to repeat to this House the experience that has been forced upon them, which experience they hope if known to you will have some weight in your judgment when you are called upon to decide the general question.

They do not come here to allege or detail stories of general distress; they do not come here to excite your compassion at their losses; or to excite the passions of the people at their wrongs: they come here simply to apprize you of the indications of coming evils which by their effect upon their interests they have been obliged to know; which, though they may be the first to feel them, will, if disregarded, necessarily be ultimately shared by millions of the people ; but which if attended to in season may be averted.

I will state what I believe to be within the possibility of proof. In the first place, I will prove that the tariff of duties that has been imposed by different countries in order to foster manufactures, and by which our manufactures are in some cases excluded and in others much prejudiced on account of the added price, was only imposed after repeated remonstrances by the Governments of those countries against our own restrictive system ; that for twenty years past in the North of Europe and before the year 1824 in America, the laws that restrict and sometimes prohibit the trade in food have been the

constant theme of complaint by those countries that
had food to offer us in exchange ; and that both
Germany and America, where our rivals are now
most prosperous, say : ' Take our corn and we will
take your manufactures.'

This has been the basis on which they have always
desired to negotiate ; and, furthermore, so averse were
the people of those countries to refuse our manufactures at first that the Governments could only reconcile them to the endurance of retaliatory tariffs by
representing to them the mischievousness and selfishness of our policy in refusing to take their food, assuming that they could not manufacture for themselves. The official journals of those countries teem
with abuse of us on this ground.

For the first great step taken by our rivals in
becoming manufacturing people in rivalry with ourselves under every disadvantage that the circumstances of our neighbourhood and established superiority placed them, we must distinctly and without
question refer to the Corn Laws. And all that we
have lost in employment and profit, and in good
will with those people, we must distinctly place
at the door of those Laws. But it is not in the
nature of the Corn Laws to be limited in their mischief; it is inherent in the operation of the system,
while it deprives us of our customers and makes
them our rivals, to give them at the same time an
advantage in competition ; for they not only have
the benefit of price added in the amount of duty that
they impose upon our goods, but they have also the

benefit of our being obliged in all matters in which the cost of living enters into the cost of production, to live at a far higher rate than they are enabled to. And your petitioners now seek to show that those people have seized the advantage that we conferred upon them ; and that in all the articles of manufacture into which the price of living enters into the cost of production they are now employing themselves in competition with us. This is no general and vague statement. They are ready here to specify the countries where this has occurred; to describe the very articles in which it has been observed ; and to verify what they allege to have been the cause of the change. They will prove that in some countries the difference in the cost of living that the Corn Laws occasion, enables the people of those countries to supply themselves with articles that we used formerly to supply ; and this in order to compete with others in neutral countries.

And here we must come to the facts that your petitioners most desire to draw attention to ; for it is not difficult to hear persons who have no interests involved in this matter prejudge the case by assuming that, whatever burdens are imposed upon the people, such is the effect of British skill and enterprise that they must be beyond the reach of foreign competition.

The first fact that I will mention to show that our ascendency may be endangered, is that our exports taken upon an average of the last five years compared with the average of the five years after the peace, are only 20 per cent. more than they were at the former period. Now though there may be some dispute as to the value of the currency at the different periods, and granted that the exports are stationary, yet the question arises, why with all our superiority and advantage over other manufacturing people, have we not kept pace with the increased demand of the world? If our Export Trade has diminished or remained stationary, has the same been the case with other countries? We find on the contrary that the exports of France have increased 50 per cent. and those of the United States 75 per cent.

But, descending from generals to particulars, let us see how far the Cotton Trade enables us to illustrate this position; for when we have seen what hangs upon this gigantic business and the fearful consequences of its loss to the country, the facts connected with it must be of the deepest concern. The primary thing to observe is that from 1770 to 1814 England had the Monopoly of the Cotton Trade: we had nothing to apprehend in competition from any country at the end of the war. America owing to a previous error in our policy had perhaps made the most advance in it; and what did she consume? Barely 100 bales. What is now the case? America at present consumes 320,000 bales; France 350,000; Switzerland 50,000; and all other countries 150,000: total, 870,000 bales, which is nearly equal to the total consumption of all England.

This will show that though we had the Monopoly

little more than twenty years ago we have not maintained it. It shows further that other countries have
been able to stand their ground and are fairly
launched in the world in competition with us, and
that we have now to consider, not whether we shall
retain a Monopoly, but whether we are in a condition
to run an equal race ; and it is for those who contend
that we are still destined to excel, to account for the
reason why other countries should have increased in
a greater ratio than ourselves ; and how it is that we
are to maintain our superiority if we do not proceed
upon equal grounds.

Here it becomes us to consider that if we have to
compete with others we must be on equal terms with
them ; for on equal competition at least we must
reckon in future, and in order to effect it we must first
institute a comparison between ourselves and other
countries engaged in the same trade.

In turning to America, we find her possessed of
two great advantages : proximity to the raw material
and cheap and abundant motive power. These have
been made the subject of precise estimate. We find
that proximity to the raw material gives them an
advantage over us equal to 7 per cent., while the
difference in their water power compared with our
steam power is as 3.10 to 12.10 per horse. Now
under these circumstances what should we expect
from the United States entering into competition
with us and imposing a duty upon our goods? Why
that in all those articles in which the raw material
enters she will have an advantage. These are her

natural advantages. What are those that we confer upon her? We tax our raw cotton, we enhance the price of flour, a vast amount of which is used in the manufacture of cotton, and by our Corn Laws we render the cost of living greater than in any other country in the world.

Let us examine the results of this. Such has been the stride that America has made in the Cotton Manufacture, that she consumes as much now as we did in 1816, and she has been increasing in a greater ratio than ourselves in the proportion of 65 to 40 per cent. We employ about 100,000 power-looms; she has now, according to a report made to Congress, about 50,000 chiefly devoted to the coarser fabrics, which is about the number we have ourselves for the same purpose.

Next let us hear what the general merchants and agents abroad say of the progress she has made in competition with us since we tempted her to become our rival. For this end I will refer to a work which has been published with the authority of the manu-facturers of Glasgow, who answer for the truth of its statements, and which contains evidence taken on oath under circumstances deserving of full credit. Mr. Kempton, a manufacturer of Massachusetts, was examined in this country and was asked :—

Could the American goods be offered at a lower price than the English goods ?—Yes ; I have understood that we have sent goods to India, where we pay an extra duty, and still undersell the English.

The same witness was examined before the Factory Commissioners :—

What is the nature of your manufactures ?—Spinning and weaving coarse yarn.

Is any of it for exportation ?—Yes.

To what markets ?—South America, West and East Indian markets.

Do you find that you can compete successfully with British manufactures of a similar kind in the same market ?—Yes, although we labour under some disadvantages.

And notwithstanding these drawbacks you can compete with us ?—Yes ; and not only so, but are gaining ground upon you, and have already excluded you from some markets.

From what markets ?—Some of the Mexican and South American. Several of our largest establishments have large contracts pending for a long time forward for those markets, at prices which would not give a fair return to the British manufacturer, but are very profitable to our manufacturers.

You say this from having ascertained, during your visit to Manchester and other manufacturing districts in this country, the exact state of the relative prices ?—Yes.

Mr. Timothy Wiggin, an American largely connected with the United States by business, and also interested in the cotton manufacture there, was asked :—

Have you been many years engaged in the cotton manufacture ?—I took an interest in those manufactures many years since.

Has the cotton manufacture in the United States prospered of late years ?—It has, it is now prosperous.

Do you think there is any probability of their being able to compete with us in any articles in a third market ?—The manufacturers of certain descriptions of cotton goods find a ready demand for their fabrics in South America, and also at Smyrna and Constantinople.

Is that the particular description of manufacture in which you are engaged ?—It is.

Mr. Joshua Bates, an American manufacturer, and also a partner of Messrs. Baring Brothers, gave his evidence :—

Do you know whether the returns of the cotton manufactures of the United States have of late been profitable, or not ?—I have various means of learning that the cotton manufactures are profitable.

That the capital invested in the cotton manufacture, some few years ago, has yielded a fair return ?—It has.

Is there not a considerable export from the United States of America of manufactured cotton ?—There is an exportation which has been very considerable of common coarse cottons.

You are aware that America possesses all the resources and elements necessary to become a manufacturing country in a very superior degree ?—Undoubtedly she does.

And that all the improvements and inventions existing in European countries will, and do, find their way into the United States ?—Certainly.

Mr. William Graham of Glasgow, a manufacturer, was also examined :—

Do you find any foreign competition that affects profits ?—Yes, we find now in all foreign markets a competition in our stouter fabrics by the American manufacturers.

What description of goods do you make ?—Principally the heavy domestic fabrics.

Do they meet you in the East Indian market ?—Yes ; within the last twelve months we have heard of their being brought into the market of Calcutta, and underselling our goods even there, where they pay an extra duty.

Do the Americans export those manufactures considerably ?—They do.

Do you find the competition of the American manufactures increasing upon you in the places to which you export ?—Everywhere.

In what parts of the world ?—In Mexico, for the last five or six years, largely ; in the Brazils considerably ; Buenos Ayres, round Cape Horn, at Valparaiso, considerably. In Manilla and Singapore they have also made their appearance ; also at St. Domingo.

Do they come into competition with you in the Mediterranean, or in the German markets?—We have done little in the Mediterranean for some years. At one time we had complaint from Malta that the American manufacturers had interfered with our sales.

Mr. Kirkman Finlay of Glasgow, a British manufacturer, was likewise a witness :—

Are you aware of the progress within the last few years of the cotton manufacture in the United States of America?—I have seen a great deal of correspondence upon the subject.

Has it not increased very much in the last ten years?—It has grown up since 1814.

Are you aware whether there is or is not an export trade in manufactured cotton from the United States?—I am aware there is.

Are you aware to what countries domestics are exported from America?—They have been trying them in all countries. They are a very active, industrious, and enterprising people, and there is scarcely any country they visit where they do not take some of them. I should say, from my own knowledge, especially in Turkey and South America, and I have understood they have taken some to India.

Looking at the United States, with reference to its advantages or disadvantages, it is your impression that nothing can prevent the progress, more or less rapid, of the manufacture in that country? —Clearly. I think nothing will withdraw them from that manufacture; that it will increase more or less rapidly, according to circumstances; and that it will be formidable.

The next witness, Mr. Wm. Gemmell, gave his evidence on oath, and it is peculiarly striking, because besides having his own establishment in Valparaiso he also spun and wove by power his own domestics in Glasgow. He deposed that for several years past he had been in the habit of manufacturing cotton domestics, a class of cotton goods of more extensive consumption than any other sent to Chili;

and that, latterly, he had been obliged to abandon the manufacture of such goods, after persevering for a considerable time in an unsuccessful competition with the manufacture of the United States, although he combined in his own works both the operations of spinning the yarn and weaving it, which enabled him to ship his goods at the lowest possible cost in this country ; and although he also had the advantage of having them sold by his own partners abroad.

I will not detain the House with other evidence on this subject, though I may say that the work to which I refer—a work published to show the impolicy of the Cotton Tax—is replete with evidence to the effect that the cotton manufactures in America are gradually progressing and coming into neutral countries in competition with us.

There is one more witness, however, who states a fact which, as it bears upon this question, I will repeat. The witness, a Glasgow manufacturer acquainted with the American market, was asked :—

Do you conceive there are any other burdens in this country affecting you, the absence of which in America enables their manufactures to come into competition with you ?—Yes ; there is another direct duty which comes heavily upon us, and that is the duty upon foreign wheat and flour used in our manufactures.

What do you suppose is the increased cost to your manufactory arising from the duty on flour ?—I should think we pay in duty on flour 600*l*. to 700*l*. a year.

To which is appended this note :—

The extra annual cost during the ten years prior to 1832, of the British cotton manufacture, for flour used in weaving and bleaching, above what the same quantity would have cost the manufacturers of the United States and the continent of Europe, estimated according to the ratio of the difference of the average prices of wheat in these countries and in Great Britain, comes out at 175,000*l.*

What I have stated here shows that the Americans are very active rivals, and that we cannot afford to fetter ourselves in competition with them.

We now turn to the Continent to see what is doing there that is to set us at ease with respect to competition. And first let us see what a country wanting in the greatest degree in our local advantages for the import of the raw material is able to effect. I allude to Switzerland, which is 800 miles from the coast ; but where, with the natural advantage of water power, living is cheap, the raw material is not taxed, and the necessaries for manufacture are not artificially enhanced. We find that though formerly we supplied her with goods and yarns, she now takes but little from us, and only the finest description of goods ; and that not only does she supply herself, but that she also exports three-quarters of what she produces, and meets us successfully in the Italian, Levant, and North American markets.

Not to weary the House with reading more extracts than are necessary—though I could draw abundantly from books that I have with me—I will undertake to say that these facts will be proved at the Bar.

Let us now turn to countries whose raw products we refuse to take ; to Russia, for example, on whose corn and timber we place high duties ; and what do

we find ?   In 1820 we exported to Russia 13,000,000
yards of cotton cloth; in 1837, 850,000 yards.
Really, when we have a case of this sort, I wish
people would pause to reflect on all the misery that
would have been spared, and all the wealth that
would have been saved, had we been labouring in
this country to supply goods and receiving corn in
exchange.   If any man seriously reflected upon the
distress that he has witnessed since the Peace, and
considered how much might have been avoided by the
employment of labour, he would come to a decision
in this case with more anxiety than some are disposed
to do.

Let us next look to the German exporters of
goods that give employment to labour, whom we
have so especially driven to be manufacturers and
who have had the advantage of our high cost of
living and their duties upon our goods.   In 1833
the yards of cotton cloth exported in Germany
were 29,531,352; in 1834, 11,045,112; in 1835,
10,037,100 ; in 1836, 7,673,020; in 1837, 5,889,957;
and in 1838 only 5,562,333.   And what consolation is it to us that our exports to that country are
swelled by the export of articles that enable other
countries to manufacture the goods that we used to
export, when we know that there is no reason why
they should not manufacture these goods in a few
years as well as ourselves ?

But, perhaps, to show what can be achieved by a
country on the Continent in competition with us in
our present burdened state, I may notice the case of

the Hosiery Trade, as this is the best in answer to all the speculations on the inability of the people of the Continent to equal the English in the productiveness of their labour. We find that though the machinery in the Hosiery Trade in England has increased 10 per cent., the machinery in Saxony has doubled every six years ; that though at the Peace we had the Monopoly of the world in this Trade, in 1838 the export of England was only 447,291 dozen pairs of hose, while that of Saxony was 1,500,000. Moreover, while we have not increased our exports for the last nine years, those of the Saxons to the United States are as follows : the exports from the Hans Towns into the United States in 1827 were valued at 96,821 dollars; in 1835 they had increased to 414,718 dollars: that is, more than 300 per cent. increase in the nine years. The comparative exports to the Havannah present much the same disparity. British exports into the whole foreign West India Islands including Cuba were in 1838, 21,270 dozen pairs ; the exports of Saxon hosiery from the Hans Towns to Cuba alone were in 1838, 69,027 dozen pairs. The exports of British hosiery to Peru in 1827 were 29,810*l.* ; in 1831, 19,605*l.* ; in 1832, 16,918*l.*; in 1833, 12,400*l.*; in 1834, 8,760*l.* sterling. All ports open equally to both present much the same decrease. And now the Saxons export to the United States alone more hosiery than we export from Great Britain altogether. But there is one fact in connection with this matter more startling perhaps than any other : though the Saxon hosiery comes into this country at an additional expense of 25 per cent., it actually undersells our own hosieries.

Now, if this be the case already in one branch of the Cotton Trade, I want to know why it is not to be the case in any other ? It proves that there is nothing that incapacitates foreigners from competing with or excelling us, and it shows that they are acting with an advantage over us. What has been alleged of the Cotton Trade I fear may be said of every other branch of trade ; foreigners are engaging with success in all of them in competition with ourselves, and it depends upon the advantages we respectively have whether we are able to maintain our ground. For there is this peculiarity about manufactures, whoever produces the cheapest must command the markets of the world.

The Woollen Trade and the Linen Trade afford the same evidence : foreigners are now manufacturers in both trades ; they are dispensing more each year with imported manufactured articles than formerly ; and they demand from us chiefly the materials of manufacture. The following statement I will read to the House, as having been drawn up by one of the persons most extensively engaged in the Woollen Trade :—

The woollen manufacture of England has already suffered materially, and is threatened with still more serious injury, from the competition of continental rivals. In proof of which the following facts are offered :—

1. Until a few years ago, the English wool-buyers at the great German wool fairs predominated so much in number, and in the extent of their purchases, over the buyers of other countries, as

to rule the prices ; but within the last few years the German and Belgian buyers have exceeded them in their purchases, being able, from the flourishing state of their manufactures, to afford a higher price for the article, and the English buyers are now regarded as of small comparative importance.

2. The exceedingly rapid growth of the woollen manufacture in Prussia, and the other countries of the German Commercial League, is shown by the fact that, five or six years since, the quantity of German woollen cloths exhibited for sale at the Leipsic fair was only 50,000 ends (an end being half a piece), whereas last year the quantity exhibited was 350,000 ends, being an increase of 600 per cent.

3. That, independent of the duty laid on English cloths in Germany, Prussian cloths are sold much cheaper than English. English fine woollens are already excluded from Germany and from several neutral markets ; and as soon as the Prussians can sufficiently extend their manufacture—which they are doing with astonishing rapidity—they will beat the English in all neutral markets, and probably in the home market of England itself, notwithstanding the import duty on foreign woollens in this country.

4. That the increase in the continental manufacture of wool is shown by the fact, that foreigners purchase a very increasing quantity of the wools of England and Ireland, of which formerly the home manufacturer had the exclusive use. The export of British wool in 1838 was of the declared value of 432,000l. ; whereas the average of the four years preceding was only 274,000l. This, therefore, shows an increase of 57 per cent. in the exportation from Great Britain of the raw material of the woollen manufacture.

5. Quantities of wool and woollen yarn, forming the raw materials of manufactures, exported from the United Kingdom.

WOOL.

Annual average of 1825, 1826, 1827— 178,035lb.
Annual average of 1835, 1836, 1837—3,744,295lb.

WOOLLEN YARN.

Annual average of 1825, 1826, 1827— 154,567lb.
Annual average of 1835, 1836, 1837—2,472,410lb.

And it not only proves an increase in the manufacture abroad, but the competition for the article raises the price to the home manufacturer.

6. The decline of the British woollen manufacture is proved by the exports of last year compared with the average of the four preceding years.

EXPORT OF BRITISH WOOLLENS.

		£
In 1838		6,157,000
Average of Four Years, 1834 to 1837 inclusive		6,543,000
Decrease		386,000

Ten or twelve years since, Belgium and Switzerland were excellent customers for manufactured goods ; and, although the French had prohibited English manufactures, vast quantities ultimately found their way into the French market, being smuggled in both from Switzerland and Belgium. Now France supplies these goods to Belgium, Switzerland, and various other parts of the Continent, as well as to the United States and South America. This applied to the finer kind of goods, on which most labour has been bestowed, and which yielded the highest profit both to the manufacturer and the work-man. We were every day doing less in fine goods ; the inferior and less profitable goods were almost the only kind for which there was any demand.

To this I may add the exports to Germany of Woollen Goods before and after the tariff.

Exports of woollen cloths from the United Kingdom to Germany :—

Years.	Pieces.	
1832	17,855	
1833	17,790	Average—15,942 pieces before the tariff.
1834	12,182	
1835	12,948	
1836	9,942	Average—9,654 pieces since the tariff.
1837	6,073	

EXPORTS OF WOOLLEN GOODS USED FOR WEARING APPAREL (EX-
CLUSIVE OF WORSTED STUFFS), FROM THE UNITED KINGDOM TO
GERMANY.

Years	Cloths of all Sorts	Napped Coat-ings, Duffels, &c.	Kerseymeres	Total of these three Articles	Three Years' Aver-ages, before and since the Tariff
	Pieces	Pieces	Pieces	Pieces	Pieces
1832	17,856	13,030	21,101	51,986 ⎫	
1833	17,790	5,530	13,562	36,882 ⎬	38,423
1834	12,182	5,511	8,709	26,402 ⎭	
1835	12,948	6,362	7,993	27,303 ⎫	
1836	9,942	7,147	6,984	24,073 ⎬	24,394
1837	6,073	11,909	3,824	21,806 ⎭	

Total woollen exports (including worsted stuffs) to Germany.
Declared value :—

Years.	£	Three Years' Averages.
1832	816,718 ⎫	
1833	694,916 ⎬	672,628*l.*
1834	565,950 ⎭	
1835	681,177 ⎫	
1836	581,837 ⎬	646,207*l.*
1837	725,607 ⎭	

I will now read a letter from a person connected
with the Woollen Trade at Stroud, which tends to
show the effects of losing any branch of trade that
affords employment to labour :—

It is an alarming fact, that in the last twelve months we
have sent many hundreds of our best workmen to foreign countries, thus having our hands and mills burdened with the aged
and disabled. In April, about 400 are expected to leave for
Australia, in consequence of being unable to maintain their
families at home. At present we have hundreds, and many
hundreds too, of good cottages vacant in this immediate neighbourhood, and I am persuaded this state of desolation will continue
to increase if the laws, as they are, remain in operation. My
opinion is, that if the Corn Laws are entirely removed, we shall,
in a few short years, require at our manufactories the surplus
population who are now starving for want of bread. But apart
from the interested view we take of the subject as men, is it not

a most wicked law to tax the staff of life which God promised to man, and to every man, if he would labour for it ; and has not Solomon said, ' He that withholdeth corn, the people shall curse him ' ?—Stroud, Feb. 12, 1839.

The Linen Trade also affords an example of the fact that the material for manufacture has been exported in greater proportion than manufactured goods :—

LINEN			
Years	Goods	Yarn	Total
	£	£	£
1834	2,443,346	136,312	2,579,658
1835	2,992,143	216,635	3,208,778
1836	3,326,325	318,772	3,645,097
1837	2,127,445	479,307	2,606,752
1838	2,919,719	655,699	3,575,418

EXPORTS OF WOOL AND WOOLLEN (WORSTED) YARN FROM THE UNITED KINGDOM.

Years	British Wool exported		Woollen Yarn exported	
	Quantity	Declared Value	Quantity	Declared Value
	lbs.	£	lbs.	£
1820	35,242	...	3,924	...
1821	34,226	...	9,121	...
1822	33,208	...	12,515	...
1823	28,563	...	6,423	...
1824	53,743	...	12,640	...
1825	112,424	...	76,961	...
1826	143,130	...	131,032	...
1827	278,552	...	255,708	...
1828	1,669,387	...	426,722	...
1829	1,332,097	...	589,558	...
1830	2,951,100	...	1,108,023	...
1831	3,494,275	...	1,592,455	158,111
1832	4,199,825	...	2,204,464	235,307
1833	4,992,110	...	2,107,478	246,204
1834	2,278,721 ⎫ Average 274,000	...	1,861,814	238,544
1835	4,642,604 ⎪	...	2,357,336	309,091
1836	3,942,407 ⎬	...	2,546,177	358,690
1837	2,647,874 ⎭	...	2,513,718	333,097
1838	...	432,000	...	365,657

But if we have reason to apprehend that we shall no longer have the advantage of clothing the rest of the world cheaper and better than any other country, have we any reason to expect that we shall retain the valuable branch of manufacture in Hardware and Cutlery ? I believe that nothing in any other branch of the question now occupying our attention would startle the House more than what an inquiry into this one would elicit. For though men are reluctant to speak out so fully as they would wish as regards the fearful competition to which they are subjected in being undersold in the other countries, for fear of advertising their misfortune, yet, as the facts are sufficiently notorious in the Trade, they could not withhold them upon inquiry. I will here read an extract from the letter of a factor who has extensive dealings with different parts of the world, and who is ready to verify at the Bar of the House any statement in the letter :—

Grainsley, Feb. 15, 1839.

My dear Sir,—With respect to our hardware articles of this neighbourhood, many are making less quantities than they were used to do, in consequence of some of the foreign markets being closed to us by manufacturing their own goods, or by prohibitory duties, such as the Prussian League affords. A great many articles manufactured in this town, and the adjacent ones, were annually exported to the emancipated States of South America ; but this market is fast closing upon us, in consequence of the rival and fast-spreading manufactures of Westphalia, Saxony, &c. Some eighteen months ago, I saw a considerable quantity of samples of locks, bolts, screws, knives, coffee and pepper mills, hatchets, cutlasses, &c., with manuscript drawings of other wrought-iron goods. These were offered for sale at a merchant's house in London, and delivered free at Hamburg. Many, indeed most, of the prices were under ours. They are much improved in finish and quality since I inspected them, and as they have increased in these qualities they have declined in prices—so much so, that they have supplanted the British artist in not only the South American market, but in North America and Western Europe. I have received a letter from the principal clerk of an establishment, informing me that the Dutch East India Company were now buying many of the articles (our hardware) from the Germans to our exclusion. The fact is, we used to supply this establishment with locks and brass foundry for the Dutch settlements, which we have now ceased to do, in consequence of our being undersold by the German makers. There are now orders in this town from Mexico, and other parts of South America, which cannot be executed, because our present prices exceed those of foreign manufactures. This is the consequence of our artisans being compelled to live on food more than 50 per cent. dearer than the foreign workman. Within these ten days I accompanied a factor to Willenhall, who had an order for sixty dozen gridirons for a foreign country; he was limited in price by an offer from a new manufacturer in Belgium to his customer, who had had this article from him before. On presenting this order to his usual workman, the man said, ' Sir, I cannot make them at the price you offer me ; iron is dearer than when I made you the last lot, and I and my workpeople are worse off, having more to give for our bread and bacon. How can you expect me to make them at the same price ? ' ' What you say is too true ; but if I cannot buy them rather lower than before, I must not send them.' After a pause, the poor fellow deplored his inability, but he agreed to ' try his hands ' (his workmen), ' for,' says he, ' they must either do this order at the price offered, or they must have nothing to do for two or three days in the week. I must get the difference out of our blood and bones (harder labour) by working fifteen or sixteen hours, instead of twelve or thirteen, as we used to do when I first began to work for myself.' Now, this is literally a fact. Our poor fellows are compelled to labour more hours for the same wages, and fare worse, as the produce of their own labour will not purchase as much food as their regular labour used to do. What, if the staff of life were equalized here and abroad (or as near as the charge of conveyance, risk, &c., would allow), would be the comparative condition of the home and foreign workman ? Why, the very article here in question was made at the same price thirty years ago, and then subject to a discount of 20 per cent., whereas now it is subject to 60 per cent. off the same rate of prices. Wheat was then about 60s., and iron rather dearer than at present. Observe, gridirons are not made by machinery; therefore labour, and labour only, pays the difference. The article of matchets, a tool shaped like a sword, for working in sugar plantations, and so of hoes, for the same purpose, are at this time manufactured in Westphalia, at from 30 to 40 per cent. under our prices, and quite as good an article. I am in possession of a foreign (Berlin) printed book of articles (hardware) manufactured in Germany, for the supply of the North and South American market, as well as the European, delivered free of carriage at Hamburg, at prices, in many instances, under ours, in close imitation of British, and on some of the articles our crack makers' names are stamped. These very things are sold by samples in London, Liverpool, Bristol, &c., for exportation, and are shipped at Hamburg direct for their foreign destination, to markets where our home-made goods—bearing the same makers' names, observe—are by such means excluded. The hardware manufactures are principally carried on at Solingen, Remscheid, and Hagen, in Westphalia, and the nearest point of access to them for England is through Dusseldorff on the Rhine. A Sheffield gentleman was with me a short time since, who had visited the manufactories of Prussia, Saxony, Westphalia, and Belgium; he assured me they were extending their workshops very fast, and improving vastly in every article they undertook. A large manufacturer in Germany, and president of their Board of Trade, assured my friend they were determined to become manufacturers on a large scale, and that they took their rise from about the time our Corn Laws began. They were smuggling goods into Russia, the Slito (I think he called the name of the town), in the Isle of Gotland in the Baltic, and the Russian authorities winked at it. There is a manufacturer of locks, &c., in Walsall, who has for some years confined himself and a large shop of workpeople to make for the South American market only. He has now very little to do, and his trade has been gradually falling away in consequence of the opposition the exporters of his articles meet with from foreign makers. Had the South American markets not been opened to our enterprise, I am persuaded this Corn Law question would have come on much sooner than it has; and, now that market is diminishing in its demand from us, we shall feel the effects sensibly every year.

Are you aware the German manufacturers have established depots at New York, Philadelphia, Boston, &c., for the wholesale sale of 'their home-made hardware goods,' and that they are supplying cutlery at prices under the Sheffield makers, as well as many kinds of our goods ? In short, foreign manufactures are increasing, and will increase, so long as our land-owners prevail and persevere in their selfish policy.

I will also read you a letter from a merchant engaged in the general trade at Birmingham :—

Birmingham, Feb. 17, 1839.

The United States now import from the continent of Europe large quantities of the following articles, which they formerly procured solely from Birmingham :—

Metal buttons, of all descriptions, gilt, plated, &c., formerly a staple article in the Birmingham trade ; now obtained almost entirely from the Continent, at a lower price.

Spectacles, of all kinds ; formerly in very extensive demand, now superseded by the cheaper German article.

Needles and fish-hooks, marked with the names of the most celebrated English makers, are now imported extensively from Germany.

Locks of all descriptions, but especially the finer qualities, are imported from St. Etienne, near Lyons. There is much more finish bestowed upon the locks and keys than the English manufacturer can afford at the same price. The present demand from this country is chiefly for the common qualities.

Fowling-pieces and pistols, of high finish, are now principally imported from France and Belgium. The manufacturers of the Continent undoubtedly excel us in those guns whose chief value consists in the workmanship.

Pins are imported from Germany in much larger quantities than formerly.

Brass battery kettles are made much cheaper on the Continent than in England, and the imports are chiefly from the former country.

Scythes, straw-knives, sickles, formerly imported only from England, are now made cheaper, and as good, in Germany ; and our sales of these articles are much diminished.

When I first visited New York, in 1826, there were, in that

city, two or three German houses, who (amongst other articles which they imported from their native country) received, every season, a few packages of assorted German hardware. The articles, however, were so inferior in finish, and so different in style and shape, from those which the Americans had been accustomed to receive from Birmingham, that, in spite of the greater cheapness of the former, the English article was still preferred.

In 1887 and 1888 I was again in New York, and discovered, to my surprise and mortification, that there were many extensive establishments for the exclusive sale of German and French hardware goods, resembling in pattern, equalling in quality, and surpassing in cheapness, similar English articles of Birmingham, Sheffield, and Wolverhampton manufacture.

The quantity and variety of continental articles now substituted for English ones are rapidly increasing.

The principal articles whose sale we have lost by the competition of American manufacturers are axes, hatchets, and many kinds of edge-tools; carpenters' hammers, gimlets, augurs, &c.; brushes of all descriptions.

I fear that the poor mechanic referred to in the former letter I read, stated what we must expect to occur if we are to experience this competition: wages will be reduced and 'the effects will be felt in the blood and sinews of the working classes.' This is the natural operation of a losing trade; and I know nothing more shocking to contemplate than the struggle that will be made at the expense of that class. How much more might I have detailed to the same effect showing that these results from competition have already commenced! But I feel that I ought not now to weary the House with further details. It is impossible to do more within the limits of a speech than to give an outline of the evidence that is ready to be submitted in support of the case;

but be assured that there are details in abundance of this kind which would both shock and startle those who would be willing to listen and who are yet uninjured. It has been my sole purpose this evening to satisfy the House that the petitioners have good ground for their application to be allowed to inform it of the operation of the Corn Laws on the manufacturing interest. I think that I have stated enough to prove that there is a case most deserving at least of inquiry.

And now I shall proceed to the last subject of my address : the ground on which the petitioners have asked you to institute an inquiry, 'not'—to use the emphatic language of the Nottingham petition— 'in the seclusion of a Committee Room, but in the face of the whole representation of the United Kingdom ;' and the grounds on which I wish to show that there is at least a strong presumption in favour of the assertion that we are compelled by the operation of the Corn Laws to engage in competition with our neighbours, fettered and on unequal terms. The request of the petitioners is in my opinion a just one ; I trust to show you that it is a reasonable one ; and I hope that you will deem it advisable to accede to it. The reason why so many are anxious for this mode of inquiry is that they believe the subject to be most important to every class of the community, and that the petitioners would be fully able to establish their case. It cannot, I think, be denied of the two modes of inquiry that this House can institute—namely, a Select Committee and a Com-

mittee of the whole House—that while the latter is
calculated to attract and excite public attention, the
other is only fitted to allay or divert it ; that while
the one is bound to satisfy those who have sought
its judgment, the other is sure, from the nature of its
composition, not to satisfy anybody.   In short, while
one is the fullest and fairest that the Constitution
admits of, the other is open to suspicion ; and I do
think that the people can come here with a good grace
to ask of the grand inquest of the country a full and
fair investigation of their grievances.

Considering the interest the Corn Laws involve,
and the time they have endured, they cannot be said
to be asking a dangerous or inconvenient precedent—
for where is the case like it ?   The petitioners cannot
be told that they are desirous of changing Laws of
which there has not been sufficient experience, or
Laws that they ever approved of.   They come here to
prove that all they predicted of their consequences
nearly a quarter of a century since has been verified,
and they have suffered all they expected from them.
And now, when they are hourly feeling their effects
in a stronger degree, they ask you only to hear the
evidence of the facts that would prove them.

Upon what possible ground can you refuse the
request ?   This really is no trifling matter, and I
trust that it will not be lightly dismissed.   It is
the great body of the middle classes—the most reflecting portion of the working class, who appeal to
this House.   They approach you in a manner the
least objectionable that is possible.   They offer you

no intimidation; they come here with no menace, with no violence; but with consideration for your supposed opinions, and even with deference to them. It is the same Parliament that refused to alter the Corn Laws last year; and they do not come now to you to ask you at once and hastily to repeal the Laws, but they request you to hear the grounds on which they demand Repeal, and on which they think you ought to reconsider your decision.

What does any reflecting man imagine will be the advantage of refusing the inquiry? Do you think that the numbers of men who have stepped out of their usual walks and left their business —can it be supposed that those who for now three months have been up here in the metropolis actively devoting their attention to this subject, will at once abandon their opinions because you reject their petition for inquiry and refuse to alter the law? Does anybody believe that those who have not the patience of the persons who seek only the repeal of the Corn Laws, but who, despairing of justice, say that there is no hope of redress from this House as it is constituted at present, will at once abandon that opinion because you refuse to hear evidence while you dispute the facts? What is the effect of this course but to teach those who yet have confidence in the House to believe that they have been wrong, and to make them heartily unite with others for its reform? They do not apply to you to do anything contrary to your forms and precedents: precedents—and there is no lack of precedents—justify the application of the petitioners. It did not require the zeal of my honourable friend the Member for Ashton to disclose the precedents recorded on the Journals. Former Parliaments have always deemed it a sufficient reason to institute a full and open inquiry when those who have represented the manufacturing and commercial interests have alleged that particular laws have been injurious to them, and have sought to prove their grievances before this House. In such cases the House has always granted the specific inquiry.

I need only refer to the Orders in Council of 1812 to find a case analogous to this. In 1812 there was a preponderating party in the House who, before the inquiry, refused to attend to the statements of the merchants and manufacturers ; who alleged the inconvenience of the mode of inquiry ; and who by every pretext sought to avoid the investigation. Every objection was urged against the proposal ; it was specifically asserted that no result would follow ; and yet I have heard from those who took part in that inquiry that numbers prejudiced against an alteration acknowledged, after the evidence had been heard, that such was the effect of the statements of the witnesses that their previous opinions had been altered by the evidence : they fully admitted the grievance and urged upon Ministers the propriety of rescinding those Orders.

And having in that case granted an inquiry, on the allegations of the mercantile, the commercial, and the manufacturing interests, will you now refuse all

tender of evidence on the present petition ? If you
do not deny the facts, but admit them to be true,
how can you refuse the consideration of the question?
If you deny the facts, how can you refuse the offer
of proof ? The petitioners in this case, moreover,
do not observe that inquiries have always been resisted from a careful economy of the public time ;
for they find that within the memory of many present you were engaged for thirteen days in examining
into the malpractices of a royal personage, and that
not sickened with the profligate details of the inquiry
you were occupied for ten days more in the discussion of the evidence and the charges.

Grant, then, but twenty-three days to the persons who in the interest of the manufactures and
commerce of the country now approach you, and I
am satisfied that before you have completed the
inquiry you will regret that it was not instituted
before : you will not repent having granted it, and
you will not rest satisfied till you have· learnt the
whole truth.

I will not, however, believe that this question will
be decided upon a matter of form ; or that the House,
with full powers to determine whether it will hear
what is offered to it or not, will reject the present application upon the mere question of precedent. Nevertheless, should the question of precedent be raised, I
have ample authority for the peculiar application that
I make. I have here a precedent that in matter and
form differs in no respect from the present case. It
is a petition that was presented on the 16th of March,

1785, to the House of Commons, from 'the gentlemen, clergy, land-owners, merchants, manufacturers,
dyers, bleachers, and others interested in the fustian
trade in the towns of Manchester, Salford, Bolton,
&c.,' against an Act imposing duties 'on cotton
stuffs, bleached or dyed, and licences for bleaching
and dyeing the same,' stating that the Act had
'involved the petitioners in the greatest distress,
and absolutely threatened that branch of commerce
with inevitable ruin, &c.'; 'that the said duty will
essentially affect labour, and will operate as a tax
upon it; at the same time that it cannot, by its
nature, be productive, it will ultimately destroy the
petitioners' trade, and diminish the public Revenue
in the same proportion as it diminishes commerce
and those various exciseable articles and duties which
spring from that source, &c.' It ends by praying
'that the petitioners may be heard at the Bar of the
House against the said Act, &c.' The complaints of
the commercial and the manufacturing interests were
not unavailing in that case, for the House at once
granted the prayer; there was no debate; and the
House ordered 'That the said petition be referred to
the consideration of a Committee of the whole House,
and that the petitioners be heard by themselves before the said Committee, upon their petition, if they
think fit.'

How any one can say that the interests now
seeking to be heard are of less importance or that
their grievances are less serious than were those of
the persons interested in the fustian trade forty years

ago, I am at a loss to conceive. Unless you admit
the facts stated by the petitioners, and do not deny
that they have already lost some trade and that they
will soon lose more, I cannot tell how you can refuse
an inquiry.

Fortified then by precedent, by justice, and by
all that is wise and reasonable in the course they are
pursuing, I trust that you will not reject their prayer;
for I cannot doubt that the impression produced
upon the petitioners and the public—thousands of
whom are paying the utmost attention to the matter
—if this application be refused, will be that there
is a fear or a reluctance in this House for the truth
to be made known and the facts to be published
to the country. No other inference is to be drawn,
or will be drawn, from your refusal except that a
majority of this House is loath to change the Corn
Laws, and that they will not receive evidence because such evidence must inevitably lead to an
alteration in them.

But not being disposed to anticipate the commission of so grave an error and injustice, I will
now submit my proposition, trusting fully that you
will concede the inquiry.

I have carefully abstained from entering into
any consideration as to the general effect of the
Corn Laws. I have confined myself strictly to the
particular effects pointed out by the petitioners
because I wished to satisfy your minds of the serious
injury inflicted on them. I now move : That
J. B. Smith, Robert Hyde Greg, and others, be

heard at the Bar of this House, by their witnesses, agents, or counsel, in support of the allegations of their petition, presented to the House on the 15th instant, complaining of the operation of the Corn Laws.

III.

HOUSE OF COMMONS, March 12, 1839.

On March 12, 1839, Mr. Villiers moved in the House of Commons ' That
the House should resolve itself into a Committee of the whole House to
take into consideration the Act 9 Geo. IV. c. 60, regulating the importation
of foreign corn.' After a debate of five nights the Motion was rejected by
342 to 195. In the debate in the Lords, March 14, on Lord Fitzwilliam's
Resolutions condemning the Corn Laws, which were rejected by 224 to 24,
Lord Melbourne said : ' To leave the whole agricultural interest without
protection, I declare before God that I think it the wildest and maddest
scheme that has ever entered into the imagination of man to conceive.'
The result of the defeat was the organization of the Anti-Corn-Law League.
The central offices of the League were established at Manchester, and its
council was formed of the executive committee of the Manchester Anti-
Corn-Law Association, which it absorbed.

IN pursuance of the suggestion that it would be convenient to discuss the subject of the Corn Laws, which
I ventured to make in the early part of the Session,
I now rise to bring under the consideration of the
House those more general consequences of the Laws
that upon the last occasion of their discussion were
kept out of view. Indeed, I consider it far preferable
to judge of a measure by its general effects, than by
what may be deemed incidental or special effects only,
and more particularly is it necessary in this case, in
which it is difficult to do justice without taking the
most comprehensive view of the subject. Still I am
decidedly of opinion that any law that is alleged to
be prejudicial to the manufacturing or the commercial
interests of this country is well worthy of deliberation
from those special points of view ; and notwithstand-

ing the censures cast upon the course that has been pursued by the manufacturers of this country, and the reproofs that have been offered to them for their impatience on a subject on which they have hitherto been represented as wanting in feeling, I cannot but think that in their respectful request to the House to take into consideration a subject that is a grievance to them, they have not only pursued a reasonable and becoming course, but also (regarding both the present and the future prospects of the question) the most judicious one that they could have adopted ; and my sole regret is that those who have openly opposed the question should have so far forgotten what is generally expected from this House by the country : to hear before deciding. But the manner in which this question is proposed for discussion to-night will elicit what the grounds are on which the House deems it expedient to refuse to hear the information that is tendered ; and whether it is that the information is already possessed and need not be sought, or whether it is that the information is still in dispute and that it is thought wise so to leave it.

The manner in which the question now comes before the House will open the widest field for the display of all the information that can be brought to its discussion ; and there will be at least this advantage (I fear that it may be the only one), it will allow the country to know upon what ground the majority of the House intend to maintain the existing Corn Laws, against the feelings and wishes of the community.

I am glad to observe, moreover, the eagerness that
my opponents manifest to enter into the discussion.
There is one so anxious to be heard that he has not
only proposed to reject my Motion, but he has also
recorded his argument along with his Notice ; an
argument, too, of so bold a character that I own I
am curious to hear its explanation.

I hope that upon this occasion we shall also hear
explained those more general views of the subject that
we on this side of the House were recently reproved
for not having taken ; and that when we are told
that this is not merely an economical question, but one
of far wider extent, we shall hear what the political,
social, and moral considerations are that can justify
the support of such laws.   Most certainly I shall not
shrink from regarding them from every point of view
because, as I have already said, I believe that the
more extensively they are studied, the more minutely
their consequences are examined, the less will persons
be left in doubt as to their policy or effect.

But still I am of opinion that the question is a
very simple one ; as simple as many of the questions
that have already been decided in this country.   It
appears to me to resemble such a question as that of
personal liberty or freedom of opinion ; and I cannot
but feel surprised that it should be left to this day to
raise a discussion on a point so easy to solve.   It is
really astonishing that at this period of our history
we should be gravely discussing whether a free, an
industrious, and a commercial people shall have a
right to exercise their honest industry in any manner

they please; whether they shall be allowed to carry on their trade in any manner that may be most advantageous to themselves and most beneficial to the State; and whether they shall be allowed to obtain their subsistence in any market at the least cost to themselves and at the best advantage to the country. It is difficult to conceive that we are debating a matter of this kind; and it will be hereafter a curious sign of the integrity and the intelligence of this House, that one Member of it should have found it important to move, ' That it is the privilege of the people to exercise their industry with perfect liberty;' and that another Member—perhaps the more successful one—should have moved, ' That it is important that the people shall be restricted in the exercise of that liberty ' and that ' the Law which has limited the amount and raised the price of human subsistence, has worked well for the interests of the country.' If the Noble Lord thinks that the House must slumber pending an inquiry into the consequences of such a law, it seems to me to be no stretch of the imagination to suppose that those who resist the Motion that I am about to make, will laugh heartily, when they go forth to a division, at the imbecility and ignorance of the people who submit to such treatment.

As I do not wish to expose myself to the accusation that was made before, of arguing this question upon too narrow a ground, and as it is proposed by the Hon. Gentleman who is to move the Amendment, to show that the Corn Laws have given protection to the productive industry of the country, it may not perhaps seem inappropriate that I should proceed to consider the effects of these Laws upon the most numerous and the most important class of the community—which I consider to be the working class, since upon their condition, and upon their contentment, the stability of the whole social fabric must depend.

And here I conceive that I and the author of the Amendment are directly at issue ; for although his language is not so plain as that which I should be disposed to use, yet I conclude that when the Hon. Gentleman uses the term 'productive industry,' he means only what I myself mean : those persons whose labour is employed in the business of production.   I would, however, suggest to the Hon. Member to be as clear and as explicit in the language he may use as he possibly can; because although nothing new can be alleged on this subject, either in point of fact or argument, yet there is one circumstance connected with it that is new : namely, that the attention of the public is directed to it.   I therefore expect that every fact, argument, and opinion that may be stated in the discussion will be closely and severely examined by those who are now interesting themselves in this question.

If I understand the Amendment that it is the intention of the Hon. Member to move, it declares that what tends to raise the price of provisions has been of benefit to the working classes of this country.   A proposition more contradictory to what might have been expected or to what has been actually experienced has never been propounded. I venture to tell the Hon. Member and those with whom he acts upon this question that it may be laid down as a principle that whatever tends to facilitate production or to increase the amount of objects of necessary consumption confers a blessing on the community, increases the wealth of the country, increases the means of consumption, increases the demand for labour, and improves the condition of every member of the community. There is nothing in the article of food that can possibly distinguish it from other articles of general consumption ; and notwithstanding the arguments that have been generally employed by the supporters of the present system, I venture to say that if any means could be discovered for increasing the produce of the land and for economizing production where cultivation admits of improvement, if any method could be introduced to increase the produce of the land and to dispense with the service of cultivators or of labourers, the Hon. Member and his party would instantly resort to such means, and laugh to scorn any person who should venture to tell them that for the purpose of protecting the cultivators or labourers they ought to forego all these advantages. The Hon. Member, if I interpret his proposal rightly, contends that the Laws that have had the effect I have stated are of advantage to the productive classes in this country.

Now I will divide the productive classes into two portions, one comprising those persons who are employed in the production of food, and the other com-

prising all those who are employed in the production
of other things ; and I tell the Hon. Member that
it is utterly impossible for him to prove that the
high price of food ever has been or ever can be of
benefit to the agricultural labourer.

What has been the result of the inquiry into the
operation of the old Poor Law? Why, that the
Commissioners were able to trace all the pauperism
under which the country then suffered to the high
price of provisions and the low price of labour,
which in 1830 had reduced the labourer to a state
as degraded as that of the slave, and one in which,
perhaps, he was even less regarded than the slave.
It was the concurrent testimony of every person
employed in the inquiry that in 1795 or 1797,
when the price of provisions rose to a great height,
the farmers first resorted to the plan of paying
the labourers out of the Rates, for the purpose of
escaping the increase of wages that would otherwise
have been rendered necessary on account of the increased prices of food.   From that time to the Peace
the price of provisions was unusually high, and the
condition of the agricultural labourer became far
worse — much worse than it was after prices had
fallen : showing that when the price of provisions is
high the condition of the agricultural labourer is bad.
The result of the high price of provisions is to lower
the price of labour by throwing a larger number of
labourers into the market, while at the same time it
increases the cost of their support.

Another proof that the agricultural labourers are

badly off when the price of provisions is high, may be
found in the fact that it is at that moment that the
employer seeks to extract from them the greatest
amount of labour.   It is known to every one who
resides in the country that whenever the price of
provisions is high, a greater number of labourers are
unemployed and may be obtained on better terms
than at any other time.   I do not state this entirely
on my own authority ; for I shall quote in support
of it the evidence given before a Committee of this
House on the Corn Bill, by a land agent and occupier
of land named Milne :—

I wished to inclose a farm at the latter end of the year 1812
or at the beginning of 1818.   I sent for my bailiff, and told him
that I had inclosed, about twenty-five years ago, a good deal of
land ; that the inclosure at that time cost me 8s. per ell of 37
inches ; that a neighbour of mine, two or three years ago, had
made similar inclosures, which cost him 5s. per ell ; that I
thought he had paid too much, and that I ought to do it cheaper.
The answer I got from my bailiff was,—that provisions were very
high—that the labourers were doing double work—and that, of
course, there was less demand for labour ; and that he could do
these inclosures last year at a cheaper rate than I had ever done
them ; and he actually executed this inclosure at about 2s. 6d.
per ell.   He again came to me, and told me that I had proposed
to him to do some ditching and draining upon another farm,
which I did not intend to do till about a twelvemonth after, from
the circumstance of not being in full possession of the whole
farm.   He requested that I would allow him to do it that
season, as he could do it so much cheaper, and that a great many
labourers were idle from having little work, in consequence of
those employed doing double work.   I desired him to go on with
that labour likewise, and he actually contracted for very large
ditches, at 6d. an ell,—which I do not think I could do now
under from 1s. to 1s. 6d., in consequence of the fall in provisions.

From inquiries that I have made in different places I can assert that this evidence corresponds with the fact.

It is said that this is a labourer's question, and that if the Corn Laws are repealed a great number of labourers will be thrown out of employment : the assertion seems to imply that the Corn Laws are necessary for retaining agricultural labourers in constant employment. I venture to say that the Corn Laws have not that effect ; they do not secure the employment of agricultural labourers ; and it is quite accidental, as experience proves, what number of labourers is employed under the present system. It has been a constant complaint in various parishes that there is a redundance of labourers. Since the Unions have been formed 6,000 persons have been assisted to go into the manufacturing districts, and upwards of 6,000 have voluntarily gone there, and have been doing well. Besides this there has been a constant emigration of labourers to the North American colonies.

Neither have the Corn Laws rendered them content ; so far from it that since the Corn Laws have been in operation, agricultural labourers have been more dissatisfied than before. In the year 1830, the Corn Laws had been fifteen years in operation, and at no period have the labourers of this country been in a state of greater dissatisfaction and wretchedness. If the principle that Corn Laws ought to be maintained because they give occupation to the labourers be good, why, let me ask, are not the advantages of the threshing machine foregone to produce the same effect? Where is there an instance of the use of machinery having been given up on this ground? And why should the land be cultivated merely for the sake of giving employment to agricultural labourers? So much, then, for the Protection afforded by these Laws to the agricultural labourer.

I have a statement to read to the House showing what has been the value of the wages of all of the other productive classes under different prices of provisions. I have selected two years previous and two years subsequent to the coming into operation of the present Corn Laws. In 1822 the average price of wheat was 43s., and a labourer receiving 31s. 6d. per week was enabled to command 23 pecks of wheat. In 1828, when wheat was at 60s., the wages amounted to 34s., and 18 pecks only could be procured. The hand-loom weaver could command 6½ pecks when wheat was at 43s.; when it was at 60s. he could command only 3½ pecks. The cotton-spinner at Manchester could command under the cheap price 16 and under the dear price 14 pecks. The stocking-maker of Leicester could command 8 pecks in the cheap year but 4½ only in the dear year. The labourer could procure 7½ pecks when the price was 43s. and only 4½ pecks when it was 60s. The wages of the printer, compositor, and persons of that class, did not vary much, and were at an average of 36s. per week; while wheat was at 43s. they could procure as much as 27 pecks, but when it was 60s. they could not procure more than 19 pecks. Since the present Corn Laws were passed the average price of wheat was in

1831, 66s.; in 1835 it was 39s. The cotton-spinners in
the dear year were enabled to command 15 pecks; and
in the cheap year 23 pecks. When the price of wheat
was 66s. the poor hand-loom weaver was able to command only 2 pecks of wheat; while the price averaged
39s., he was enabled to command 4 pecks. The
cotton-spinners at Manchester received 30s. per week,
and could obtain 14½ pecks; the stocking-makers at
Leicester when they had 7s. per week could obtain
3 pecks; and when in the dear season they received
8s. they could obtain 4½ pecks. The labourer obtained
when wheat was 66s., 4 pecks; and when 39s., 6 pecks.
The printer when it was 66s. obtained 17, and when
at 39s., he obtained 28.

And this is the practical result of the Laws that
give Protection to productive industry, and by maintaining the high price of provisions place the working
classes in a better position!

But what is to be said for such Laws when
their indirect effect on the manufacturing classes
is considered? What is the ground on which
Protection is claimed under them according to the
author of the Amendment? It is that the productive classes are not able to compete with the
cheap and light-taxed living of other countries.
This is the very case of the artisans and the manufacturers : they say that they cannot compete with
the cheaper living and lighter taxed artisans of the
Continent ; and they ask for the Protection of cheap
living here in order that they may compete with their
foreign neighbours. They are employed by a foreign

employer who cares not by whom he gets his work done—whether by English, Italians, Swiss, or Belgians, provided he can procure it at the cheapest rate; and he finds that the artisans of Belgium and Switzerland can produce their work cheaper than those of England, because the cost of their living is less; therefore he chooses to employ the inhabitants of those countries; and therefore it is that Englishmen ask to be put upon as good a footing as the foreigner.

There is a difference, however, between the Protection claimed by our artisans and the Protection that the supporters of the Corn Laws claim; the artisans do not ask for a law to make food cheap, but the repeal of the Laws that make food dear. The manufacturer says that he cannot compete with the foreign workman because his food is taxed. I ask whether this is justice to the English manufacturer. The difference between his circumstances and those of the foreigner is this: the Englishman is obliged to pay dearly for his food while the foreigner can get his cheap; and his difficulty lies in competing with the foreigner who can live cheaply. Now you claim the Protection of your interest because you say that you cannot compete with the foreign grower who is so lightly taxed. What pretext, I would ask, is there for your Protection that is not as good for the Protection of the manufacturers?

I will not refer again to those details of foreign competition that I mentioned on a former occasion, because it seemed to be admitted that this competition did exist and must continue. But every year the

English manufacturer is called upon to produce the article that he has been in the habit of producing at a lower cost than he ever produced it before ; and the merchant factor who receives orders from the foreigner, receives also directions that if he cannot execute the orders at a certain price he is not to execute them.   So that he has no alternative but to execute them at a lower price or not to execute them at all; and, consequently, he is constantly obliged to tell his workmen that they must work at lower wages or not work at all.

Well, this has been going on now for five or six years in this country; and it has had the effect of throwing many of our artisans out of employment. The House will see that such a state of things must continue to exist so long as the circumstances of the country as compared with those of foreign nations, remain unaltered ; and I want to know whether you can expect us to be able to compete with foreign manufacturers whilst they can produce articles at a cheaper rate, in consequence of cheaper living, than we can.   I am aware that it has been urged against me by some persons in support of the Corn Laws that we must not depend upon Foreign but upon Home Trade.   I do not deny that the Home Trade is beneficial : this indeed is my case; for I say that the home consumer should be put in the best possible condition; but the home consumers are not the landlords only but all others, and the cheaper the people can procure their means of subsistence the more they will have to spend in manufactured goods ; by the Corn Laws, however, you are diminishing the means of the home consumer for the benefit of the landlord alone.

It has not been usual in discussing this subject to put the case of the labourers prominently forward ; and it is perhaps new to this Session to hear that this is a labourers' question.

It is another class whose claims for Protection have generally been put forward as a defence of the Corn Laws ; the claims of what is called the British farmer, the English grower. Now I really hope that the case of the farmers will receive the fullest consideration because I feel assured that this very valuable class of men is under a considerable delusion on the subject of the Corn Laws; but I am aware also that their attention has been called to it, and I think that they will attend to this discussion of the question with advantage. They will expect something more than vague declamations of their importance, or exaggerated statements of their distress. They are to hear, it seems, from one side that the Corn Laws have protected their interests; but they will also hear from the other side that the Corn Laws have not shielded their interests, but, on the contrary, that they have in fact occasioned their distress. I wish indeed that the whole question turned upon this part of the subject —I mean the interests of the farmers; because this is the only plausible plea, it appears to me, that has been advanced in favour of the existing system.

I am very anxious not to be in error in anything I may say in reference to this part of the question ; and I hope that I shall be corrected should I

make any mistake in my statements. I want to
know whether the farmer can be considered in any
other light than that of a person who having a
certain property wishes to employ it as capital in the
cultivation of land; and whether he does not proceed
to business with the same spirit and purpose with
which any person might hire a vessel of the owner,
or borrow money, or engage in any other commercial
transaction. He is a capitalist and he proceeds in a
commercial spirit. Can there then be any doubt that
the price at which he is able to obtain his land must
be determined by the value of the produce of the land
and the competition of other capitalists? Those
capitalists who are in the same trade will not allow
him to obtain more than the average rate of profit;
and, on the other hand, the land-owners will not permit
him to procure his land at less than the market rate.
Therefore, if a law were passed professing to fix the
produce of the land at 84s. or 64s., it will not be
denied, I suppose, that the capitalist taking land would
reckon the value of his returns in accordance with
the fixed legal price.

But it is said that there are certain local charges
and burdens that press heavily on the farmer; and
that it is in respect of these that Protection may
justly be claimed. These charges however do not
arise after the occupation of the land. They are in
existence beforehand; they are precisely estimated
and are as well known as those that are incident
to the occupancy of a house. If a man has not the
capital to occupy the land and to pay the charges that

would in the course of things arise, what business has he to undertake to occupy it? If he takes the land with all these charges upon it, if the charges are high and the value of the produce is high, a larger amount of capital is required than otherwise would be. This appears to be so evident that it will not perhaps be disputed; but then it is said that these charges place our agriculturists under much disadvantage compared with the foreign agriculturist; and all the time it is the very mode in which the farmer is supposed to be indemnified that renders the payment of them more onerous. I have no hesitation in asserting that the manner in which the farmers have been indemnified, as it is called, for these local charges has had the precise effect of enhancing them. Look at the outgoings of the farmer: with the exception of rent there is scarcely one that is not increased by the high price of provisions. Look at the County Rate, the Poor Rate, the taxes on servants, the taxes on horses, the assessed taxes: which of these is not increased by adding to the cost of provisions? If these local charges are too high for him, his business is to go to the person from whom he took the farm and to procure an abatement in his rent: it is clear that he has no interest in the outgoings being higher than is necessary.

But perhaps it will be argued to-night that it is very true that the farmer has no interest in high outgoings, but that somehow or other through the bounty of heaven or the munificence of landlords, the farmers of this country have done well since the Corn Laws were passed; and that it would be a thousand pities to disturb what appears to work so well. If this has been the case it would not be difficult to characterize the statements that have been made about every other Session on the subject, by Members who have been in the habit of declaring their inability to express in adequate language the sufferings of the farmers!

A Noble Duke whose friendship to the farmers is well known, has frequently brought forward the question and commenced his remarks by saying that he regretted that he had to detail again the same sad story that he had so often repeated. A year after the Corn Bill had passed, the Board of Agriculture reported that 'the present deplorable state of the national agriculture, bankruptcies, seizures, executions for debt, imprisonment, and farmers becoming parish paupers, are matters particularly mentioned by many of the correspondents. There are great arrears of rent, and, in many cases, tithes and poor rates unpaid; improvements of every kind generally discontinued; live stock greatly lessened; tradesmen's bills unpaid; general pauperism in the agricultural districts: these circumstances are expressed in language denoting extreme distress.' Within twenty years five Committees have sat on what was termed the 'unparalleled distress of agriculture.'

I have looked into some of the Reports that have been made and I find that only about four or five years after the Corn Laws passed, an inquiry was instituted into the sufferings of the agriculturists; and if I collect anything from this cir-

cumstance it is that these distresses were produced
by the Corn Laws themselves. The Corn Laws
were denounced in these Reports as delusive in
principle and calculated to ruin every one connected
with the trade in grain. In 1826 the law was not
altered, and again there was distress. In 1828 the
law was altered, but the same principle was maintained in the Corn Laws of 1828 that had existed in the
previous Laws. In 1833 and 1836 complaints were
again made to this House and a Committee again sat
upon the subject. On looking through this inquiry
I find many details and much evidence of the sufferings of the farmers; and although it may be seen that
leading questions were put as if to invite evidence
upon the subject of distress, yet the statements that
were made before the Committee corresponded with
those that had been made out of the House.

I was anxious to ascertain whether any great
land-owner was called to say whether he was suffering from distress; I looked in vain for any such
evidence. It has indeed been said that the farmers
have been compelled to pay their rents out of
their capital; but I see no evidence of the landlords reducing their establishments, their horses, or
their dogs, or of their quitting the country before the
usual season.

My conclusion from these circumstances is that
the promises made by the Corn Laws have been
delusive as regards the farmer, and that they have
caused the distresses that have occasioned these inquiries. The Corn Laws proposed to fix a price

that was to be remunerative. In 1815, Parliament told the farmer that he should have 80s. for his wheat; and the farmer trusting to the promises of the House of Commons arranged to pay rent with reference to that price. But how far did the law realize the expectations it had raised? Four years after this price had been fixed it was reduced to 37s.; but the farmer had already contracted with his landlord; and therefore he found himself in distress and compelled to pay the rent out of his capital: and then the landlord in full receipt of his rent comes to this House to detail the distress of his tenant and gets a Committee to collect evidence of what we already know.

This, incontestably, is the history of most of these Committees of Inquiry. I say, then, that the same principle that was adopted in the old Laws is preserved in those now existing. Under the old Laws the promised price was 80s.; it is now 64s.; the Act of 1828 promised that 64s. per quarter should be the price; and I find that amongst the witnesses before the Committee of the House of Lords in 1836 there was one farmer who declared that if the farmers had been aware of what would happen they never would have entered into the engagements they had made. They expected that the price of produce would have been maintained, and they had taken their farms in 1828 upon that understanding; but in 1832 and 1833 they found that wheat had fallen from 30 to 40 per cent.: they were therefore unable to meet their engagements; and then their ruin began.

Such are the consequences of this system : the farmer incurs expenses and has large outgoings all calculated upon a certain price being returned for his produce ; he finds himself paying rent according to the price that had been promised but not receiving the price. The House of Commons professes to regulate the price ; but this they cannot do unless they also limit the quantities, which they dare not do. The attempt to combine the two only ruins the farmer and angers the people. You tantalize the people with food under their face at half the price, which they are forbidden to touch ; and you encourage the farmer to believe that foreign corn shall not be introduced. Then comes a bad season in the country, which produces no benefit to the farmer because the quantities are less though the prices are higher than usual, and in the end, a quantity of foreign grain produced at a much less cost than that which has been grown at home, is let in and the farmer finds himself ruined by the fall that takes place in consequence.

If there happen to have been a bad season abroad as there has been at home, then the farmer hears the Laws denounced by the people in every town and city; and he knows not what engagements to make from the uncertainty of what may occur. And this is the man for whose benefit it is said that the Corn Laws were enacted ! The man who only cares to know how he stands, that he may get a steady demand for his produce, and ascertain what terms he should make with the owner of the land ! One year he procures 120s. for his corn amidst the curses of the people ; the next it will probably be sold at 37s., through the intervention of the sheriff who has seized it. And yet the maintenance of the Laws is said above everything to be important for securing a steadiness of price !

Within the last four years we find a fluctuation of 100 per cent. in the price of corn. And the system of the Corn Laws is maintained in face of all this ; and in spite of the experience gained during the period between 1773 to 1791 when the ports were open upon paying a nominal duty of 6d.: then there was more agricultural improvement going on, more general contentment, less complaint of distress, and less fluctuation than had existed at any other time ; and this was the result of opening the ports.

I really pity the farmer as one of the industrious and productive classes who wastes his labour in fruitless efforts. He is a man of peculiar habits and feelings, and I cannot help believing that he has been practised upon in the passing of these Laws— that he is in fact the victim of the Corn Laws. He is strongly attached to the soil on which he was born and which his forefathers dwelt on; he is a man of little education; he is not what is usually termed a man of business; he is unable to engage in any other occupation than that to which he was brought up; he is averse to leave the place in which he was bred; he is apt to make contracts that are not justified by prudence; and he is willing to agree to any terms that the landlord proposes. The landlord is aware of this ; and then begins that dreadful struggle in which the farmer anxious to retain his occupation is unable to meet his undertakings. The landlord exacts too much rent; and the tenant, desirous of keeping his word and expecting redress from the Legislature or that things will turn out better—deluded in fine by various circumstances, is constantly undertaking to do that which he cannot do.

I am not speaking without proof; I am almost repeating the statements that the farmers have made upon the subject. I deny that there is any foundation for the argument that the effect of the repeal of the Corn Laws would be to throw the greater part of the land out of cultivation. It is a mere idle tale to talk of much land being thrown out of cultivation when it is known that before the land of the country could go out of cultivation every sixpence of rent must cease. The farmers are now generally in arrears, and, therefore, it is difficult for them freely to express their opinions on the operation of the Corn Laws; but they are every day growing more enlightened respecting their interests, and it will not be long before they will declare themselves opposed to restrictions the sole effect of which is to raise the value of land.

I have dwelt on the probable effect of the repeal of the Corn Laws on the farmer somewhat more at length than the relative importance of this branch of the subject deserves; but I have done so because I feel that of all the grounds of opposition that can be urged against my Motion, this is the one that affords the supporters of the present restrictions the most plausible plea.

I now come to that view of the question which I

conceive to be paramount to all others, because it is
really the only one that ought to be regarded in
any question : namely, the effect of the Corn Laws
on the community at large.   But I must confess that
I approach the consideration of this branch of the
subject with a feeling akin to humiliation.   Is it
in this enlightened age to be made a matter for
doubt and grave argument whether or not it is for
the advantage of the community to have the necessaries of life in abundance, and to be able to obtain
them at the cheapest rate ?   The position is really an
absurd one.   Surely it is as clear as that the sun will
rise !   So clear, indeed, that if the persons interested in
denying this advantage to the people were not a very
powerful class they would be met with ridicule and
contempt for attempting seriously to raise the question !   In fact, were it not for the powerful interest
that one part of the community feels with respect to
this subject and the ignorance of another part, it
would be unnecessary to enter upon the discussion.

The loss sustained by the community from the
existence of the Corn Laws is exactly in proportion to
the loss that the supporters of Monopoly contend they
would suffer if it were put an end to.   If the landed
interest can justly oppose Repeal in order to avert loss
from themselves, the opponents of the Corn Laws are
fully entitled to claim consideration for the equivalent
loss that the community now suffers by reason of
the privation of cheap food.   If the supporters of
the existing Laws oppose Repeal because the effect
would be to lower vastly the price of produce, is not

their opposition a proof that the community are
now sufferers to the extent of the difference between
the present price of produce and that reduced price
the advent of which the landed interest so much
fears ? Taking the calculations of the least sanguine
or prejudiced persons, it appears that at the very
lowest estimate the loss to the community by reason
of the continuance of the Corn Laws amounts to ten
millions a year. This is equal to a poll tax of 8s.
a-head, or a tax of 2l. on each family in the kingdom.
With a large class of labourers it amounts to a
month's labour ; or, taking the number of hours of
labour during the day, on an average, at ten, a tax
of ten millions a year obliges the working-man to
labour three-quarters of an hour each day more than
he would have needed to labour if no such tax on
food existed.

The calculation that I have used applies to the tax
on wheat only ; but the effect of the tax on oats also
must be added to the loss sustained by the labourer,
because in many parts of the country oats are more
in request for general purposes than wheat. It is, moreover, a mere calculation founded upon such data as are
within the reach of the opponents of the Corn Laws ;
but in order to ascertain the full amount of the injury
inflicted on the community by the existence of these
Laws I must first hear the calculation of loss anticipated by the landed interest from their Repeal. The
one will be the best evidence of the other.

I now come to the consideration of the effect of
the Corn Laws on local and general taxation. First as

regards local taxation ; take the Poor Rates.   In the
Poor Law Unions already formed, 8,000*l.* a week is
spent in flour alone.   But if flour be now double
the price it would be if the Corn Laws were repealed, is not the difference between this 8,000*l.* a
week and the reduced price of corn incident on Repeal
just so much taken out of the pocket of the rate-
payer ?   If the Guardians of the poor could put their
hands into the warehouses and take the flour at the
reduced price, would they not save an enormous
amount to the ratepayers ?

The case does not stop here ; because all money
unduly taken from the ratepayers for the maintenance of the poor is so much deducted from the
amount that would be spent in labour.   In any
given district this might be made the subject of strict
calculation ; for instance, in a Poor Law Union.   The
whole amount of the Poor Rate is four millions and
a half ; and therefore looking at the subject pur-
posely in a practical point of view I really do hope
that as Hon. Gentlemen opposite are so anxious to
make this question a labourers' question, they will
also make it a ratepayers' question and consider
the vast amount that might be saved to them in
Poor Rates alone if the Laws were repealed.   I hope
the ratepayers themselves will make it their own question and that when about to pay their rates they will
ask why they are called on to pay such large sums
when by the repeal of the Corn Laws they might get
bread for the poor so much cheaper.

Then as regards the County Rate : 100,000*l.* a

year is expended in feeding the prisoners of the
different bridewells throughout the country ; and
this portion of the County Rate, from which the
landed interest not long since applied to be exempted
and which they succeeded in transferring to another
fund, is nearly doubled in consequence of the high
price of provisions.

The same remark applies likewise to all asylums
for lunatics, to hospitals, schools, and generally to all
public institutions.   It is a most important consideration in the expenditure of such institutions whether
bread is dear or cheap.

But if this argument is forcible as applied to
local taxation, it becomes far more powerful when
applied to general taxation.   There is scarcely a department of the Public Service in which a reduction
in the price of bread would not be felt.   On the
Army, Navy and Ordnance, eighteen millions a year
are expended.   As regards the Army, the amount
depends on the price of food in an additional respect
—every soldier being guaranteed the repayment of all
that he pays for bread above 6d. a loaf.   It is obvious
that if the Corn Laws were repealed this additional
expense would not fall on the public, because they
would not have to pay more than the 6d. per loaf.

The Miscellaneous Estimates amount to two
millions a year : in this branch of the public expenditure also, a great change would be produced by
the repeal of the Corn Laws.

Now when the immense weight of the burden of
general taxation is considered ; when it is borne in

mind what would be effected for the country by a
reduction of taxation ; when, too, it is recollected
that the great bulk of these taxes is raised from the
consumer, and that seventeen millions accrue from
the Excise alone, what argument of force can be
adduced against the reduction of expenditure by
cheapening the price of bread, accompanied as that
must necessarily be by an increase of commerce ?
There are many imposts that ought to be reduced
or taken off where the claims on the consideration of
the Legislature are very strong. Take the case of
the Post-Horse Duty. The utmost anxiety has been
evinced that this impost should be taken off, because
those who pay it are in the course of being ruined by
the changes brought about by the great improvements
made in the internal communication of the country.
The sufferers by these changes, however, did not,
when they were about to be made, come to the
Legislature for Protection against the locomotive
engines or against the railroads ; but they come now
for relief because they find that the tax presses too
heavily on them. But if the Corn Laws were repealed the keep of their horses would not cost them
what it now does, and so they would be better enabled
to bear what at present almost prevents them from
exercising their trade.

To take another and a greater branch of the
public economy—the Post Office. It has long been
desired to effect a most important alteration in the rates
of postage : one that would afford the public an advantage more to be wished for, perhaps, than any other

that it is in the power of the Legislature to grant.
What is the obstacle to the immediate adoption of this
arrangement ?   The impossibility of withdrawing
from the Revenue the difference that would be
hazarded by the adoption of the new plan. The
amount that might be saved in those branches of
the public expenditure to which I have referred
would in all probability enable the Government to
consult the wishes and interests of the public in
regard to the transmission of letters at a low and
uniform rate. Do the opponents of Repeal imagine that
the people do not observe these inconsistencies ?   Do
Hon. Gentlemen suppose that now that the attention
of the public is aroused, calculations are not made
of the amount paid for the public service over and
above what would be necessary under a system of
non-restriction ?   Is it supposed that the public disregard these matters ; that they are not growing
discontented with a state of things that while it
much increases the taxation of the country, deprives
them at the same time of advantages which they
might enjoy under a better system ?

    To turn also to the effect of these restrictive
Laws on the Shipping Interest. If any Hon. Members connected with that interest are present, they
will be able to inform the House with more detail
than I can command, what are the injuries inflicted
on the Shipping Interest by the existence of the
Corn Laws. For my own part, I believe that one of
the most striking arguments in favour of Repeal
is founded upon the grievances of the Shipping

Interest. They suffer not only from the increased cost of provisions for their ships, but also from the loss of the useful business of conveying the foreign grain which under a different state of things would be consumed in this country.

An illustration of these evils came under my notice a short time since when I was in Hamburg. I there saw ships loaded with flour, the provisions for which had been purchased at from 40 to 50 per cent. less than the English merchants could have purchased them at home. And whither does the House think that those ships were bound ? They were actually conveying to our own colonies—to Newfoundland in particular, flour that had been ground at Hamburg ; ground too at mills that were erected there in consequence of the rejection of the measure introduced by the Hon. Member for Dartmouth to facilitate the grinding of corn in bond here for the purpose of exportation !

And these are Laws for the protection of productive industry ! What would any foreigner think of the intelligence of England if on asking how she contrives to support the weight of so enormous a debt— a debt larger than the debts of all other civilized nations put together, the debt of the East India Company included—he were to be told that the only way in which we can bear the existing burdens of the country is by proposing and maintaining another burden of still greater magnitude ? Yet such is substantially the argument of those who plead that the maintenance of the Corn Laws is necessary in order to enable us

to collect the interest of the National Debt. Their
position clearly is this : ' We have already two great
burdens on the country—the National Debt and
the expenditure necessary for the Public Service.
And the only way in which we can support them
is by protecting the landed aristocracy and maintaining the restrictions on the importation of corn,
which keep prices high.' But is it a safe, just, or
honest principle of legislation, to limit the resources
of the nation in order to afford an exclusive advantage to a particular class? The Corn Laws may rob
A to benefit B ; but they do not create wealth ; they
do not benefit the public generally. And when it is
borne in mind that in order to afford the exclusive
Protection to one class, we are ruining the manufacturers and contracting the commerce of the country,
it is surely time for the Legislature to interpose and
to consider whether the danger and national loss that
would accrue from the contraction of the commerce of
the country would not be much greater than any that
could possibly arise out of a Repeal of the Corn Laws.

How could we meet our national engagements,
and support the public burdens ; how could the
credit of the country be maintained were it not for
our Foreign Trade? By our Foreign Trade we were
enabled to support the expense of the long wars that
gave rise to this debt ; by our Foreign Trade we
were enabled to maintain the public credit under the
burdens that this debt imposed upon us ; and it
will be by facilitating and extending our Foreign
Trade that we shall ultimately, if ever, be enabled

to clear ourselves from this debt. The maintenance
and increase of the commerce of the country then
ought to supersede all other considerations. How are
the twenty-two millions collected from the Customs,
if not through the employment of the capital of the
manufacturer? Do we export the produce of the
soil? How, then, are the imports got, if not by
reason of the exported manufactures? Yet the
landed interest, and those who support the existing Corn Laws, are endeavouring to undermine our
commerce !

For my own part, I believe that but for the
restrictions that the Corn Laws have imposed on the
commercial activity of the country, we should have
been almost able to discharge our public debt, and to
have indefinitely extended our commerce.

It required such a scheme as the Corn Laws to
give a check to our career of commercial prosperity ;
and the promoters of them have fully effected this
disaster. They have lowered the price of labour ;
they have reduced food in particular countries to
a mere drug in the market, while they have raised
the price of it at home ; and thus they have offered
a premium to foreigners to engage their capital in
manufactures. If they persevere in this course the
evils will continue, and the capital and the artisans
of the country will be yearly leaving it in larger
amount and greater numbers than they now are.
On the other hand, I am satisfied that if the Laws
were repealed, the progress of the existing evils
would be arrested; English capital would be pre-

vented from leaving the country ; and foreign capital
would not be further invested in manufactures abroad,
because the demand from our market for agricultural
produce would give employment to their capital in
agriculture. The price of labour would also be raised
and the foreign manufacturers would no longer have
the advantage of superabundant labour at too cheap
a cost.

One most important consideration in connection
with the present agitation of the question is that
there is now just time to correct the greatest error
into which this or any other country so circumstanced
ever fell : I allude to the fact that the tariffs of the
Zollverein and those of the United States will both
cease in 1841. In that year the States united in
the Zollverein are to reassemble with the view of
determining whether they shall continue united ; and
it will much depend on the arrangements that we may
then be ready to make as to receiving the produce of
those States, how far the tariff to which they shall
then agree will be prejudicial or favourable to our
commerce. If in the meantime we prepare ourselves to take their raw produce—their timber, and
their grain free from restrictions, we shall not only
check the investment of their capital in home manufactures (an operation that is rapidly progressing
under the system of mutual exclusion), but we shall
also gain by their importing our manufactures that
they now exclude.

Again, as regards the United States : our conduct
with respect to the restrictive duties may determine

American capitalists in the course they will adopt—
whether they will invest their capital in agriculture
to supply the demand of our markets, or whether
they will persevere in their home manufactures.
Surely, then, when we consider the enormous advantages that would arise from the establishment of
commercial relations with Europe and the United
States on the solid basis of national interest—advantages which it is almost impossible to exaggerate—
it will be acknowledged that the time has arrived
when the Legislature ought to take into consideration
what steps will secure those advantages, and avert the
injury that our commerce and manufactures must
sustain if the system recently adopted by foreign States
in consequence of our Corn Laws be continued.

A more important object than the extension of
our trade with foreign States cannot, I apprehend,
occupy the attention of the Legislature. It cannot
be denied that it is more reasonable to expect the
preservation of peace, the increase of commerce, and
the prosperity of manufactures, by interesting the
productive classes and capitalists of other countries
in our favour, and by affording them the means of
wealth, than by manning our Navy, or by making
treaties, or forming merely personal alliances with
foreign princes.

I cannot conceive a higher duty for the Minister
who presides over the trade of this country or the
Minister who has the charge of the Foreign Department, than to devote their best attention to the means
of extending our commercial intercourse with other

nations. Such a course would not only have the effect of increasing the national wealth, but it might possibly allay the apprehensions that are now rife lest the peace and security of our foreign possessions should be disturbed.

We are constantly alarmed by intimations that the Northern powers are opposed to our interests and policy. Now, it would be impossible to have a better opportunity than the present for conciliating Prussia. If we were in a situation to offer to that power the establishment of commercial intercourse on the basis of non-restriction, the Prussian Government could no more resist the will of their people when they request to be allowed the advantages that we should offer them, than the general Government of the United States was able to bend the inhabitants of South Carolina to the adoption of their tariff.

Perfect freedom to all men to exchange their industry wherever they can get the utmost of what they desire in return, is the best possible security for the preservation of permanent peace. The acceptance of this principle would be a great mark of that advanced civilization to which all men are looking forward ; resistance to it will prove us to be still under the dominion of the unreflecting selfishness that, in all ages, has marred the various stages of human progress.

I have at last arrived at the least satisfactory portion of the question : the obstacles existing in this country to the adoption of a wise course of policy. Though it be not whispered in this House or even surmised in another place, it is nevertheless a fact that, wherever persons not directly interested in the maintenance of the Monopoly are assembled, it is broadly and openly stated that the landholders of this country are the persons who are opposed to Repeal ; that they are in possession of the Legislature, in which their authority is unchecked and uncontrolled ; that they believe themselves to have a direct interest in the maintenance of the Corn Laws ; and that nothing but actual fear will induce them to consent to Repeal.

We cannot conceal from ourselves that if the working classes had been less anxious about the shadow than the substance, the Legislature might at the present moment be acting under the most degrading influence to which men who have a public duty to perform can be subject : the influence of fear.

I should be the last to desire that such an influence should be brought to bear on the supporters of the Corn Laws. But in the absence of fear, it is said that the landed interest will only consent to Repeal if they can be shown that they will not be injured by it.

In the meantime, however, the people have an undoubted right to hear distinctly the grounds on which the land-owners of this country are prepared to maintain the Corn Laws. If it be on the ground of the pressure of local taxation, let them submit to an inquiry, and abide the result. If it be the pressure of general taxation, then let them at once say whether they are prepared to give up their Monopoly for a commutation of taxation. Whatever the grounds may be, the public are entitled to claim that they should now be specifically stated.

If the pressure of local taxation is alleged, then I have a point from which I can start ; and I would refer to what fell from one of the most intelligent and, on this subject, one of the best informed of his party—the Right Hon. Baronet the Member for Pembroke. The Right Hon. Baronet on a former occasion stated that his assent to the Protective policy was identified with his concurrence in the policy that left a portion of the local taxation to be borne by the landed aristocracy. Further, in the discussion on the Malt Tax, he said he felt that if the Poor Law continued in operation, and if Tithes were commuted and the expense of county prosecutions were charged on the public funds, there would then be nothing left but the Malt Tax to justify the maintenance and continuance of the Corn Laws ; and that if the Malt Tax were reduced or taken off, the repeal of the Corn Laws might be irresistibly urged on the House of Commons.

These were the sentiments of the Right Hon. Baronet. I presume, therefore, that I am justified in contending that they are to be considered as the sentiments of the supporters of the Corn Laws generally ; and hence I conceive that I have a right to infer that the Malt Tax is the only ground on which the continuance of the Corn Laws is justified. For the other conditions named by the Right Hon. Baronet have been severally fulfilled : the Poor Law has

reduced the rates 60 per cent.; the expense of criminal prosecutions has been transferred from the counties to the Consolidated Fund; and the Tithes have
been commuted. Seriously, however, does the Right
Hon. Baronet suppose that the Malt Tax of four
millions and a half, which falls only indirectly on the
landed interest, is any indemnity to the public for the
enormous loss they sustain from the existence of the
Corn Laws? Upon what principle is it that because
the consumer does not consume barley enough to
satisfy the landed interest, we are to tax his bread
in order to enable him to consume more? Was ever
such a principle recognized as this: because there
exists a tax on one thing, there ought to be a tax on
half a dozen others? If any Protection were wanted
on account of the tax on malt, the natural and
corresponding indemnity would be to lay a tax on
foreign barley; not on foreign wheat, oats, or rye.
And is not foreign malt taxed? I have accepted the
statement of the Right Hon. Baronet as being in
accordance with the sentiments of the party of which
he is so distinguished a member, not thinking it necessary to pay much heed to the arguments or assertions of others who know less of the matter; and,
consequently, I have proceeded on the assumption
that the Malt Tax is the only existing obstacle to the
repeal of the Corn Laws.

Since, then, we have this distinct declaration of
the opinions of the landed interest on the question to
go upon, I ask, would the Monopolists be willing to
relieve the country of the burden of the Corn Laws

if the Malt Tax were taken off ? For of this I am sure, that all those who are now injured by the existence of Monopoly would be ready, nay, anxious to get rid of it by acceding to those terms. The produce of the Malt Tax would be lost to the Revenue no doubt ; but I am perfectly satisfied that the public credit would not be endangered by such fetters on the industry and commerce of the country being removed. Four millions and a half are a small sum indeed compared with what might be raised through the medium of taxation if the energy of the country were allowed its full and natural play.

If the landed interest are not prepared to agree to this compromise, then it is their bounden duty at once to declare on what terms they are disposed to give up the Monopoly they enjoy through the effect of the Corn Laws.

I cannot conceive any compromise to be politic in this case, save that of compensation or the commutation of taxes. The question, however, is : Are the Monopolists entitled to either ? Do they expect compensation like the slave-owners ? Or do they complain that they are unfairly taxed ? Whatever may be their right, it is the interest of the country to concede it. Feeling as I do that no interest ever required Protection until it was unable to support itself, my objection to the Laws is that they are perpetuating evil to the country. To support and protect such interest at the expense of the public and to the detriment of the community would be to support and protect a positive evil. If there be a question of compensation, let it be at once entered into ; let there be no delay.   If, at present, there really exists any ground of claim, to postpone inquiry would be but to add to the evil.   Twenty years hence such claims will be still stronger ; interests not known now will then have grown into existence.   I do not hesitate to declare my conviction that if the discontinuance of the Monopoly of Corn could be attained by the course, it would be a bargain were the country to purchase every one of the acres that the landed interest have declared would be thrown out of cultivation, and were we to support at the public expense every labourer who it is said would be thrown out of employment by Repeal.

But I would venture to suggest to Hon. Gentle-men opposite that it is treading on somewhat delicate ground for them to plead exclusive taxation as a reason for the maintenance of the Corn Laws ; because if an inquiry were gone into as to whether they are more or less taxed than other classes, it would raise the question of what exemptions from taxation they now have.   I will state one fact alone to show the sort of inquiry you would subject yourselves to : 50,000,000*l.* have been paid out of personal property since the imposition of the Probate and Legacy Duty, not one sixpence of which has been borne by the landed interest.   Thirteen millions have been paid under similar circumstances on other taxes in which the landed interest bore no share.   I have a list of duties, including those on horses, servants, the auction duty, and other duties, from the payment of all of which the landed interest are

free ; and this, it appears to me, is a great injustice to the rest of the community. When also we
consider (and I think that we are bound to consider
it as being matter of great importance) that the
principle of Protection or Prohibition applies to the
importation into this country of all articles of animal
food (for the importation of beef, mutton, and other
raw animal produce is actually prohibited), the House
will, I presume, agree with me that there is a very large
balance not on the side of the landed interest.

It is not my business to inquire what would be
the probable extent to which the landlords would
suffer from the reduction of rents by the repeal of
the Corn Laws ; for when I learn the enormous
losses to which the community at large is exposed
by their continuance it is my care not to let a single
hour elapse without seeking to stop that loss.

But the landlords must know that great exagge-
rations are put forth as to the effect that the importation of foreign wheat would have on prices in the
English market. I have made inquiries as to the price
at which wheat could be imported if the ports were
opened. I have learned that in the Channel Islands
they export all their agricultural produce ; and that
all the wheat and other corn they consume they import from the Baltic. I find that the difference
between the price of produce in this country and in
the Channel Islands varied in eighteen years about
30 per cent. This difference decreased in proportion
as this country imported wheat from the Continent.

But if it should only be a difference of 30 per

cent. in the price of grain when it is imported free into Guernsey, as compared with what it is sold for here, why is the community here to pay that 30 per cent. ? And can it be thought that people will continue to do so when this question is thoroughly understood ? Is it in keeping with the state of things in the present day for the public to submit to any impost of this kind unless assured of its necessity ? I ask the landlords of this country whether really they see no 'signs of the times' that should make them pause before they determine to uphold a system that is opposed by the industry, the commerce, the intelligence, and the masses of the country, and that they cannot, beyond a limited time, be expected to retain ? Can they blind themselves to the fact that the people who now are chiefly demanding the repeal of the Corn Laws are those who have hitherto placed confidence in the present Legislature, and who have relied on its adequacy to redress the wrongs and reform the abuses of which they complain ? And can they suppose that the people are so weak in purpose or so meek in mind that they will sit down quietly under disappointment and rebuff; or that they will be diverted by the obvious reflection that they have misplaced their confidence in this House ; or that in vindication of their opinion and under a sense of wrong they will not call for those changes in the Constitution that will place it more in unison with their interests ?

Surely, then, it is a matter of serious consideration for the land-owners to determine whether they will, for the paltry profit which the Corn Laws afford them, forfeit the respect and esteem of large classes of their fellow-subjects, and place in jeopardy the great social and political position that, though accident has conferred it upon them, it is yet in their power by their conduct to confirm and maintain. I must say that if after all that has been said on this subject, and after all the important consequences that have been traced to these Laws, the land-owners should now refuse to consider them, they will be taking a step the importance and responsibility of which they cannot appreciate.

I conclude by moving : That the House resolve itself into a Committee of the whole House to take into consideration the Act 9 Geo. IV. c. 60, regulating the importation of foreign grain.

IV.

HOUSE OF COMMONS, July 9, 1839.

On account of the mischievous effects of the Protective Duties on
foreign timber, Mr. Villiers, July 9, 1839, presented a petition from
Wolverhampton for their repeal, and moved for a Committee of the whole
House to consider the duties levied on foreign and colonial timber.   Mr.
Poulett Thompson, then President of the Board of Trade, said that, ' looking over the whole customs of the country—or, indeed, of any country—he
did not believe that any other article would be found to which such an exaggerated Protection was applied as that applied to timber ; ' he concurred
generally in the opinions and statements of Mr. Villiers, expressed his sense
of the necessity of drawing public attention to the very important subject,
and his special satisfaction that Mr. Villiers had brought it under the consideration of the House ; and then dwelling with regret on the apathy of
Parliament to questions of the kind, he stated his belief that so long as
such apathy existed it would be idle for him to introduce a measure dealing
with them, and that under existing circumstances it would be useless to
press the Motion to a division. After a short debate Mr. Villiers, in reply—
having stated that had he considered the taste and feeling of the House to
be identified with the interests and wishes of the country, he should not
have obtruded his Motion on their attention, and that he brought it forward for discussion believing that by repeated discussion only the country
would be brought to see the great interest it had in the alteration of the
existing system—said that in the present state of the House he did not
think it advisable to press his Motion to a division.

In seeking to draw the attention of the House to the
subject on which I have given notice of a Motion, I
am aware of the disadvantages under which I labour.
I know the distaste that the House has for matters
of this nature ; and I know how difficult it is at
the present season to win serious attention to any
question of public importance.

Still, as the subject is a momentous one, and as I

am constantly reminded by those who placed me here
of the mischievous effects of restrictions upon industry and commerce, I feel it a duty to submit it to
the attention of this Parliament.

And, moreover, I must claim for it some degree
of opportuneness, since not only are we at this moment
about to review the relations in which we stand to
those provinces in America that are connected with
the trade in timber—in the hope of placing them
upon a footing more suited to the true interests of both
countries than that which they now stand on, but
we are also fresh from hearing a statement from the
Financial Minister by which it appears that we are
in a course of expenditure in excess of our income ;
and the case that I have to submit to this House
is one in which the resources of the country are,
perhaps, more prodigally, uselessly, and mischievously
wasted than in any other with which a parallel can
be instituted.   I believe that as regards the correctness of this view, there is more unanimity of opinion
than in any other in which particular interests are
opposed to public good.

Indeed, the question of the policy of these duties
has been decided.   They have been condemned by
every Administration that this country has had
for twelve years past ; they have been pointed at
by every independent politician ; and even that last
expedient has been resorted to with regard to
them by those who are beaten in fact and argument : namely, a Select Committee to inquire into
facts already known, which has been attended with

the usual result of eliciting further facts in confirmation of the mischiefs alleged.

The story of these duties was told in this House
about eight years since. It is fortunately a short
one, and I will now only repeat it with the utmost
brevity.

I need not, perhaps, tell the House that this article
of necessary consumption is not produced in the
United Kingdom in quantities sufficient for the demand, and that the deficiency equals about 1,200,000
loads of timber annually. The countries that supply
us with timber are those in the North of Europe and
those in the North of America; but whilst the wood
imported from the North of Europe is good and cheap,
that from the North of America is inferior and dear.

The House has now to learn in what proportions
the timber so characterized is imported into this
country. It is as follows: three-fifths of the timber
are from the country where it is bad and dear; and
two-fifths, or somewhat less, from the country where
it is good and cheap.

A stranger to our policy, it seems to me, would
naturally ask by what contrivance it is that we
are induced to act in a manner so opposed to the
usual dealings of sane men. The answer to such a
question is that the Legislature causes a duty of 55s.
a load to be laid upon the good timber and one of
only 10s. upon the bad.

I believe that I am safe in making this statement
respecting the character of the wood that is imported
into this country; for those who would maintain

the duties do not, if I understand them, dispute it ; they do not contend that the community is as well supplied from Canada as from Europe ; but they say : ' Do not alter the duties, lest every consumer of timber in England should resort to the European market, where he would get the article the cheapest and the best.' But, not to allow anything to depend upon bare assertion, I will read a short extract from the Report of the House of Lords on the subject, which, I presume, will be received as an authority. The Report says :—

North American timber is more soft, less durable, and every description of it more liable to the dry rot, than timber from the North of Europe. Red pine, however, which bears a small proportion to the other description of timber, and the greater part of which, though imported from Canada, is the produce of the United States, is distinguished from the white pine by greater durability. On the whole, it is stated by one of the Commissioners of his Majesty's Navy most distinguished for practical knowledge, experience, and skill, that the Canada timber, both oak and fir, does not possess, for the purpose of ship-building, more than half the durability of wood of the same description, the produce of the North of Europe.

Mr. Copeland, the most extensive builder and timber merchant in London, also said in evidence before that Committee that 'the timber from the Baltic in general,' speaking of Norwegian, Russian, Prussian, and Swedish, ' is of a very superior quality to that imported from America, the bulk of which is very inferior in quality, much softer in its nature, not so durable, and very liable to dry rot.'

This evidence respecting timber, given nearly twenty years since, was confirmed in every particular before the Committee of 1835 ; attached to the Report of which will be found most instructive evidence on the whole subject ; and none more so than that given by the Honourable Member for Bridport,[1] who in his testimony has nearly exhausted the question.

But, in case any doubt should be cast upon individual opinion, there are corroborating circumstances that must satisfy every one : for instance, Canadian timber is excluded from the dockyards ; and, also, in all building contracts there is special provision that none shall be used. There is one other fact, however, that is more conclusive than any other : for the woods admitting of comparison there are two prices in the same market, the European timber fetching the higher price.

The next point to notice to the House is the pecuniary loss that the use of this inferior timber at high price causes to the country, which it is not difficult to estimate ; for having the different prices in the market we can estimate the loss from quality, and taking the duty from the gross price we learn the difference of price. Now, examining the current prices of the woods of the different countries in the modes in which they are rated and brought to this country, I find that on every load of pine timber we lose 2*l.* 5*s.*; on oak timber in the same proportion ; on every hundred of deals we lose 17*l.*; and on every thousand of staves, which are so much used in this country for packages, staffs, &c., 38*l.* Applying this measure of loss per load to the whole quantity im-

---

[1] Mr. Warburton.

ported from the North American colonies, I reckon the total loss—after deducting about 100,000 loads of yellow pine which we must always get from Canada— to equal the sum of 1,500,000*l.* ; an estimate that will be found to correspond closely with others that have been made.

For instance: Sir Henry Parnell in his work on financial reform, which was published when we imported much less timber than we do now, stated the loss to be probably above 1,000,000*l.*; and a most able and intelligent witness, Mr. Norman, in his evidence before the Committee on Manufactures, Shipping, and Commerce, stated that the trade must have cost the country not less than 30,000,000*l.* in the last twenty years.

I should also mention, perhaps, that, owing to the peculiar mode of adjusting duties on timber in the log and deal, the Revenue further sustains a loss of about 12*s.* a load, without any advantage or convenience to the consumer.

Now, I contend that this sum of 1,500,000*l.* is not a sum that should be taken from the community, unless it be applied to the purposes of revenue, or unless it be shown that the loss is a necessary loss, or that there are countervailing advantages. But it is the peculiar enormity of these special duties that not one sixpence of the sum goes to the Revenue; it is not at all necessary or advisable to continue them ; and not any of the advantages that are pretended to result from them are at all adequate to the evils they entail.

It is, moreover, a peculiarity of the proposed changes in the mode of levying the duty that they can be effected with benefit to the consumer, and without injury, nay, with some advantage to the Revenue; or with some advantage to the consumer, and great benefit to the Revenue—for a given amount of timber will be imported. Whereas a duty such as is now collected cannot in any way be satisfactorily adjusted: so little profitable is it to the Revenue or the consumer as it exists at present.

I own that when I consider that timber is a considerable element in production, and that to all classes of producers, whether manufacturing, agricultural, or the labouring classes, it is of the utmost importance to have it good and cheap, I regret extremely that it should have been deemed a fit subject for taxation at all; but as it has been, the Revenue ought certainly to derive the full benefit of the tax without prejudice to the public.

This subject is one of far more consequence to the labouring classes than it is usually judged; but if we bear in mind the miserable dwellings of many of the labouring classes of this country, and the degrading influence of a wretched dwelling upon every poor man, we shall at once perceive that it is impossible to overrate it.

I have obtained a copy of a Report on the dwellings of some of the poorer classes in a large manufacturing town, which I will just refer to because I believe that it describes their condition in nearly every populous manufacturing town in the kingdom.

It is a Report made of the dwellings of 1,384 families in the borough of Stockport:—

Statement of the number of families dwelling in cellars, and also of the number of families dwelling in single rooms, in Stockport. Extracted from the rate-book, June, 1839.

1839.	REMARKS.
Families dwelling in cellars in Stockport . 1,253	These cellars are mostly without drains, cold, damp, and very dark. The poor families who occupy them are subject to fevers, and often lose their health and cheerfulness, whereby they are unable to get a living. There are instances of two families, and lodgers besides, being huddled together in one cellar.
Families dwelling in single rooms in Stockport . 131	These rooms are seldom more than 12 feet square ; and in that space there are (in some
Families . . 1,384	instances) two families and two lodgers—that is, ten or twelve persons in one room.

I am led to connect this statement with the price of the materials of building, from the account I get of the condition of the poor in countries where timber is cheap. I was much struck by a passage in the work of an intelligent traveller in Norway—Mr. Laing—who observes upon the comfortable dwellings of the peasants, and is led into reflections on our Timber Laws in consequence. He says :—

This population, also, is much better lodged than our labouring and middling classes, even in the South of Scotland. The dwelling-houses of the meanest labourers are divided into several apartments, have wooden floors, and a sufficient number of good windows; also, some kind of outhouse for cattle and lumber. Every man, indeed, seems, like Robinson Crusoe, to have put up a separate house for everything he possesses. Whoever has observed the condition of our labouring population, will admit the influence of good habitations upon the moral habits of a people. The natives of New Zealand have dwellings more suited to the feelings and decencies of civilized life than the peasantry of a great proportion of Great Britain and Ireland, who live in dark, one-room hovels, in which not only household comfort and cleanliness are out of the question, but the proper separation of the sexes can scarcely be maintained. It is from the operation of our Timber Duties that the working class in Great Britain, and particularly in Scotland and Ireland, is so wretchedly lodged— an evil by which the whole community suffers. The timber of America is not adapted, either in size, strength, durability, or price, for the woodwork of small houses; for the beams, roof timbers, or other parts in which there is strain or exposure, it is considered totally unfit; and were it stronger, the waste in reducing its logs to the proper dimensions prevents the application of it to such small buildings. The duty upon the kind of wood alone suitable for the poor man's habitation—which is the small-sized logs, deals, and battens of Norway or the Baltic coast— renders it impossible for the lower, or even the middle classes, to lodge themselves comfortably, or even decently. It affects the price, not merely of the good building material which these countries could furnish at a cost lower than the duty now levied upon it; but it raises our own wood, which no prudent man can use in any work that is intended to last for twenty years. If our labouring classes understood their own interest, they would find that the Timber Duties press more heavily upon their comfort and well-being than even the Corn Laws.

And now, having traced the evil effects of these duties upon this country, I come to the question, What excuse is there for their continuance? I am, of course, prepared to hear those old watchwords of Monopoly—Ships and Colonies—started again upon this occasion, and to be told the old story that the British Navy depends upon her Commercial Marine;

that this particular Monopoly looks to the colonies, and that the colonies are the natural customers of the manufacturers ; that without the continuance of this and other monopolies they could not purchase our manufactures.   And seeing the success with which these silly fallacies have been urged hitherto, I should shrink from attempting to battle with them, if I did not daily observe the advantage of discussion ; and if, moreover, I did not believe that by means of discussion the truth will prevail.

After having given a careful attention to all the information that can be obtained on this subject, I must say that there is not any point on which I would speak with more confidence than that the British Navy is in no way dependent for its efficiency upon that part of the Mercantile Marine that is employed in the Timber Trade ; and with respect to the colonies, that their prosperity has been greatly deferred, and that they have been seriously injured in being tempted, by means of these duties, to divert their capital and industry from their more natural channels of employment in order to devote them to the most hazardous, gambling, and demoralizing business in which they could have engaged.

In examining the evidence before the Committee already alluded to I find that some witnesses, who from their local acquaintance with our North American Colonies seem to have been thoroughly competent to speak on the subject, and who also were unbiassed by any local interest, have given important evidence to this effect: I allude particularly to Mr. M'Gregor

and Mr. Revans. They state that the colonies
have ample resources to enable them to support
their trade with other countries ; and that nothing
but the bounty that we have placed upon their
timber has prevented them from giving to those
resources a more ample development. Many products
are enumerated for which each seems to have its
appropriate section in British America. Canada has
its agriculture; Newfoundland its fisheries; Nova
Scotia its mines ; while New Brunswick would by
this time, probably, have become one of the finest
grazing countries in the world, but for the seduction
of the timber bounty which has left it now to depend
for its resources on British America. And it is urged,
with some force, that unless these colonies had other
resources than the Timber Trade it would be a species
of fraud practised upon emigrants to tempt them to
settle as agriculturists.

But it appears that the colonies are far from
depending upon the Timber Trade alone for the purchase of imports. In Canada, for instance, the imports amount to 1,500,000*l.*, of which not more than
450,000*l.* can be paid for in timber : the rest being
paid for by the expenditure of our Government and
that of emigrants who bring out money with them,
and by products other than timber.

It is stated that this trade is a hazardous and
gambling one. Some of the risks of it are pointed
out in the evidence given before the Committee. For
example, the fluctuations in price here are upon the
whole price of timber; but any variation of price

must, in fact, fall upon the original cost of the timber,
which makes the speculation in every consignment
much more precarious.   In Newfoundland no timber
is exported ; and in Nova Scotia it is the least item
of her exports.   New Brunswick seems to be the province most interested in the Timber Trade ; and this
is chiefly on account of its greater proximity to the
mother country ; but it is the misfortune of the
colony that it is so.   There is also great hazard
attending the floating of the timber down the river
to the ports of shipment ; so great indeed that the
general belief in Canada is that one-third of this
timber is lost before it reaches port.   This of course
enhances the value of the cargo that reaches its destination in safety ; and this is the sort of prize that tempts
many to venture their capital in the lottery ; but
though some realize fortunes in it, it is the ruin of
hundreds of others who engage in the Timber Trade.

Now, with respect to the influence that this
employment and its accompanying circumstances
exercise over the character of the people engaged as
lumberers, there appears to be but little difference
of opinion.   I can conceive no greater nuisance to
a well ordered community than to have periodical
visitations of such people as the lumberers are described to be.   They go in bodies, and live in the
woods together ; they are not subject to any of the
social influences of civil life ; and perpetually yielding
to the greatest temptation to the use of ardent spirits,
their constitutions are impaired, and they become reckless in their morals and habits.

It is another fact, I believe, also no longer in dispute, that the business of lumbering offers no advantage or employment to the emigrant on his first arrival : besides being unskilled in felling the wood, his object is to settle as an agriculturist. And, in truth, the Timber Trade affords employment to those only who going out without any means of their own, succeed in finding work in some of the lumbering establishments about the ports. But, as most of the emigrants leave this country because people have not the means of employing them here, what policy is it that should tax this country 1,500,000l. in order to find them employment across the Atlantic? It would be far better for the people to keep their money in their own pockets.

Is it not idle, moreover, to talk of people being destitute of other employment in Canada, and of the necessity of establishing this Monopoly for the purpose of affording it ? Why, the future well-being of the colony depends upon a constant tide of emigrants flowing in from this country and occupying the land; and, as it might be expected, evidence was given before the Committee of the demand for labour existing in Canada. It was also stated that all the more recent and flourishing settlements in Upper Canada are quite independent of the Timber Trade. In short, so clear is it that the prospects of these colonies are not increased by the Timber Trade, that gross injustice is seen to be inflicted by it ; and therefore what remains to be done is, to ascertain how to get rid of the Monopoly with as little injury as possible to the capital vested in the Trade.

The more this part of the question is examined, the greater are the facilities for solving it that present themselves ; for fortunately there is, as it were, a trade in wood springing up with the United States ; and the forests in the States of New York and Vermont are now so much cleared that it is better economy for those States to import wood from Canada than to resort to their own forests. This gives employment to some of the principal saw-mills in that province, which is the most valuable kind of capital I find engaged in the Timber Trade.

But there is little reason to believe that the majority of the people in Canada attach any importance to the Timber Monopoly ; they appear to me to care far more for good government than for any such adventitious advantage as we give them by such means ; and in my opinion our chance of retaining those colonies depends far more upon the system of governing them, than it does upon the maintenance of the Timber Monopoly.

Of one thing I am sure : the people of this country will never tolerate the continuance of an annual loss of 1,500,000l. to satisfy the colonists by means of Monopoly, concurrently with the payment of nearly an equal sum for the purpose of ruling them by force. The present appears to be a favourable moment to redress, on the one hand, their political grievances, and, on the other, to establish commercial relations on a sounder footing. And really it is difficult to conceive (with the example of our trade with the United States as it exists at present) how any person can venture to say that we cannot have an unpro-

tected commerce with the countries immediately
adjoining.

The class that I expect will be found most eager to
maintain the Timber Monopoly will be what is termed
the Shipping Interest; for that is the class apparently
the most tenacious of the advantages gained by it.
Nor will I deny that if we were to import less timber
from Canada it would affect the capital of some ship-
owners engaged in the Timber Trade—in the same
way that other people are constantly affected by
changes and improvements that supersede their employments. But that the trade in bringing timber
from Canada can be maintained, without a most culpable sacrifice of the public interest to private advantage, if we can get timber from elsewhere at a lower
freightage, I emphatically deny. And as we are told
that the Shipping Interest is at stake in the maintenance of this trade, I cannot now do better than
produce evidence to show the proportion and character
of the shipping so employed.

In the first place, there are not more than 1,816
voyages made to this country by trading vessels
employed between North America and the United
Kingdom. Of these about 447 are made for the
transport of other things than timber, which being
deducted from the total, leaves 1,369 for the freightage of timber. But, as every vessel makes two
voyages, in order to ascertain the number of ships
employed in the Timber Trade, the number of voyages
must be divided by two, which gives us 684. And
as from the special qualities of the North American

pine we should always require about 100,000 loads of Canadian timber, equal to 222 cargoes, the number of the 111 vessels used to carry them would have to be deducted from the 684, leaving only 573 that, if the anticipations of the ship-owners were realized, would be deprived of employment in the event of the cessation of the presently existing Canadian Timber Trade.

And, granted this loss of employment, what proportion does the House suppose that these ships bear to the whole Mercantile Navy of the country and her dependencies? The number of registered vessels in 1836 amounted to upwards of 25,500 ; and it is to prevent the subtraction of 573 ships from the whole amount of British tonnage that we are told that the Shipping Interest of the Kingdom is in danger, and are required to submit to an annual loss of 1,500,000*l.* to avert it.

The annual consumption of the shipping of this country from wear and tear and casualties of all kinds is, I believe, estimated at 1,200 ships or thereabout. But what is it but gratuitous assumption to assert that the loss of the business thus entailed will be sustained by the Shipping Interest of this country if the Timber Monopoly were abolished? It proceeds upon the idea that foreign shipping will engross the whole of the increase in the Baltic trade, on the supposition that we should obtain all our timber from that quarter. Why, this was the old cry against Mr. Huskisson when he altered the Navigation Laws. It was said then that the Shipping Interest was to be

ruined ; that we were to be beaten out of the seas by
foreigners ; and that the Prussian Navy would ride
ascendant on the ocean! I should have thought that
the alarmists upon that occasion would have lost
their credit as prophets for ever in this country, considering the results that attended the change. For what
happened, contrary to all that was predicted? Just
this : more ships were built and employed in a given
period after those laws were changed than before ;
and while foreign shipping has since increased $11\frac{1}{2}$
per cent., English shipping has increased 29 per
cent. And not only this, but the Mercantile Marine
of Prussia has diminished in a most marked manner
since the period when the Reciprocity Treaty was
signed.

From experience, then, there is little reason to
expect the results that are predicted in the present
case. On the contrary, there are reasons that render it
peculiarly improbable ; for the ships that are usually
employed in the Timber Trade are ships that have
become unfit for service of any other kind, and that were
built and employed for other purposes. Now to meet
an increased demand for shipping, it is far more likely
that an adequate supply of cast-off ships would come
from this country, which has the most extensive
marine in the world, than from countries that have
hardly enough to meet their own wants.

What has been the case lately with respect to
grain that has come chiefly from the Baltic? Has
the carrying of that fallen entirely into the hands of
foreigners? Or is it not the reason of the extravagant

freights that the ship-owners have been lately getting,
that they have had an extraordinary demand for
vessels for this purpose?

There are only two reasons why foreigners should
navigate their ships cheaper than we do: one is that
the cost of materials for building their ships is less ;
and the other is that the provisioning of their ships
is cheaper.   Now the obvious effect of reducing the
duties on timber would be to lower the building materials of ships.   And with respect to provisions, the
cost would be the same to all ships trading in the
Baltic.

But, in truth, the only just conclusion at which
we can arrive from past experience is that there are
at present no people that we know of who can compete with us in navigation.   The only people in the
world who could—and who will eventually, if any do
—are the Americans.   Yet what is actually the case in
America?   Why, that whereas in the year 1821 the
proportion that our shipping bore to that of the
United States in the trade with the United Kingdom,
was 7½ per cent., the proportion of our shipping now
is 35 per cent., so that even there we have been
gaining ground.

It might be asked why, if they have such decided
advantages over us, foreigners do not supersede us
where the trade is open to them as well as to us?
And why we command the trade, as we do, between
Europe and the South American States?   Or, indeed,
why before the Navigation Laws were altered the
preference was invariably given to a British ship

whenever the trade was free? There is, in fact, a decided superiority in our vessels and our seamen ; and—which everybody else can see but a ship-owner, who has always got Monopoly in his eye—nothing can benefit the ship-owner more than to extend our commerce in all quarters of the world. This can only be done by removing from it restrictions of every kind ; and it really is lamentable to see a class of men like the ship-owners siding so frequently with those who take narrow and selfish views of their own as well as their country's interest.

I believe that it is usual on these occasions with those who uphold the Timber Monopoly, to urge in its behalf the interest of the manufacturers who it is said are anxious to preserve the Monopoly for the sake of the colonial market. I do not believe that the manufacturers are so foolish. I believe that they are too wise to distinguish between foreign customers and colonial customers ; and that what they feel the most is, that they have been deprived against their will of their foreign customers by these and similar restrictions upon their commerce. And more especially do they complain of the duties on timber, which have tended so materially to disturb their intercourse with the North of Europe. It is my firm opinion that no step could be taken that would be more satisfactory to English manufacturers than one that would tend to revive again a trade with those countries : they feel, and most justly so, I think, that every hour that this commerce is suspended, fresh manufacturing rivals are springing up there ; and that nothing would stay that competition more than greater facilities being afforded for the introduction of our goods.

I am glad to see that my Hon. Friend the Member for Leeds has a notice of a Motion this evening on the subject : the time is now at hand when the countries, united in the Zollverein, are about to agree upon the terms on which they wish to rest their commercial relations with other countries in future ; and I believe that it will just depend upon what we are disposed to agree to in the matter of corn and timber, whether we shall be excluded still farther than we are at present from their markets.

Bearing in mind, therefore, the great importance that belongs to this question, the vast issues that it involves for the productive classes of every kind in this country, and having shown, as I consider, that those who seek to continue the Timber Monopoly have no public or national ground on which to rest their claim, I hope that the House will consent to the Motion, which I now propose to it : That this House do resolve itself into a Committee of the whole House to consider the duties now levied on foreign and colonial timber.

V.

HOUSE OF COMMONS, April 1, 1840.

The financial state of the country in 1840 was very serious ; whilst expenditure was increasing, the deficiency of revenue was no less than a million and a half. Depression in trade continued without a prospect of improvement ; and the sufferings of the people were so heart-rending, that the members of a deputation which waited on Lord John Russell to seek relief for them in the Repeal of the Corn Laws, utterly broke down in attempting to detail them. It was under these circumstances that Mr. Villiers, seconded by Sir George Strickland, brought forward his third Annual Motion on Wednesday, April 1. After two adjournments, the debate—in which the Earl of Darlington, Mr. Labouchere, Lord Morpeth, and Sir Robert Peel amongst others had taken part—came to an end on the Friday following. Between one and two o'clock in the morning, after many of those who would have voted with Mr. Villiers had gone away in the belief that the House would not be divided, Mr. Warburton moved the adjournment of the debate until the following Monday. This Motion was, however, pressed to a division and lost by a majority of 116, the Noes being 245 and the Ayes 129. Mr. Warburton, to avoid a division on the main question, then moved the adjournment of the House, and this being agreed to the original Motion became a dropped Order.

IN rising to propose the Motion of which I have given notice, I beg to apologize to the House for its postponement till this evening. I assure the House that the delay proceeded from a cause that I could not control : it arose from indisposition. An excuse that I could, indeed, offer with great force this evening, and one that together with several other considerations present to my mind makes me regret more than ever that it is still in my hands to bring this question before the House ; but having learnt that many persons expected it to be discussed this week, I determined that, if possible, no other delay should occur on my account.

The question is now assuming a very serious aspect in the country. It is arousing the interest and engaging the attention of the great mass of the community ; and, whatever the House may think, questions of this character, affecting as they do the commerce, the employment, and the condition of the people, excite among them an interest far exceeding any other. I wish, therefore, that the present Motion were in the hands of those who could do more justice to it than myself ; and still more that it were in the hands of those who have the power to do justice to the people.

I hoped, moreover, that ere now the landed proprietary of this country, in consideration of the deep distress that pervades and bears down the productive classes of our community, would have given some sign of an intention to relax the rigours of their Laws ; and that what has hitherto been denied to the claims of justice would have been granted on the grounds of mercy. But three months have passed away since Parliament assembled, and not a whisper of such an intention has been heard. On the contrary, the same querulous note has been sounded in another place about agitation, and the same haughty and ill-placed observations respecting its object have been uttered ; while in this House we have seen the usual efforts made to produce some proof of opinion in favour of the Corn Laws, which reveal with tedious sameness the influence commonly used by landowners over their dependents, and their determination to maintain the Corn Laws unchanged.

However, as I mooted this matter before in this House, some confidence is placed in me that I will not suffer it to slumber. I cannot, therefore, allow more time to elapse without asking the majority of the House to reconsider the decision they gave on it last Session, and seriously to review the grounds on which they rested their decision. These grounds I apprehend to have been that the Corn Laws work well; that they have satisfied the purpose for which they were enacted; and that they ought to be maintained.

It was a bold thing to pronounce such a conclusion last Session; but it will, I think, require more courage to repeat it. And therefore I shall re-state some of those facts and arguments that led me to the conviction that the Laws are bad; that they have worked ill; that they have caused and are still causing great loss and suffering to the productive classes; and that they now cast upon the community a fearful addition to those burdens that it is at all times compelled to endure. Were I to state further what it is that prompts me to press this matter again on the House, I should say that it is because of my conviction that not a day has passed since the last discussion on the Corn Laws on which, either from personal suffering or greater intelligence, fresh converts have not been made to the repeal of these Laws; while, at the same time, I do not believe that one human being could be produced who, having been either indifferent or opposed to the Corn Laws before, has since become a convert to their continuance. I regret the importance that I must attach to this circumstance. But it will greatly outweigh any argument that I could adduce on the subject; for I cannot persuade myself that unless there were a general impression in both Houses of Parliament that either great ignorance or general indifference prevails among the people on the question, those who take a prominent part in these discussions would utter the things that we hear said about it. Not only do we hear that the Corn Laws are a necessary evil, but also that they are a positive advantage; and thus the advocates of Repeal have it cast upon them to prove once more that an abundance of the essential of life, which gives further means of satisfying the wants of life, is better than the dearness and scarcity that deteriorate the condition of the mass of the people.

Still, if the task has to be performed again, the present moment is perhaps favourable for the purpose; for it is difficult to believe that those who argued against the Corn Laws last year would have made the statements they did make could they have known how quickly events would follow that would completely refute them; and it is scarcely credible that their decision would have been what it was had they foreseen the sad advantage that the distress in the country gives us this year.

Nevertheless I am not going to deny that there

has been great misapprehension on the subject of the
Corn Laws; that mystery has been artfully thrown
round it; and that thousands have only now come
to view it in the true simplicity of its character. On
this account I shall discuss it with all the calmness
and deliberation that should be devoted to a matter
admitting of dispute; and I shall, as I have done on
former occasions, first proceed to consider the object
of the Laws.

The object of the Corn Laws may be simply
stated to be the limitation of the quantity of food
imported from abroad, for the purpose of raising and
maintaining the price of that which is grown at
home. This is the object as it is to be collected from
the avowed purpose as well as the provision of the
Laws. The policy of such legislation seems to belong
to the present century; and we are now living under
the third legislative experiment that has been made
in it. In 1804 Mr. Western's Bill passed into law;
this was followed by the Corn Law of 1815; and at
the present time we are bound by the enactment of
1828. Each one of these measures has professed the
same end : namely, to maintain lands in cultivation,
to keep the people in employment, and to secure to
the cultivator a certain price for his produce. To
each, also, have the same objections been offered :
namely, that such policy must be at variance with the
public good; that the interests of the community
must be sacrificed by maintaining particular soils in
cultivation; and that, as the price of produce depends
upon circumstances beyond the reach of legislation,

such a Law is calculated only to mislead those who rely upon it.

The justice of such objections with respect to two of these laws is now matter of history. Mr. Western procured his Act by stating that without such a measure thousands of acres would be thrown out of cultivation, and that a proportionate number of labourers would be thus rendered destitute. Now, I believe that I state the fact accurately when I say that after the passing of that Bill the ports were never closed; and that, so far from land going out of cultivation from this circumstance, within six or seven years afterwards produce had risen nearly 300 per cent. above the price that he had fixed as remunerative.

The Corn Law of 1815 proposed to make the community always pay for its food the price that it had reached during the war and a depreciated currency. I have a right to say that this was the deliberate intention of the Legislature, because there was an Hon. Member at that time in the House whose eager and able exertions on the occasion to expose what he called the iniquity and injustice of the Law excited general attention ; and he made a distinct proposition that if such a law were to pass it should not exist beyond the time when we should place our currency on a more sure basis—in short, when we should resume cash payments. I need not say that I allude to Mr. Baring, who has since become Lord Ashburton. He made this proposition to the House ; but it was rejected.

It is no longer matter of dispute that the Law

of 1815 was a failure in every respect. It failed to give profit to the producer; it failed to give plenty to the people; it failed to maintain steadiness of prices; and it failed even to do that which might have been expected from it: namely, to give wisdom to those who projected it. It was introduced amidst the curses of the people: it expired without favour from its friends.

Nevertheless in 1828 its failure does not appear to have been ascribed to its object, but only to the means adopted for its attainment. It was still thought possible to fix by law the price at which the produce of the land could be sold, and to secure the cultivator the price that he expected. It was maintained that the means had simply not been discovered by which this object could be attained; and it was in 1828 that the discovery was thought to have been made, when the scheme of a Sliding Scale was suggested in order to meet the wishes of the agriculturists.

We must now consider whether this scheme, devised in 1828, has succeeded or not. There are some who think that it has worked well, that it has accomplished every object intended; and it is for them to prove their case. I certainly am of opinion that it has but verified every prediction of evil that was likely to attend it; and I think I can show that it has done so. I do not think that the public require much information on the subject; but they are watching this discussion, and I trust that they will ponder well on which side the truth prevails.

Now, I contend that the present Corn Laws are a

complete failure ; and when I say so, I refer to their avowed object rather than to that which may have been intended though not avowed : I contend that they have failed to benefit agriculture, though they may have succeeded in greatly raising the value of land.

And here it is very important to distinguish clearly between what is called agriculture and the ownership of land. These interests are in many respects distinct ; but because they are the same in some respects, the land-owners claim for themselves all the arguments usually advanced in support of the Laws that have reference solely to agriculture. The fact is, the connection between the cultivation of land and its ownership is not nearer than that between a house and the business carried on in it ; or that between the merchant and his banker who may lend him the capital to conduct his business ; or that between the manufacturer and the person of whom he pur- chases the raw material. These respective interests are in some material points distinct, and nobody con- founds them ; and there is no more reason for confusion between the interests of the cultivator and the owner of the soil than between the other interests. The land-owner may hardly know where his property is ; he may be unable to distinguish one kind of produce from another ; he may live abroad, and know no one connected with his property but the receiver of his rents. The cultivator, on the other hand, may be equally ignorant of any of the circumstances con- nected with the ownership of the land beyond the price he pays for its use.

This distinction is so obvious that I should not have troubled the House by stating it but for the singular confusion of the interests of owner and cultivator which is made in arguing for the Corn Law of 1828, though they are in many respects different and it is important that they should be so viewed; and because under the general term agriculturists we hear the most exaggerated pretensions put forward, based on the assumed identity of the interests of landlord, farmer, and labourer.

With regard to the necessity or policy of legislating at all for the particular interest of the agriculturist or the farmer, what does it consist in? What would he desire the law to do for him if it could do anything? Probably to enable him to get the return for his capital that he expected; and this, I suppose, is what every capitalist would wish. He would like to be made sure in his calculations, and to obtain the profit he expects; and this in truth is what the Corn Laws promise to do for him : they do hold out the prospect of something like certainty and steadiness on these points.

We have now to examine how far they have realized the expectations they raised. The first fact to be observed is, that since the passing of the Corn Laws there has been every variation in the price of produce and the farmer has experienced great distress and disappointment, which at least seems to lead to the conclusion that these Laws have not averted the evil apprehended by the agriculturists. The question therefore is, whether this variation, this distress and disappointment, have been actually caused by the Corn Laws. That this has been the case can, I believe, be proved almost to demonstration. . I deduce my evidence from the agriculturists themselves. Not to have referred to their opinions collected by this House seems to have been an omission in the previous discussions upon the Corn Laws. Those who complain of these Laws have usually been so much occupied with showing their gross injustice that they have as yet paid little attention to the evidence against them by those for whose interest they are professed to be maintained. But there has been a great body of evidence collected by the House, and given under circumstances that compel us to credit it, to which public attention ought to be directed ; for I am sure that if there is one conclusion before another to which a candid inquirer would arrive after reading this evidence, it is that the Corn Laws are extremely prejudicial to the farmer, and that they have occasioned distress and disappointment to all of that class who have trusted to them.

This is a grave consideration, because there are many who now distinctly see the injustice of the Laws, but who from fear of the consequences of their Repeal to the persons who have invested capital upon the faith of their continuance, are yet slow to call for it.

At the risk of wearying the House, and hoping to be excused by the importance of the subject, I shall proceed to read some extracts from the evidence collected in 1836 by the Agricultural Committee appointed in that year.

The first person whose evidence I will advert to is Mr. Ellis, a Leicestershire farmer, who was asked whether the distress of the time had any connection with the Corn Laws. He said, in reply, that he thought the duty too high because it gave a fictitious value to land and gave the farmers an expectation of something that could never occur; and thus fictitiously maintained the value of land. The question was then put to him whether he thought the Corn Laws induced the tenants to make larger offers than in the result they had been able to pay. He answered in the affirmative; and said that farmers were prone to expect high prices, and had been anticipating returns that they were not likely to get.

Mr. Parker, an Essex farmer, was asked :—

Do you consider that the distressed state of those farmers can be at all attributed to the rents not having been lowered sufficiently in time ?—I should say very materially, the landlords not prudently lowering their rents earlier than they have done.

The farms would have been in better condition ?—Yes; it has been by persisting in the high rents that the farms would have been worked out of condition, and then no person would take them except at a very low rent.

Do you think that they (the Corn Laws) hold out hopes of a continuance of a higher rate of price than can ever be realized? —The Corn Laws have been in operation but a few years, they commenced with large foreign supplies; we have been only put on our own growth the last four years; I do not think if the present Laws continue that we should be often interfered with by foreign supply.

Take the whole of the farmers in the county of Essex, do you think that they are possessed of as much capital now as they were in 1821 ?—Certainly not.

Then they have been labouring now for fifteen years, and have expended a great deal of industry, and skill, and capital, with no return at all, as a body ?—They have been parting with their capital, a great many of them, to their landlords, and to other persons, whose charges upon them were excessively high.

Mr. Cox, of Buckinghamshire, gave his evidence :—

For the last three years you have been farming that land to a profit ?—Decidedly not to a profit.

Should you say that the cultivation of Buckinghamshire has fallen off within the last eight or ten years ?—I should say so, in the neighbourhood in which I live.

In what respect ?—The land is getting very foul and over-cropped ; in some places driven further than it should be.

Mr. John Houghton, a gentleman of great experience, was also examined :—

Have you not arable farms in the county of Buckingham, over which you are steward ?—Yes, I have.

What is their state now compared with the state of the grazing farms to which you allude ?—On the heavy clay lands the distress is very great, more than it is on the turnip and barley lands, or grass land.

How do you account for that distress upon the clay lands ?—From the low price of wheat.

Do you find that the capital of the farmers has been diminishing ?—Certainly ; I think the great distress has been on the heavy land farms.

Have the farmers been paying their rents out of their produce, or out of their capital ?—If you take the heavy clay land, certainly out of their capital.

Then we have the evidence of Mr. John Rolfe, a farmer of Buckinghamshire :—

Do you use wheat for any other purpose but that of human food now ?—I have not done it ; some have ground wheat for the pigs ; some have given it to their horses, but that was principally the grown wheat of the last harvest but one.

What is the cost of the cultivation of your farm per acre now, as compared with what it was some years ago ?—The cost of cultivation is very much the same; there is a little difference in the price of labour.

Can you state how rents are paid in your district ?—Rents have heretofore, till the last two years, been very well paid.

How have they been paid since 1833 ?—They have been paid very badly.

Even on the light soils you speak of ?—Yes.

There is more wheat grown upon land now ?—Yes.

Supposing there should not be a corresponding demand for wheat in proportion as that class of land increases, it must make the heavy clay land less profitable ?—Yes.

You do not complain of the price of mutton now ?—No.

Of wool ?—No.

Of barley ? you cannot expect much increase in that ?—No, not much.

Oats ?—Oats we should wish for a little increase.

Beans ?—If we had 4s. a quarter more we should not have much fault to find.

The chief complaint is on account of the depression in the price of wheat ?—Yes, that is where the farmer is suffering most ; that is where he looks for his rent in the spring of the year, when he should have the price of his wheat to raise the money for his rent ; when he is looking for a large sum of money to meet his payments ; when he comes to thresh out and carry to market, his expenses almost take the whole price.

What will become of the landlord ?—We shall be all beggars together.

Mr. John Curtis, another Buckinghamshire farmer, was next examined :—

Has the capital of the farmers in your opinion diminished ?—I should say considerably.

Will you state in what way farmers are worse off ?—In the first place, they have cropped their land hard, and it is now getting into bad condition ; it is getting foul, and the stock diminishes.

Now looking at the different descriptions of soils ; first of all the grass, has the produce of your grass enabled you to pay the rent upon the grass land ?—What little grass I have is very good ; that is the best part of my farm.

You have stated that the condition of the labourers is good ;

you mean those that are employed ?—Those that are employed ; and there are very few out of employment.

Has the Poor Rate been reduced lately ?—Yes ; the Poor Law Bill works well with us.

And Mr. John Kemp, an Essex farmer, equally bore testimony to the decreasing capital of the farmer :—

Do you consider, then, that the quantity of wheat in the market has been the cause of the depression of the price ?—I should say so.

Has the capital of the farmers in your neighbourhood, and under your knowledge, diminished or not ?—Very much diminished.

What was the rate in your parish previous to the passing of the Poor Law Bill, and what is it now ?—Our expenditure in the parish used to be 1,600*l.*, and last year it was not more than 1,200*l.*

What is the state of the small farmer about you ; the man who rents a hundred acres ?—As bad off as the poor man.

Are farmers paying rents from their profits or their capital ? —From their capital.

Taking the labourers as a body, are they as well employed as they used to be ?—They have been very well employed for the last three years.

Do you think that upon the average, the higher price, from a scarce season, compensates the farmer for the deficiency of his crop ?—No ; for at the time when corn was so high, about six years ago, during the wet seasons, we were certainly worse off than we are now, and wheat was much higher.

I now turn to the evidence of Mr. Thurlwall, of Cambridgeshire :—

What, in your opinion, is the condition of the tenantry gene-rally in your neighbourhood ?—I think verging on insolvency, generally in the most desperate state that men can possibly be.

Mr. Charles Page, of Essex, farmer, was asked :—

Have you lost or gained this last year upon your farm ?—In fact, I have lost every year since I have been in business.

Have you lost principally upon the wheat or the barley crop? —The loss upon the wheat crop I think is the most material.

And Mr. George Babbs :—

Do you believe that the farmers are paying their rent out of capital, or out of the profits of their farms?—I believe the farmers have been paying their rents out of the capital they employ.

Is that your case?—It has been my case.

Has the land been cropped harder in your neighbourhood than it used to be?—I think it has.

Nothing more hopeful is to be learned from Mr. Charles Howard :—

Taking the period since the last Committee sat in 1833, what do you consider to be the comparative state of the farming interests now and at that time?—Decidedly and progressively worse.

Do you take into your consideration every species of land, or one species of land more than another?—I think upon the sheep-farms, the upland farms, from the increased demand which there has been for sheep, the distress has rather decreased; sheep have been very high.

Then with respect to the lowland farms?—Their situation has been progressively much worse.

You stated that in consequence of the depressed state of the farming interest of that county, the landlords have permitted a considerable portion of the old grass lands to be ploughed up; has that tended to precipitate the affairs of the tenant, or otherwise?—It has kept the tenant longer upon his legs.

But it has more materially deteriorated the condition of those farms upon which the permission was given?—Decidedly so.

Either you think that the land will go out of cultivation and produce a diminished supply, or you think that the Legislature will interfere in some way so as to produce a rise in price?—Exactly.

And you think that is the view of those persons that buy those farms at present?—I do believe it is.

Mr. Robert Hope, a Scotch farmer, cannot cer-

tainly be quoted as a favourable witness for the present Corn Laws :—

Have you ever thought anything about the present Corn Laws, whether they are beneficial to the farmer or not?—Yes, they have been often discussed, but it is a very general feeling among those that pay corn rents, that they have not been hitherto beneficial, but the very reverse of beneficial.

What is your reason for that opinion?—It induced men to offer more than has been well realized by the price of corn, because it was generally expected from the Corn Laws that prices would be kept up to something like what they promised ; that the import of foreign corn would be restricted, and by that means keep up the price of the home growth to 70s. or so.

How has the Corn Law disappointed your expectation?— Because it led those that took farms at money rents to give a much higher rent than they would have done.

Then is it the opinion of you and those other gentlemen that have considered the subject in the way you mention, that the present Corn Law ought to continue, or do you think that any change would be beneficial to the farmer?—From what we experienced in the year 1831, I am disposed to think that a change might be more beneficial to the farmer, by reducing the scale at which foreign corn is imported.

You have stated that you consider the existing Corn Law is prejudicial to the farmer ; is your opinion founded upon the circumstance of there having been a miscalculation as to the effects to be produced by the Corn Laws, or upon the working of the Corn Laws themselves?—I think by the present working of the Corn Laws that it may run prices too high for the interest of the farmers in years of scarcity ; before any foreign corn can be admitted into the country, prices may be run up so high as to be prejudicial to the interest of the farmer, because, in such a year as we had in 1831, we could not grow so much wheat as we had to pay in rent.

If the result of this Corn Law should be to produce great fluctuations in price, you would think that effect would apply to all farmers?—I think it has been prejudicial to those that even pay a money rent, because I am sure that if it had not been for the Corn Laws they would not have given so high a money rent.

Mr. James Tison, an English farmer, gave this evidence :—

What causes have there been to depress the state of the farmers of stiff land ?—High rents ; it is my opinion, founded on the testimony of farmers themselves, that many of them are farming under war rents, while they are selling their corn at peace prices.

The consequence of the rents being kept up too high has been that the land has been overcropped ?—Yes ; when I have conversed with farmers, this appears to be the conclusion they have come to, that they have paid their landlords what they ought to have paid to the labourers. If they had paid it to labourers they would have had value for the money ; whereas they paid it to the landlord, and, of course, received nothing back, and they had so much less to lay out upon their farms.

On the light soils, have the tenants been met by the landlords with a reduction of rent ?—They have not needed so much reduction as they have upon the heavier soils.

It appears from your evidence, therefore, that it is a question very much between landlord and tenant as to the present condition of the farming interest ; that is to say, that the landlord has more in his power than can be done by the Legislature ?—Decidedly ; I do not see what the Legislature can do, except with respect to the Poor Law, to benefit the agriculturist effectually.

Looking at Mr. Coke's estate, in Norfolk, could any number of his tenantry afford to give him any rent whatever, with wheat at 5s. a bushel ?—Yes, I think with a good crop they could.

Then you think that the want of intelligence and the want of skill has gone a great way towards producing the depressed state of the farmers ?—According to my view of it, such is the state of society in this country, that for a person to do well in any branch, whether in agriculture, manufacture, or in commerce, there must be a combination of intelligence, practical skill, capital, and industry ; and if any of those be wanting, whether it is in agriculture, or in mercantile affairs, a person is almost sure now to go wrong ; and when I have traced a great number of cases of individual distress among farmers to that cause, one of those has been wanting.

What do you conceive to be the effect of the present Corn Laws upon the consumer ?—I think they have a very unfavourable effect ; they operate as a very great hindrance to the extension of trade, to the manufacturing and commercial interests, because, under the present system of Corn Laws, we can receive nothing in return from those countries which would take our manufactured goods, if they could send us their corn in return ; for instance Prussia ; our trade would be immense with Prussia if we could take their corn in return.

What do you think is the average price which may be fairly calculated upon by the farmer under the existing Corn Law ?— Under 50s. a quarter for wheat.

Mr. Thomas Bennett gave his evidence :—

Do you think, with reduction of rent, and the reduction of prices, the farmer can cultivate his land at a profit ?—Looking to the seven years back, and having taken those farms under very low prices, I have not a question that some may do it profitably, and I have no doubt some will.

At what price do you estimate wheat for the next seven years ?—If I was going to take a farm myself, I should not expect, nor would I calculate for the next seven years, to have wheat above 5s. to 6s. a bushel.

Will the Duke of Bedford's tenants, who have retaken those farms, be able to pay the rent for which they have just agreed, with wheat at 5s. a bushel ?—I think they will. I think the majority do not expect to see it at much more.

The disappointment and ruin attested by Mr. Andrew Howden, a Scotch farmer, are deplorable :—

If you had been sold off in 1820, do you think you would have been better off than you are now ?—I do not know that mine is a fair case to be taken as a general case, because I started very poor in life, and I have had a hard struggle, and other circumstances that contributed to assist me. I am the only remaining farmer in the parish where I was brought up ; except myself, there is not a farmer, nor the son of a farmer, remaining within the parish but myself.

What is the reason of their having all gone away ?—The money rents that were exacted of them. They all conceived that they were to have 80s. a quarter, and their calculations were made upon that. It soon appeared that that could not be realized, and they were not converted, and ruin has been the consequence.

VOL. I.   M

Then there has been a great change of tenancy in your neighbourhood?—There has.

And that has been caused by the fall of prices?—Yes, and the want of accommodation on the part of the proprietors.

In your opinion did the Corn Law that was made in 1815 deceive both the landlord and the tenant?—It did. I believe that the calculation upon which they took at that time was almost universally 4*l.* a quarter.

The Corn Law having promised a price of 80*s.*, failed to perform it?—Yes.

Mr. William Bell, a Scotch farmer, was opposed to the Sliding Scale :—

What is your reason for supposing a fixed duty would be preferable?—By the present Corn Law, when the price approaches near the rate at which the foreign corn can be brought into the market with a profit, the prices may possibly be run up to that rate by artificial means. Thus a great quantity of corn would be improperly liberated and thrown upon the market, and this might probably depress the market for the whole season. Now, at a fixed duty, that could not take place.

I must not omit the evidence of Mr. George Robertson, another English farmer :—

Supposing that mutton had borne the same proportionate price when wheat fell to 40*s.*, do you think the Scotch farmer would then have been enabled to make a good living?—The Scotch farmer would have tried something else than wheat; he would have extended his grass cultivation, and that would have tended to reduce the price of meat still more, no doubt.

And if the price of barley had been also reduced?—Those are all regulated by the demand of the manufacturing and commercial classes.

Do you know anything of the sale of the manufacturing and commercial classes?—My belief is, that they were never more prosperous.

How long has that been the case?—It has been gradually coming on for years.

In the face of that increasing prosperity, has there not been a decline in the price of wheat?—That may be accounted for by the great additional average crops for a series of years.

Are you able to perceive a great increase in the demand of the operative classes?—Very great in flour and meat, and I have no doubt the increased price of barley is caused by a demand for malting in England.

Supposing the supply and demand for labour to remain the same, will not eventually the price of labour fall in proportion to the fall in the price of food?—At present the demand for labour for the manufacturing interest is so great, that we can scarcely get hands for necessary operations of agriculture.

You have been asked, with reference to the price of wheat governing the price of meat, can you anticipate a very great falling off in the price of meat, when you consider that the population of this country is increasing so rapidly, and that the manufacturing employment of that population is so great as it is at present?—No. I think the price of agricultural produce must keep up; that is to say if the manufacturing classes prosper and live as they are doing.

And now I will not trouble the House with any further extracts. It is impossible to read this evidence without being convinced that the farmers are induced by the Corn Laws to promise for their land rents that they are unable to pay; and that they are tempted by the price that these Laws profess to guarantee them, to devote much of their capital to the growth of wheat; and therefore, as wheat is the most expensive crop they can grow, the loss they experience is proportionally severe if they are disappointed in the price they expect. And this, Sir, I think I may venture to state with confidence to the House, since I find in the admirable address that you published to your constituents that it is the conclusion to which you arrived, after devoting more attention and time to the Committee of 1836, and to

the subsequent consideration of the evidence, than
perhaps any other Member. I find it to be your
conviction that the Laws are actually prejudicial to the
farmer, and in the manner in which I have stated
them to be so ; and you, Sir, also seem to agree in the
conclusion to be drawn from much of the evidence
given by agriculturists themselves : namely, that they
must not depend for good fortune upon the adventitious aid of such legislation as the Corn Laws, but
upon what all other capitalists must rely—upon the
skill, experience, and intelligence that they bring to
their pursuit.

But now I wish the House to mark the consequence of the farmer's being tempted to direct his
attention chiefly, or to apply his capital largely, to
the cultivation of wheat, and, by neglecting the
culture of other produce, and by the overproduc-
tion of wheat, to reduce its price below the sum
that would be remunerating : he becomes suddenly
alarmed and disappointed at his loss, and withdraws
much of his capital from such employment. Thus
he narrows the breadth which he sows with wheat ;
and then we see how the supply of the community
with food at a reasonable rate—another purpose
which the Laws are supposed to have—is fulfilled.
The first result of growing less wheat has been, of
course, to raise the price, which occurring simultaneously with a bad harvest, has inflicted distress
on the public for the last eighteen months ; and now,
after paying a great additional price for their food,
they are suffering from an unusual deficiency of it,

and have not any prospect of an improvement. There
is, in fact, every probability that prices will keep up,
and that great sacrifices will yet have to be made by
the people for food.

But supposing that all the assertions about the
present season, and all the usual predictions respecting the coming harvest, were true ; and that the price
were to fall greatly in consequence of the rotation
of the crops being disturbed by a greater breadth of
wheat being sown this year than was ever sown
before ; how would it benefit the farmer ? We
should have the same story of distress over again,
and see agriculturists as badly off as they were in
1836. This, indeed, is the regular operation of the
Corn Laws : they either ruin the farmer or greatly
prejudice the public. Yet these are the Laws that
it is sought to identify with all the cherished institutions of the State ; and if anyone assails them he is
charged with designs against the Constitution itself.
But who is benefited by the Laws, if the farmer is
thus injured and deceived ?

It is usual to say in these discussions that by
making prices high particular soils are kept in cultivation, and employment thereby secured to the
labourers ; that wages rise with the price of food,
and therefore the labourer is better off with high
prices because he can earn more money. This was
said deliberately last year. Will it be repeated ? I
trust not. I do not think it creditable to have urged
it at all : it certainly is not true. It is cruel to the
labourer who can have no doubt of the privations

he endures from a high price of food, misleading to others who do not know that ; and, there is not the least pretence for asserting that when provisions are high the agricultural labourer gets high wages. The contrary has always happened whenever such has been the case.

In 1797, the great scarcity and high prices then prevalent, so far from leading to high wages, gave rise to a system of pauperizing independent labourers, previously unknown ; and a heavy burden was thrown upon the Rates for the express purpose of avoiding precisely that which is said to be the advantageous result of high prices : that is, a rise in wages proportionate to the price of food.

Again, in 1810, 1818, 1830, there were—as there are at the present time—great complaints of the sufferings of the labourers ; and during each of these periods the prices were—as they are now—high. But it is a fact not less striking, in contradiction to what is assumed, that whenever provisions have been low the labourers have been well off ; that there has been a great demand for their labour ; and that their wages have given them a greater command over the necessaries of life. This certainly is not astonishing to any person who reflects for a moment on the subject, because it is clear that as everybody is more or less an employer of labour, and that he is so according to his means, in proportion as his means are greater or less so will be his demand for labour ; and so, consequently, will be the wages of the labourer, since it is the proportion that their number bears to the demand for them that must determine their condition.

But if there can be any doubt as to the influence of high prices on the condition of the people, it will be well to view what really is the case at this moment. I own that as far as my own inquiries have gone I can learn nothing but that either the wages, though raised, have not risen in proportion to the price of food, or that, not having risen at all, the labourers have in many cases endured the greatest privations.

And here I will just read to the House a report of some cases that occurred a short time ago. The cases first appeared in a provincial paper. I inquired into the truth of them, and I give them simply to show how incautiously it is asserted here that the agricultural labourers are not affected by the price of food :—

In the southern part of this county 6s. a week is commonly given to agricultural labourers. Within the last fortnight at the petty sessions held at Salisbury, a farmer, living at Durnford, was summoned by a labourer named Blake for refusing to pay him 6s. 6d. for a week's work. The complainant stated that he worked on 'the Stem,' sometimes for one master, sometimes for another, at 6s. 6d. *a week, the rate agreed to by the farmers at a vestry meeting.* His employer had refused to pay him more than 6s., which Blake would not accept, as it was not sufficient to maintain himself and wife. The master, in his defence, told the magistrates that the farmers of Durnford had 'stemmed' the surplus labourers of that parish *at* 6s. *per week, which was as much as they could afford to pay.* The Bench expressed their surprise—as well they might—at the practice pursued by the farmers at Durnford towards the labourers, and ordered the defendant to pay Blake the full amount of wages agreed on, 6s. 6d., and to remunerate him for his loss of time in seeking redress. This week we will take a different district, and name Rushall, a parish standing comparatively in favourable circumstances, where the poor have advantages which in many other places they do not enjoy. This parish is divided into three large farms, the land is chiefly arable, and of excellent quality, producing on an average, certainly not less than eight sacks of wheat, and ten sacks of barley per acre. On this fertile spot the highest wages of able-bodied married labourers with families are only 9s. per week (we except harvest work, for which, of course, more is paid) ; those without children, and single men, although equally able, aye, and willing too, to do a good day's work, are put off with 5s., 6s., and 7s. a week. We do not understand why this is ; it appears to be an act of injustice, and we should be glad to know upon what principle the distinction is made :—If an able man's services be worth 9s. a week, then is the single man deprived of his due by being paid only 5s. ; but if an able man's services be worth only 5s. or 6s. a week, then must the difference between that and 9s. be considered as parish allowance for the children ; it is high time this were properly understood, for if the latter be the case, the *real* rate of wages is much lower than it is represented to be. Of course, with such wages, destitution and distress abound. Many families are unable to obtain more than *one* meal a day, and in many instances that one meal consists of *potatoes and salt*, without meat, and with only a small quantity of the coarsest bread. Very few even of those who are the best off get wheaten bread, but are obliged to have recourse to a mixture of barley and wheat, the latter being of a very inferior description—tail wheat. Meat is hardly ever eaten by any of the labourers, they never buy any.

I think I have a right to refer to such cases when I read addresses to the peasantry such as have been made by a noble Duke [1] who takes a lead in maintaining the Corn Laws, asking them to believe that while they maintain those Laws they will ever be prosperous. Why, if it were for no other reason than that they tend to make land dear, the Corn Laws are prejudicial to the labouring classes, who are always better off when land is accessible to them ; nothing tends more to their contentment and comfort than the possession of land.

Another circumstance that I might mention to

[1] The Duke of Buckingham.

show that the people are now badly off and discontented in the agricultural districts is that there
have been a greater number of agricultural labourers
who have sought to avail themselves of the provision for emigration this year than ever before. Why
should this be the case if the people were well paid
and well employed? The fact is, there is less means
for employing labour this year because the price of
food is so high; and the poor are driven from the
farmhouse to the poorhouse, and thence to the State
to implore it to send them out of the country. And,
really, if we will not allow the food to come to them,
it is only merciful to send them where the food is
produced. But, in God's name, why are they to be
driven from their homes, when if provisions were as
low as they were in 1836, they would get plenty of
employment as, on the admission of the farmers themselves, they did then?

Who is it, after all, whose interests are benefited
by the Corn Laws? In the first place I say that none
can be permanently so at the expense of the rest of
the community; but immediately and for the while,
there is no doubt whatever that the owner of the land
has an advantage in them. And it is an advantage
in this way : they enable a certain class of inferior
soils to be cultivated with wheat which unquestionably
could not yield any profit if the produce of better
foreign soils were brought into competition with it ;
and this class of soils being thus artificially enhanced
in value tends to raise the value and consequently
the rent of all other land ; and the owners of land,

therefore, without reference to their effect upon other classes of the community, have a certain interest in the Laws.

It is well that the truth should be known and avowed, and that it should be acknowledged that the owners of land have a temporary advantage in the Corn Laws.　For unquestionably they have, though the farmers and the labourers cannot benefit by rent being thus artificially raised.　And it is to the land-owners alone to whom we most turn for redress ; to them we must appeal on the score of injury and injustice done to the community at large, and of injury done to themselves ultimately through the impaired fortunes of those on whose custom they must depend for the permanent value of their estates.

It is reasonable, therefore, to direct our whole attention to this class, for I am certain, notwithstanding the delusion of some of the farmers on the subject, that if some of the more distinguished of the land-owners in both Houses of Parliament were to rise in their places and express an opinion that the Corn Laws ought to be changed, all alarm among their tenants would at once be dissipated.

I am not, however, inclined to join in any wholesale denunciation of the land-owners of this country. It would be unjust to do so ; because there are among them men of great intelligence, high-minded men, men of generous feeling : some are ready and anxious to change these Laws knowing them to be prejudicial to the country at large ; and others seeing their own advantage in them will not nevertheless adhere to them at the expense of their country. Hence it is right to discriminate between them; but certainly it is also fair to fix upon those who obstruct and oppose all change of the Laws the full responsibility and all the consequences of such a course.

And I say this the more confidently because it is not in their power to show that the Laws rest upon any ground of justice or of public good. The landlords in any other country but this might allege that they were exclusively taxed, that they bore more of the burdens of the State than any other class, and were entitled to have a law that should give an artificial value to their produce. In this country they cannot allege it. Will they go into an inquiry? Is there any particular burden they bear from which other classes are exempt? Can they say that they are not exempt from burdens that others have to bear? They are not entitled to this Protection on the ground of advantage to the community. It cannot be shown that there is one burden borne by them that other classes do not equally bear. What, therefore, is the ground for their exclusive Protection? What is the ground that they themselves take? They say : ' If you allow the produce of foreign countries to come into competition with our own, you will throw out of employ many of the labourers on our own land.' What is the principle implied in this assertion, supposing it to be true? Are the interests of the country to be sacrificed that certain' lands shall not forego a particular cultivation? We wish for the benefit of the community to resort to soils more

productive, whence we shall get food cheaper, and
the land-owner forbids us on the ground of Protection. What might the mechanic not say ? What
says the hand-loom weaver ? They might say, do
not introduce a machine that shall make labour
cheaper. They do say, tax machinery. The principle is the same. There seems to be no difference in
the policy. What is the truth then? The proprietors
not being exclusively taxed, but, on the contrary,
being rather exempted from taxation, have no ground
in justice for claiming Protection whatever may be
their power for enforcing it.

Before I quit what may be called the agricultural
part of the question, I shall, perhaps, be allowed to
refer to another argument that in the course of this
discussion will probably be adduced in support of the
Corn Laws : namely, that Ireland is an agricultural
country and that it is an advantage to Ireland that the
present Laws should be continued. I should be sorry
to let anything fall from me that could possibly give
offence to Ireland, we have done enough to offend
that country already ; but I must say that of all
pretences for supporting these Laws, Ireland seems
to me the most groundless and unreasonable : Ireland that of late years has been sending us less and
less wheat ; Ireland where the mass of the people
are too poor to consume wheat, where husbandry is
the worst in the kingdom, where the landlords have
a larger share of the produce for rent and spend it
more out of their own country than any other landlords in Europe ; Ireland, moreover, where agricul-

ture would thrive better without than with the cultivation of wheat; Ireland that would benefit more
perhaps than any other country from the introduction
of manufactures or from the prosperity of manufactures
here. For Ireland has always and instantly felt the
benefit of the prosperity of manufactures in England.
And what condition would she now be in, with her
new liability to maintain her poor, if English manufactures were to decline? That is a question for
Irish landlords to consider. But in the Report of the
Committee on Agriculture to which I have referred,
there is positive evidence that where Irish agriculturists have prospered it has been attributable to
their abandoning the culture of wheat and applying
the soil to other purposes. How, then, are the real
interests of Ireland consulted by Laws that, in the
price they promise, offer peculiar temptation to the
cultivation of wheat? If I thought the present
Corn Laws of advantage to Ireland that would have
great weight with me. But what is to be gathered
on this head from the avowed opinions of men who
have studied and sought to promote the interests of
that country? I allude more particularly to the
opinions of Mr. Sharman Crawford and the Member
for Dublin—gentlemen differing on many matters but
agreeing in condemning the Corn Laws as tending to
make land dear and to repress manufacturing enterprise in their country. I cannot believe under all
these circumstances that Ireland offers us any ground
for upholding the Corn Laws.

I think that I have said enough with regard to

the wisdom of these Laws in their relation to agriculture, to show how far that interest can be said to have thriven under the influence of Monopoly. I must now turn to the great and general question involving the principle that should be the test of every law : its effects upon the community at large. Hitherto I have examined the effect of the Corn Laws on the class interest alone for which it was professed that they were passed. But one of the things that the public expect to learn from this discussion is the general effect of the operation of these Laws ; they want to know how far they are affected by the higher or lower price of food in this country. And this can be shown them.

It is indeed among the advantages of the agitation of a great question of this kind, that it brings very many intelligent minds to its consideration, and so tends to elicit truth where doubt previously prevailed. And here I am glad to be able to point to an admirable work entitled 'Influences of the Corn Laws,' recently published by Mr. James Wilson ; for this author appears to me to have made some very faithful and accurate calculations respecting the effects of the Corn Laws. He takes as the basis of his calculation the amount in quantity and the rate at which the people have been annually paying for food for the last seven years. He adopts the general estimate as to the quantity annually consumed which is sixteen millions of quarters ; and the average price of the last seven years which has been about 52s. a quarter. From this it will be found that the annual cost of wheat to the community is 41,600,000*l.* It follows, therefore, that whatever is paid more or less than this sum, is lost or gained to the community ; and hence it can be proved what this has been of late years, and what is the amount now lost to the community. Mr. Wilson shows in one carefully prepared table what has been the sum paid at home and abroad for wheat during the years 1834, 1835, 1836, 1837, 1838, 1839. For instance :—

Years.	Total Cost of Wheat. £	Cost of Foreign Wheat. £
1834	36,933,333	101,750
1835	31,400,000	34,654
1836	38,800,000	51,177
1837	44,666,000	499,480
1838	51,666,000	4,594,014
1839	50,533,000	7,515,800

It thus appears that during the last three years we have as a nation spent more in wheat grown at home by 45,793,000*l.* than in the three preceding years ; and paid more by 12,420,000*l.* during the first named period for foreign wheat than during the latter. The illustration, however, will be still more simple, if we compare the two last years : namely, 1838 and 1839. In the beginning of the year 1838, we find the price of wheat was at an average of 52*s.* a quarter. In the autumn of the same year it suddenly rose to 75*s.*—being more than 20*s.* a quarter higher. Therefore, taking the annual consumption at 16,000,000 quarters the country in September, 1838, was suddenly called upon to pay 300,000*l.* a week more for food than it paid in the six preceding months; and 450,000*l.*

a week more than it paid in 1835. And this increased sum was paid during the whole of the following year. This, then, is a sum that was suddenly abstracted from the capital and income that, under existing arrangements, was finding useful and convenient employment elsewhere ; and it must thus be considered as lost to those departments of industry in which it was giving employment.

It seems, moreover, that what invariably attends a high price of food in this country is importation from abroad, the amount of which in late years has been stated. But under our present relations with the corn-growing countries, we are compelled to export Bullion Currency to pay for grain. We have, therefore, on these occasions a certain amount of the Currency of the country invariably abstracted to make this payment. And thus we have an additional abstraction from the means usually devoted to employment at home : a very important consideration in a commercial point of view since the absence of so much bullion is of necessity followed by a contraction of the Paper Currency. Hence the public have to consider the Corn Laws in connection with a twofold evil—high price and a contracted Currency ; and thus doubly checking the operations of capital and labour.

To prove the connection between the price of food and the Currency in this country the same author has collected in a tabular form the annual amount paid for wheat, the amount of bullion and the amount of deposits in the Bank of England, and the amount paid for foreign wheat during a period of above twenty years. From this table there appears a close correspondence between the different amounts of bullion and the deposits in the Bank, and the different amounts paid for wheat at home and abroad : the former declining as the latter increased. And this with such regularity as to render it impossible not to conclude that a necessary connection exists between them. From 1817 until the present time, as grain has been imported from abroad and prices have been high, the deposits and the bullion have declined. The diminution of the deposits would result from the increased payments required for food, which lessens the amount of surplus capital in the country ; and the amount of it in the Bank of England would indicate pretty much what surplus was in the country generally. In support of which I quote the opinion of a mercantile man :—

When money is everywhere abundant and prosperity general, the resource of the Bank of England must be very great; at such times the surplus of every man throughout the country finds its way to his banker; a portion of the surplus of the bankers throughout the country finds its way to their agents in London for employment; and the surplus of these agents, as well as all the London bankers, finds its way to the coffers of the Bank of England, as the most accredited place of safety ; and thus constitutes an index, not of the wealth and capital of the Bank of England, but of the extent of surplus capital possessed at any given moment by the whole country.

It seems reasonable to expect that if great and sudden demands for the national means were made, they would be manifested in this way ; and the facts to which I have referred seem to establish that they are. Now we observe that from the end of 1838 till October 1839 there appears to have been a diminution from month to month of bullion and deposits, and during the whole of that time we were importing food from abroad. We know further how bitterly the commercial classes complained during that time of the contraction of the Currency. The great importance of this circumstance to the public is that they may know the truth respecting the sources of those fluctuations in the value and amount of the Currency which occasion such serious and alarming embarrassment in this country ; and though I do not stand here as the apologist of the Bank of England (against which if judged only according to the rules that it has laid down for itself, there is abundant ground of complaint), it is well to show that what is imputed entirely to its mismanagement must in great measure be referred to the operation of the Corn Laws.

And now after having proved that there has been a contraction of the Currency, an increase in the price of food, and a large sacrifice of the national means to meet it, it is necessary to consider what has been the effect of these circumstances upon the commercial interest of the country.

I will first allude to the Cotton Trade. The facts that I am about to state will, I believe, prove that whereas there has been a greater export of manufactured goods, the consumption of manufactures at home has been less. I quote them to show that the whole trade of the country was worse in the years in which the price of provisions was high. I take the years 1838 and 1839. The quan-

tity of cotton exported in 1838, was 269,000,000
lbs.; in 1839, it was 262,000,000 lbs.: being a decrease of 7,000,000 lbs. In 1838, the home consumption of cotton was 155,000,000 lbs.; in 1839, it was
122,000,000 lbs. : being a decrease of 33,000,000
lbs. Of wool, the home consumption, in 1838, was
56,000,000 lbs.; in 1839, it was 53,000,000 lbs.: being
a decrease of 3,000,000 lbs. But the export of
woollen goods had increased. In 1838, the quantity
exported was 6,000,000 lbs.; in 1839, it was 6,600,000
lbs. Of flax, the home consumption, in 1838, was
1,600,000 lbs.; in 1839, it was 1,200,000 lbs., and so
on with respect to many other articles which I will
not stay to enumerate.

It appears also that the articles that contributed
to these staple manufactures of the country had also
greatly fallen off in consumption. From the returns
that I have quoted the House will perceive that whilst
the goods entered for home consumption had materially
diminished in amount, the quantity of manufactured
goods exported had increased. Doubtless some persons in the House will think that this proves the
country to have been prosperous. I advise such
persons to consult their manufacturing friends or
any competent authority connected with our Foreign
Trade, and to inquire whether the increase of exports was a sure sign of prosperity ; whether it was
not compatible with the manner in which business
is conducted in this country that the exports should
increase when the consumption at home was declining—the manufacturers being driven by necessity

to procure somewhere a sale for goods cast back, as it were, on their own hands; whether it was not usual for them in such circumstances to consign these goods on their own account to houses abroad to be disposed of; and whether this has not, from distress, been done during the last year to a very great extent.

Indeed there is evidence of it in the complaints that come from different countries, of the sales of our manufactures which we are forcing on their markets. In a letter addressed to one of our most influential journals, its correspondent abroad, speaking of the extraordinary quantity of British goods brought into foreign markets, says: 'I would wish to give a hint to those British manufacturers who continue to send over goods to be sold at forced sales at any price; if that practice be continued the loss will be enormous.' Mr. Biddle, who is well known in America, in a letter addressed to this country last year, spoke of the injurious extent to which British merchandise was forced into the American markets. And I might quote much more to show that goods are frequently exported for want of the market at home for which they have been produced, and which for some reason has failed: in this case I ascribe the failure chiefly to the heavy payments that have been required for food.

Another proof that I might give of the depression at home would be the diminished consumption of certain articles on which revenue is collected, as shown by the amount collected in the different quarters ending in January 1839 and 1840. I will take four articles of ordinary consumption:—

	£				£
Hops in 1839	298,348	in the year ending 1840			280,079
Malt ,,	5,211,798	,,	,,	,,	4,845,948
Soap ,,	1,047,545	,,	,,	,,	740,000
Spirits ,,	5,451,792	,,	,,	,,	5,442,477

But I can fortify my opinion that there has been a diminished power of consumption at home owing to the influences that I have traced to the Corn Laws, by the authority of a gentleman whose name will, I am sure, be received by the House with great respect: I mean Mr. Jones Loyd,[1] who in a pamphlet recently published inquires into the causes of the commercial distress of the last year in this country. He places first in order:—

The succession of two bad harvests in a country afflicted with laws which render such an occurrence peculiarly oppressive to the community, and by a peculiar felicity in mischief, contrive to make monetary derangement, and consequently commercial pressure, the inevitable accompaniment of the misfortune of the seasons. The poison of impolicy is thus thrown into the fiendish cauldron of injustice,

> For a charm of powerful trouble
> Like a hell-broth to boil and bubble.

In referring to this gentleman I am not naming a person likely to express himself rashly or incautiously, or one who has no stake in the country, as it is called ; but I am referring to one who is probably the possessor of more property than any of those who will take part in the discussion this even-

---

[1] The present Lord Overstone.

ing—property of every description, not only in money but also in land ; and whose judgment is held in high esteem wherever he is known.

And now we will just consider what are the consequences of this monetary derangement and commercial pressure of which Mr. Loyd speaks ; for there ought to be something to correspond to them in the actual condition of some of our manufacturing towns if these things are true. A trustworthy Report from one of those districts that I have here will enlighten the House upon the subject ; and I will therefore read from it the result of an inquiry made at Bolton a few weeks since :—

In the cotton mills alone about 95,000l. less have been paid during the last twelve months. Many of the mills have been entirely stopped for all or part of the time, and with only two exceptions all have worked short time for a considerable portion of the past year. I have made a very careful calculation from extensive personal inquiry, and assert most confidently that altogether there must have been at least 130,000l. less paid in wages in the Bolton Union. Now, add this 130,000l. less in wages to the 195,000l. more for food, and there is a total loss to Bolton of 325,000l.! What are the consequences? There are now in Bolton 1,125 houses untenanted, of which about fifty are shops, some of them in the principal streets. Here is a loss to the owners of 10,000l. to 12,000l. a year. The shopkeepers are almost ruined by diminished returns and bad debts. There were, a short time ago, three sales of the effects of shopkeepers in one day. Distraints for cottage rents occur daily. The arrears of cottage rents, and the debts to shopkeepers, are incalculable, but they must amount to many thousand pounds. The pawnbrokers' shops are stowed full of the clothing, furniture, and even bedding of the destitute poor. Fever is also prevalent. Mr. R. S. Kay, one of the medical officers of the union, and a young practitioner of great promise, lately took the infection of malignant typhus fever, and last week fell a victim to his harassing duties.

He had latterly worked almost day and night. A short time ago 590 persons were relieved by the Poor Law guardians in one day, in amounts varying from six to eighteen pence per head per week. In many cases two or three families are crowded into one house. In one case, seventeen persons were found in a dwelling about five yards square. In another, eight persons, two pair of looms, and two beds, in a cellar six feet under ground, and measuring four yards by five. There are scores of families with little or no bedding, having literally eaten it, *i.e.* pawned or sold it for food! The out-door relief to the poor is three times greater in amount than on the average of the three years ending 1838. South of Bolton, four miles, a large spinning establishment, giving employment to 800, and subsistence to 1,800 persons, has been entirely stopped for nine months. The proprietor has upwards of 100 cottages empty, or paying no rent, and, although possessed of immense capital, finds himself unable to continue working his mills to advantage. Entering Bolton from Manchester, another mill, requiring 180 hands, has been entirely standing for eighteen months. In the centre of the town, another, 250 hands, stopped several weeks. North of Bolton, one mile, a spinning, manufacturing, and bleaching establishment, on which 1,200 persons were dependent for subsistence, has been entirely standing for four months. Several machine makers and engineers are now employing one or two hundred hands less than usual, at wages varying from 15s. to 40s. a week. A public subscription, amounting to nearly two thousand pounds, has just been raised to mitigate, in some degree, the sufferings of the destitute poor ; in fact, to deal out a scanty pittance, just sufficient to keep them from actual starvation, to a body of workmen who possess, perhaps, greater skill and industry than any population of similar numbers on the face of the globe, but who are forbid, by the inhuman policy of our land-owners, to exchange the produce of their labour for food in the open market of the world !

And that really was the cause of their distress. And this melancholy state of things is unfortunately by no means confined to the Cotton Districts, as I myself know well from information that I have procured from the place that I represent. Is it not strictly in point, I would ask, to bring these matters before the House? I am not one who would advise the Legislature to interfere simply because of the existence of distress ; but when great evil and great distress can be traced to the law, then I think that it is the duty as it is in the power of the Legislature to interfere. I believe that in this case it is in the power of the House to give instant relief; I believe that it is possible to give permanent relief. The people are now suffering from the high price of provisions ; and they are suffering for want of commerce with those countries where the food is grown cheap. The warehouses here are full of foreign grain ; and the countries where it is grown are ready to negotiate with us for a regular interchange of products. But nevertheless the people are starving and we forbid them to touch the cheap and abundant food within their reach. The people want employment and we refuse to allow them to work for corn-growing customers and employers. Our manufactures are stopped because payments from abroad are not made for goods already supplied, owing to the scarcity of money. Abroad they offer us flour in payment for our manufactures, and our manufacturers are willing to take it and would at once be willing to execute fresh orders upon receiving it ; but the law forbids the people to touch it without payment of the duty, and thus stops the payment that would be readily made by the merchants in America to the manufacturers of this country. This is no mere opinion, it is the fact. America owes a large debt to our merchants in this country ; be-

cause of its own monetary embarrassments it has no
means of paying this debt, but large quantities of
flour have been sent to this country on American
account ; could these quantities of flour be admitted
not only would the debt be paid and relief thereby
be given to our manufactures, but the manufacturers
would be ready to execute fresh orders and thus give
employment to our people who are starving for want
of it.

We are, moreover, now left without a pretence for
saying that the States from which we might import
corn have not always been and are not now ready to
admit our manufactures on terms of reciprocity.   I
do not understand the denial of it if it proceeds from
any authority.   Is it intended to imply that the late
President of the Board of Trade stated what was false
when he said that besides the official communications
that he read to the House, he had perused many other
letters from foreign Ministers all showing willingness
on the part of the several countries they represented
to reduce their tariffs on our applying the same principle to their products?   And what does the able
Report of Dr. Bowring but distinctly confirm the
impression made by the official documents read by
Mr. Thomson, and prove even at this hour the
readiness of those countries to trade with us?   I
believe what is contained in Dr. Bowring's Report,
for it corresponds exactly with the information that
I procured myself when in those countries, and I have
since heard no reason to question its correctness.

Already the effects of our system in compelling

those States to employ their population in manufacture may be seen in the following official statement taken from the first and last year of the tables of the Board of Trade relating to our trade with the corn-growing countries :—

MANUFACTURED GOODS EXPORTED TO RUSSIA, GERMANY, AND PRUSSIA, IN 1832 AND 1838.

	1832. £	1838. £
Cotton Manufactures . .	1,273,355	946,433
Hosiery	359,157	197,615
Linen Manufactures . .	6,429	25,111
Silk	20,888	17,629
Woollen	952,450	815,785
	2,612,279	2,002,573
Deficiency, notwithstanding a great increase of population		609,706

To enable these countries to employ their population in manufacturing clothing, to make up the deficiency of their imports, the following statement, from the same source, shows the yarns exported to them in the same years :—

	1832. £	1838. £
Cotton Twist and Yarn .	2,935,775	3,502,186
Linen Yarns . . .	65	29,871
Woollen	137,082	229,572
	3,072,922	3,761,629
Increase of Material to work into cloth . . .		688,707

But as it is needful, in order that these countries shall successfully rival England at home and in neutral markets, that they shall have our coals, iron, and steel, and more especially our machinery and millwork ; the following statement, from the

same source, shows the progress of our exports of these materials
in the same years to these countries :—

	1832.	1838.			
	£	£			
Coals . . .	27,790	56,350	increase	100 per cent.	
Iron and Steel .	75,295	190,222	,,	250	,,
Machinery and					
Millwork .	7,863	97,479	,,	1,250	,,
Total .	110,948	344,051	average	300	,,

The result is a reduction in the export of manufactured goods,
which would employ our labour ; an increase of yarn to employ
their own labour ; and an increase of machinery of 1,250 per
cent., to render them perfectly independent of us in their own
countries, and to rival us in neutral countries.

But it is not only with the German State that it is
important for us to negotiate at this moment ; it is
also the moment yet left to us to engage in fresh
treaties with the United States and Brazil. And here
I must express a hope that the President of the Board
of Trade will tell us exactly the truth on this matter ;
and that he will tell us whether the general impression is correct that the present tariff of the United
States will cease in 1842, that about the same time
our present treaty with Brazil will expire, and that our
future relations with those countries will very much
depend upon the terms that we may be enabled to
offer them. I trust that the people will be under no
delusion on the subject, and that if we are to continue
these fetters on our commerce it will at least be done
deliberately and with our eyes open. The future
well-being of this country must depend upon the
extension of our commerce ; there is no other mode

of providing for our population or averting the decline of the nation. The foolish and impolitic fetters
with which we restrict it are now pressing upon the
vitals of the people ; and their cry for relief is to be
heard in the Motion before the House.

There are some who think that our Foreign Trade
has been carried too far, and that we should have been
better without it. This may or may not be true ;
but in any case the complaint comes too late ; our
Foreign Trade is now essential to our existence, and
we cannot lessen it or destroy it without jeoparding
our whole financial and commercial system. We must
look to it for the maintenance of our Credit and the col-
lection of our Revenue. And most certainly this is
not the moment to weaken the sources of our Revenue:
when our expenditure has increased and is increasing
by the price that we pay for our sustenance and by
the steps that we are taking to subdue our colonies, I
cannot, indeed, see how the deficiency in the Revenue
is to be supplied. The great sources of our Revenue
are found in the capacity of the people to consume
the articles that are taxed. I fail to see how it is
possible to expect that any fresh tax upon the daily
consumption of the people can be levied. For while
the price of provisions is enhanced by the Corn Laws
and the prospects of Trade remain as they are, how
can it be supposed that if a fresh tax were imposed
some other branch of the Revenue would not fall off?

The only resource that in wisdom or justice I can
think it would be possible to have recourse to would
be a property tax. In the year 1830 the country was

tending to the condition in which we now find it. The price of food was high and the taxation was grievously felt by the productive classes. Mr. Huskisson then in a most able speech (the last that he made in this place) on the state of the nation drew the attention of the House to the sources of our Revenue, and to the difficulties that would exist in collecting the same amount of revenue if trade declined and the productive classes remained depressed ; and he pointed to the imposition of a tax upon property as our only alternative. These were his words :—

The more general considerations to which I now claim the attention of the House are these. First, that no other country in Europe has so large a proportion of its taxation bearing directly upon the incomes of labour and productive capital. Secondly, that in no other country of the same extent—I think I might say in none of five times the extent of this kingdom—is there so large a mass of income belonging to those classes who do not directly employ it in bringing forth the produce of labour. Thirdly, that no other country has so large a proportion of its taxation mortgaged (in proportion to the amount of that mortgage are we interested in any measure which, without injustice to the mortgagee, would tend to lessen the absolute burden of the mortgage). Fourthly, that from no other country in the world does so large a proportion of the class not engaged in production (including many of the wealthy) spend their incomes in foreign parts. I know I may be told that by taxing that income you run the risk of driving them to withdraw their capital altogether. My answer is, First, that ninety-nine out of every hundred of these absentees have no such command over the source of their income. Secondly, that the danger is now of another and more alarming description—that of the productive capitals of this country being transferred to other countries, where they would be secure of a more profitable return. The relief of industry is the remedy against that danger.

I believe that the people will now turn their

attention to this same mode of obtaining relief ; and certainly I doubt if any new tax but that on property will be submitted to.

I am afraid that I have exhausted the patience of the House by so far detailing the mischievous results of the Corn Laws, and I will proceed no further ; but I cannot conclude without exhorting those who have hitherto opposed any change, to pause well before they pronounce their decision again upon this question. I ask them whether they perceive anything in the appearance of circumstances around them to encourage the belief that the people will adopt the views they have hitherto expressed? Do they think that any change of opinion has occurred in the public mind since the last Session? Do they not, on the contrary, know that great numbers have come forth and declared their opposition to the existing Corn Laws who were silent before? Are there not many classes who have never spoken before, now eager upon the subject? I draw the attention of the House to the fact that some of the most cautious and conservative persons in the community, men who were supposed to preside over the monetary system of the country and who were most averse to any change, have come forward and declared their opinion that these Laws are extremely injurious to all the great interests with which they are connected. Have not a greater number of the working classes now pronounced their opinion upon this subject than ever did before? I want, therefore, to know what it is that is expected to result from the rejection of this Motion.

The Hon. Member for Rutland has declared his determination to oppose it ; and I certainly admire the bold injustice of the Hon. Gentleman more than the insidious proceeding of the Hon. Member for Cambridge, who has proposed an amendment and left the real mischief of the Laws untouched.   What do these gentlemen expect to gain by such a course?   Do they expect that all those who have come forward and devoted their attention to the subject, who have sacrificed their property in the cause, and who have pledged themselves for the future to agitate this question until it is brought to a satisfactory conclusion [Opposition cheers]—yes, I think it is a strong test of the earnestness of men when they devote their money to promote an object—do Hon. Gentlemen who oppose my Motion expect that by its rejection all those persons of whom I have spoken will go home and admit themselves to be in error?   Do they expect that those persons will say : ' We certainly did think we were right, but we have found after discussion that we are wrong ; that all those who have agitated the question are in error ; and that the Corn Laws are a gain and a blessing to us.   Let us forget our folly, and never revert to the matter ' ?   Is it reasonable to suppose that the great mass of the people will altogether reverse their language upon this subject, and adopt that quiescent and convenient course, if this Motion is rejected?   If Hon. Gentlemen do not expect this what is it that they conceive will be the consequence of its rejection?   Why, the people will return to their homes in the conviction that they are right, and at the same time satisfied that the House of Commons will not do them justice. And what prospect does this present? Will it decide the question? If there is difficulty now in making arrangements in the settlement of property, will the mere rejection of this Motion facilitate the views of those who reject it? Will it allay the anxiety of the public mind on the subject? What is there to induce the people to admit that they have been wrong? They do not doubt themselves that they are cruelly injured by the Corn Laws. What eminent authority, what person of any kind has lately appeared to shake them in this conviction? And yet, what year has passed that some fresh person whose interest or intelligence entitle him to credit has not appeared to denounce the Laws? On all other great questions men of ability advocating opinions in favour of the proposition advanced as well as in opposition to it have appeared ; but with respect to this particular question there is hardly a single man of eminence and intelligence who has undertaken to write in support of the present Laws. [Ironical cheers from the Opposition.] If any able publication has appeared in favour of the views of the Hon. Gentlemen opposite, I am unaware of the fact, and I should certainly feel great pleasure at having an opportunity of perusing it.

But while there is comparative silence observed by the advocates of the existing system, men of the greatest talent and most extensive information are coming forth daily with publications of their opinions against it. What, then, can Hon. Gentlemen expect to result from their resistance to any change? I pray the House to pause before it comes to a decision to resist all inquiry. I have abstained from stating my own views of what, consistent with justice and policy, should be substituted for the present Corn Laws. I have been satisfied with pointing out the evils that result from these Laws. And consequently there is no pretext for resisting the Motion on the score of the known opinions of the mover.

But supposing that the House should now resist all inquiry, how long will those who vote against it abide by their vote? Let them reflect how soon it may be that they will be called upon to vote in the directly opposite way. And whether such conduct will reflect credit either upon the House as a body, or themselves individually. For this reason if for no other I ask the House to pause before it opposes all change. It would be of no use to say that because I proposed this Question the House would not assent to it ; or that because I wished to see the Corn Laws totally repealed those who had the power to resist all change, those who had the power to determine the precise amount of change would not consider the subject. The people would not be deluded by such distinctions and pretences as these. The Motion is now made by one who has a perfect right to make it ; and those who vote against it will be very justly considered the friends and advocates of the Corn Laws.

And let the House bear well in mind who they are that are arrayed against them. This is no mere dispute between land-owners and manufacturers. Such an assertion is the weak invention of the enemy and uttered for the purpose of throwing discredit on the subject. No ! The Question before the House is, above any other that could be named, one in which the great majority of the community are interested one way, and a comparatively small section of it deem themselves interested the other way : the advantage in it enjoyed by the minority is due to their position in the Legislature where their power greatly prevails. But is it wise to rely solely on this power? As far as I have been able to collect the opinions of that great and intelligent portion of the population termed the working class, they rest their claims to the Suffrage chiefly and with emphatic distinctness on these grounds : that their interests and those of the community at large are not duly represented in the House of Commons ; that they are bound by laws enacted and maintained by those who have no fellow-feeling with them ; and that the general conduct of the Legislature is their strong argument for widening and altering the character of the Constituency. And as far as I can collect the views of the many thousands of this class who have petitioned for the repeal of the Corn Laws, they have done so as a sort of test of the character and consti-tution of the House to which they may point hereafter as a ground for the assertion of their claims.

But do the working classes stand alone? Have not other classes attached themselves to them? Are not the classes immediately above them acting cor-dially with them upon this occasion? The working

classes certainly speak with confidence of the House
not doing them justice in this matter ; but for the
moment they consent to act with the middle classes,
whose language to those below them generally is :
' Act with us, petition the House respectfully, pray
for the redress of your grievances patiently, do not
believe that Parliament will reject your prayer and
refuse you justice, we will join you.' And they have
petitioned patiently ; but it is well known that every
working man who has signed the petitions this year
has declared that if they prove abortive they are the
last that he will sign for the repeal of the Corn Laws :
the next will be for the reform of the House of Commons itself.

There is now upon the question of the Corn Laws
perfect union between the middle and the working
classes. Do Hon. Members believe that under common
disappointment there would not be union as firm and
cordial between them upon the other, the ultimate
question that would then be raised? If this Motion
is rejected, I believe that three years will not elapse
before such an alliance will be formed for the purpose
of a further reform in the constitution of this House.
The middle classes experience the mischief of these
Laws, and they call for their repeal. The working
classes suffer from them equally—I believe in a much
greater degree ; but they say that it is useless to call
upon this House to repeal them ; and they tell the
middle class that it is for this reason that they want
the Franchise. They do not call for change for the
sake of change, but because no advance will be made

in the House on these questions of national interest until they can throw their weight into the political scale. Does the House suppose for one moment that it is able to change an opinion thus deliberately formed and strongly maintained, by the rude rejection of the present Motion?

A few months ago I attended a meeting of the working classes at Manchester, when I witnessed the most gratifying spectacle of upwards of 5,000 working men who had just quitted their daily avocations, assembled together at dinner to express their opinions upon this vital question. A more orderly, respectful, or attentive meeting, and one where those decent observances requisite in public assemblies were more regarded, I never witnessed. Nothing could have been more striking in contrast with the conduct of many other meetings composed of persons who are accustomed to discredit and disparage the people, than the decorous deportment of that vast assemblage. I do not doubt that a similar feeling and conduct would be displayed throughout this kingdom wherever the working people might assemble.

Once more, then, let me ask, What does the House think would be the effect of the rejection of this Motion on these men or any others in their circumstances equally endowed with qualities entitling them to respect? Is it to be supposed that they would tamely submit to the injury and affront that you would offer them by refusing an inquiry into the working of the Corn Laws? Would they believe that they were in error, because those who are interested in the Laws asserted them to be? Let the majority of the House make it a matter of calculation with themselves and ask what they will gain by persisting in the maintenance of the Laws as they are, and incurring all the odium that attaches to such a course? Whatever its opinion really is the House should look at this question practically. Granted that the repeal of the Corn Laws is an evil, is it not an inevitable one? The people believe that the Laws are an intolerable evil ; does the House, in anything it says, prove to them that they are not? And do they not hear, and have they not heard, from some of the most distinguished men in the land that they are right in their belief—that the Corn Laws are unjust and unwise and that they rightly refer their sufferings to them?

Still I fear that these considerations are not weighing with the majority of this assembly, and that this Motion is to be rejected. If it is I shall then only say that the responsibility of all the consequences that follow from such a course must be fixed upon the majority. Whatever happens, whatever disturbance follows, whatever evils occur, be they social or political or of a physical kind, if they result from these Laws the whole blame and responsibility must attach to those persons individually and collectively who give their vote this evening against my Motion.

The people are now enduring great physical suffering, which on weighty professional authority I ascribe to the miserable food to which the Corn Laws condemn them ; discontent, springing from a sense of injustice inflicted on them by this House,

pervades the working classes throughout the kingdom ; their attention once reluctantly is now habitu-
ally devoted to the consideration of political subjects ;
and their feelings, from these several circumstances,
are becoming hourly heightened by the agitation of
the question of the Corn Laws.   The House has at
the present moment an opportunity of allaying the
excitement by relieving the people from the pressure
that is bearing them down.   Will they throw away the
opportunity?   Let them! and they will be indebted
to fortune alone should they be enabled to regain it.

I will no longer obtrude upon the attention of the
House.   If I have expressed myself with too much
warmth I regret it.   If I have done so, it is because
of a very strong conviction on my part that I am
right on this subject and from a grave apprehension
that the House may be guilty of the egregious error of
resisting the Motion.   I now move : That the House
resolve itself into a Committee of the whole House
to take into consideration the Act 9 Geo. IV. c. 60,
regulating the importation of foreign grain.

VI.

HOUSE OF COMMONS, May 26, 1840.

Determined not to be thwarted by the expedient resorted to by the upholders of the Corn Laws on April 1, Mr. Villiers renewed his Motion on May 26, after he had presented petitions with a quarter of a million signatures attached to them, in addition to those signed by a million and a quarter presented on the occasion of his previous Motion. The moment he began to speak a firm determination not to give him a fair hearing was shown by the House. A most disgraceful scene of uproar ensued: the Speaker's orders were totally disregarded, and it was not until the dinner hour had reduced the House to about a hundred Members that Mr. Villiers was allowed to proceed without interruption. As soon, however, as the House began to refill, the noise and confusion recommenced. Mr. Strutt could scarcely make himself heard. Mr. Warburton was interrupted by loud cries of 'Divide,' and when Mr. Mark Philips, representing the most important manufacturing community in the kingdom, rose, the clamour was so great that it was found impossible to carry on the debate. A Division was taken, and the numbers were 300 against, to 177 for the Motion.

THE House is, I believe, fully aware that it is in consequence of the extraordinary course which it thought proper to adopt with regard to my last Motion on the Corn Laws that it has now become my duty again to propose the subject for its consideration. I trust that Hon. Members feel that whilst that course was unsatisfactory to the public, offensive to those interested in the discussion, and almost cruel to the much larger number who refer their recent sufferings to the operation of these Laws, it has also been unattended by any advantage or convenience to this House.

I, for one, am not sorry to see that when the House shrinks from a fair decision or a full discussion on a question vitally important to the people at large it derives no advantage from its wrong-doing.

I know that it may be said that the immediate occasion of the course to which I have referred was the Motion of the Honourable Member for Bridport. [Cries of 'Hear, hear!' from the Opposition benches.] But I ask when was it that my Hon. Friend moved the adjournment of the House? Why, when this House had decided that the debate should not be adjourned at all, which it did after six hours out of the seven hours during which the debate had lasted, had been occupied by persons opposed to the Motion; when the last speaker only closed his address at past one in the morning, after the Members for the most important and most distressed of the manufacturing districts had been referred to and the interests of their constituents misstated, and after thirty or forty Members had left the House on the faith that the debate would be adjourned—then it was that the House insisted on dividing and that my Hon. Friend thought that it would be more expedient to resume the discussion at a future time when a fair decision might be taken upon it.

The majority, therefore, have to thank themselves for any disadvantage accruing to their cause by an adjourned discussion; for I do not suppose that it can be very politic in those who desire to maintain these Laws to invite public attention to them more than is possible. And if I am to judge of the

scornful manner in which the Member for East
Somerset referred to the mode in which I had introduced this subject, when, as the House remembers,
he complained with so much impatience that gentlemen like himself should be kept from their avocations
in the country to listen to such dull treatises on the
Corn Laws—I say that taking that gentleman to
represent the taste and temper of the House, I do not
suppose that at this season, when there is even more
to divert the mind of the House, it can be more
agreeable to hear another essay on what affects the
poverty and privations of the humbler classes.

And I hear, again, that I have but ill chosen the
moment for renewing the discussion. I should like
to know when it would be agreeable to a majority
of this House to discuss the matter. The avocation
of the Member for East Somerset was, as I understood him, to attend some local Bench of Justice that
was used to profit by his learning. This time I am
told that it is the season when gentlemen quit the
Bench and enter another department of service, and
tenants, converted into troops, pass in review before
their lords. And the grievance now is that gentlemen are again brought to London from the country
to listen to another dull discussion. As far as I am
concerned, I am sorry to disturb their manœuvres,
feeling sure that they are more innocent away than
in this House ; for it will not be in my day that I
shall satisfy them that respect for the House would
be better insured by a patient consideration here
of Laws proved to be bad than by a display of

incompetence for the Bench or inefficiency for the
Field elsewhere.

However, whether it be thought a trick or a
triumph to have disposed of the question before, I
shall not complain of the circumstance since it has
enabled us to discuss it again ; and I have seen too
much of the advantage of discussion on this subject not to value very highly its continuance. Discussion has, in truth, done nearly all that can be
expected of it : it has disclosed the truth and exposed what is untrue in the matter. And notwithstanding the fallacy and vague generality with
which it has been attempted to perplex it, discussion
has certainly cleared the question of confusion, and
brought it back to the point from which it was at first
advanced : namely, what right or reason there is for
one class of proprietors to impose a heavy burden
on the rest of the community for the purpose of
swelling their own fortunes. This is the question
the people ask ; this is the question that has not
been answered ; but it is a question that must be
answered if the public are not to be left in the
belief that the Corn Laws rest upon nothing but the
rude right of power—a reckless, ruinous, heartless
enactment, maintained for the interest of a few,
though really injurious to all. Such is the opinion
of the great body of the people so far as public
sentiment can be collected ; and it has been elicited
by that opinion being denied. It would be well for
the House to reflect upon the progress of opinion
on this matter.

In 1837 either despair of justice or dread of conflict had produced what is called apathy on the subject of the Corn Laws ; few petitions were presented to this House relating to it ; and a county Member thought it decent and safer, when I rose to speak upon it, to attempt to count the House out. In 1838 I brought the subject forward ; and then it was asserted that the manufacturers were indifferent to it ; that they were in no way injured by the Corn Laws, but rather that they partook of the benefit that it was asserted others derived from them. Mark the result of so treating the subject.

Before the Session of 1839 there was hardly a Chamber of Commerce that had not petitioned this House, and hardly a manufacturing town that had not appointed its delegate to proceed to London and respectfully ask the House to listen to the facts that they were ready to detail in answer to the strange misapprehension of their interests which seemed to prevail in it.

How did you deal with their petitions ? On what ground did you dismiss their prayer to be heard in the face of the country and the world at this Bar ? You thought it convenient to assume that what they said was true ; but you denied the policy of changing the Laws, which you declared rested upon a general regard to the interests of the community. You said that the working classes were not of the same mind with the petitioners, and that it was a mere selfish manufacturing question. Now, what followed from this assertion ? Why, that there was scarcely a town of any note in Great Britain where there was not some meeting assembled or some petition signed by the working people against the Corn Laws as if for the purpose of recording, at least, their opinion respecting them ; and although they may never again petition the House on the subject (many have declared that they will not), they have by the sentiments expressed in their petitions left no one in doubt as to their views of the justice, humanity, or policy of such laws.

And how stands the question now ? What has been the result of all the agitation and discussion that it has everywhere excited ? No less than this : that all the pretences on which it has been sought to defend the Corn Laws have been thoroughly sifted and examined ; and that at the present moment there is hardly a mechanic or a schoolboy in any town who is not familiar with the fallacies that have been used for the occasion, and the refutation of them. I have listened to many debates on this subject ; I have looked through those that have taken place in Parliament at former times ; and I find that they all resolve themselves into some three or four phrases which, though they may be varied in expression, are simply repetition of the same things. I shall now merely refer to them with the view of noting them to the public and the hope of preventing their repetition this evening.

First, there is the notion that the high price of food occasions a high rate of wages, and that the people have therefore an interest in the continuance of the Corn Laws. Next, that by the landlord's receiving a higher price for his land, he becomes a better customer to the manufacturer. Then, that it is part of the system of this country that when an interest cannot maintain itself it should be maintained, and that the Corn Laws are the mode of affording that support to the land-owner by law. And lastly, that it is unwise for a country to depend upon other countries for food.

If any person will examine the arguments urged for the Corn Laws he will find them comprehended in one or other of these sentences. I am very glad that such things are put forward, for it has forced upon the public the discussion of matters deeply interesting to the middle and working classes from which their attention is usually diverted by the absorbing interest of individual affairs. It has, moreover, led to a particular consideration of the circumstances that influence the condition of the working class in this country ; and it has fairly brought all the fallacies advanced on the subject to the test of common sense and experience.

Now, what may be said with truth to have resulted from the inquiry into the connection between the high price of food and the condition of the labouring class ? Why, the unpleasant disclosure that a greater mockery of their misery could scarcely have been devised or uttered by any person than to say that the high price of food has been productive of anything but sorrow, misery, and wretchedness to the poor ; that in the progress of society in this country, in proportion as the food of the people has become more scarce their condition has become worse ; that the agricultural labourers are in some respects worse off now than they were three centuries ago ; and that during the last eighteen months, when food has been very high, their sufferings have been greatly aggravated. In making this statement I am supported by an authority which may be supposed to be quite unprejudiced : I allude to Mr. Hallam, who, inquiring into the history of the labouring classes, is compelled, after allowing for the many advantages that modern inventions have procured for them, to conclude that their condition has deteriorated in comparison with what it was in past ages. I will quote his words :—

> I should find it difficult to resist the conclusion that, however the labourer has derived benefit from the cheapness of manufactured commodities and the inventions of machinery, he is much inferior in ability to support a family than his ancestors were three or four centuries ago. I know not why some here suppose meat was a luxury seldom attained by a labourer ; doubtless he could have procured as much as he pleased, but from the greater cheapness of cattle, it seems to follow that a more considerable portion of his diet consisted of animal food than at present. It was remarked by Sir J. Fortescue that he thought the English lived far more on animal food than their neighbours the French, and it was natural to ascribe their superior courage to that circumstance.

It is strictly relevant to point to this circumstance since we are called upon to judge of the policy of these Laws by their influence on the condition of the agricultural labourers.

A paper by Arthur Young in the ' Annals of Agriculture ' further confirms this view, and shows that the wages of the labourer formerly commanded a larger amount of the necessaries of life than they can do at present.

However, the matter need not be in doubt : it is within the power of every person to know what wages the agricultural labourer receives, and what they will procure for him. My statements were questioned as to one county to which I referred ; and subsequently to the debate I made inquiry on the point, and merely found that to be generally the case in the county which I had adduced as occurring in some parishes of it only. Married people with families rarely get more than 9s. a week—the maximum appears to be 11s. ; and young unmarried men, as able to work as the married men, earn only 6s. or 6s. 6d. I own that I was wholly unable to learn where it was that these men preferred 6s. to 10s., of which fact, however, we were assured by the Member for Wiltshire. Now, when the House refers to one of its very recent Reports upon the working of the Poor Law, and finds there that a married man has to spend nearly 7s. 6d. a week in bread and flour, it may judge how his family must fare with regard to the other wants of life.

But perhaps a more astounding argument has been recently advanced for the Corn Laws than even that of their being advantageous to the labourer : I mean the assertion that the change is sought solely by the master manufacturers in order to reduce the wages of the labourer. This has actually appeared in a publication of a society that has just been

instituted for the professed purpose of protecting
British agriculture ; but, in truth, for the purpose
of upholding the present Corn Laws.   It is stated in
the prospectus of this society—patronised doubtless
by the nobility, gentry, and clergy—that the manufacturers wish to lower the rate of wages in seeking
to repeal the Corn Laws.   It would be curious to
learn whether this is stated in ignorance or with the
knowledge of its being untrue.   Do they know or
have they inquired into the condition of the people
in the manufacturing districts ?   If they have, can
they say how, under any change of the law, their
wages could be lowered ?   And, if the object of the
manufacturers is simply to reduce the wages of these
men, could they fare better than at this moment when
wages are at their minimum ?   Have the wealthy
patrons of this society ever read the Reports of the
Commissioners on the hand-loom weavers ?   These
unfortunate people, amounting in number to 800,000,
cry out for the repeal of these Laws on the ground
that they are the great cause of their suffering ; and
yet this Agricultural Protection Society would imply
that Repeal is a matter affecting only the masters,
and that the interests of the men are against it !
[Sir C. BURREL : ' Hear, hear ! '] I hardly know
how to explain that cheer of the Hon. Baronet ;
but if it be to affirm this charge against the master
manufacturers, I must repeat my question to him :
How does he explain the complaints of the masters
when the men are nearly starving ?   The Hon.
Baronet should learn the condition of the people

under the operation of his Corn Laws before he talks of its being possible to make it worse by their repeal.

But if any man wishes to understand the bearing of this question on the manufacturing interests let him read the answers of these poor weavers to the Hand-loom Commissioners. If men wish to learn that with which they ought already to be acquainted, let them study those blue volumes containing the opinions, and referring to the interests, of these working men. I was really startled at their shrewdness and sagacity; and I was in consequence led to ask one of the central Commissioners what he thought of those replies. He admitted that he, like myself, had been struck with the just and sagacious views the hand-loom weavers took of their interests. What is their simple reasoning on this subject? They say: 'These Corn Laws act as a great restraint on trade in this country; and whatever extends the trade increases the demand for labour, and with that demand our wages rise. Whenever that demand increases we find ourselves better off; and we now feel that these Laws are injuring us by diminishing that demand and by increasing the cost of food.' It is true they refer to other remedies than the repeal of the Corn Laws to meet their case; and we find among their suggestions one for taxing machinery and another for universal suffrage; but these are not urged altogether without reason. They say: 'We have as good a right to have a tax imposed upon machinery as the land-owners have to a tax upon the produce of more fertile soils. The country in the last case is taxed for the benefit of a class : we have an equal claim to a tax on machinery ; for the principle is the same : it is taxing the community for the benefit of a few.' And they certainly do further say that if the Legislature will neither act wisely as regards the public and repeal the Laws, nor consistently towards them by taxing machinery, then they will seek to be represented more faithfully in this House than they are at present. They claim the Suffrage with the view of getting justice to themselves ; and I own that I see nothing inconsequent in such reasoning.

Before I quit the question of the influence of the Corn Laws upon the working population, I must adduce something in support of my position that scarcity and dearness of provisions tend to generate disease and accelerate death among them. For this purpose I cannot do better than quote a letter entitled to credit, from a Member of the College of Surgeons now practising in an important manufacturing town. Dr. Ryan, of Stockport, writes :—

I take the liberty of addressing you on the necessity of cheap bread for our artisans and their families. As a medical man, I feel that the results of my experience may, with propriety, be added to your information on the subject. My practice is much among the poorer classes in this populous town and neighbourhood ; for, in addition to my private engagements as a professional man, I am the medical officer to the ' Stockport Board of Health,' consisting of upwards of 3,000 members. I find, Sir,—1. That a large amount of the labouring population in this neighbourhood is insufficiently fed and clothed ; that the scarcity of clothing arises from the high price of provisions, which thus absorbs, for the support of life, nearly all the hard-earned wages of each family; and that the cause of the insufficient diet is the high price of flour. 2. I find that the scarcity of good substantial food is productive of many very fatal diseases, and much misery among our people, and especially among poor children, whose sustenance ought to be principally farinaceous. 3. That among many—very many—families, portions only of whom can at present find employment, the small amount of wages accruing weekly is consumed in the purchase of oatmeal and potatoes; that whole families subsist, week after week, on meal gruel; and that payment of rent, and the purchase of fuel and clothing, are out of the question; and that the result too frequently is, the confiscation of their household goods and removal to the workhouse. 4. That to avoid the disgrace of seeking parochial relief, the most extreme misery and starvation are constantly endured by families in this town; and, although the standard of wages is continually falling, the necessaries of life are advancing in price, and therefore the ratio of misery is perpetually increasing. Such, Sir, are the impressions I have received in going from house to house, among our labouring poor. Day after day am I compelled to witness the most heartrending scenes of misery and privation, such, in fact, as none but medical men are allowed to behold, for the decent pride of an Englishman ever prompts him to conceal the full extent of his poverty from the public view. I have given you, Sir, no laboured details, no speculative theories, no proposed methods of amelioration. I leave, Sir, the remedy, with confidence, in the hands of men like yourself, who, prompted, I trust, by the principles of sound and unflinching philanthropy, will never rest until laws unnatural as the Corn Laws are, be for ever erased from the Statute-book.

I have also been supplied with a table showing the effect on the population of a high and low price of food. I regret that the table has not been completed down to the last year; but it is sufficient to enable us to form an opinion on the subject. I will not read the whole table to the House, but merely a portion of it showing the total number of deaths in seven of the manufacturing districts of

England at four different periods, together with the average prices of wheat per quarter at each period :—

Years	Average Price of Wheat per Quarter	Deaths	Excess of Deaths above those of the year 1804, when wheat was 60s. per quarter
	s. d.		
1801	118 3	55,965	11,171
1804	60 1	44,794	—
1807	73 3	48,108	3,314
1810	106 2	54,864	10,070

This shows that in the ratio that food was cheap the health of the community was good.

Is it not something shocking for the Legislature deliberately to persist in maintaining Laws that are ever spreading disease, occasioning death, and weighing down industry ; and all this for no other purpose than to add to the wealth of persons who do nothing themselves to add to the wealth of the country ? I do not mean to say that the wealthy classes are more unfeeling or hard-hearted than other people : the fact is they are not aware of the extent of the evil and of the misery occasioned by the Corn Laws, being misled by those who ought to know better. I believe that if they knew the real consequences of these Laws they would meet the question in a very different way from that in which they now meet it. But under the circumstances, would it not be worse than idle to let it be contended that the Home Trade is benefited by these Laws, when men have hardly the withal to buy bread, and consequently are obliged to forego the purchase of manufactures ?

The manufacturers' case is, in one respect, that

the Home Trade is injured by their customers being deprived of their ordinary means of consumption ; and though their case may have been misrepresented, it has not yet been disproved that by the Corn Laws you deprive them of customers both at home and abroad. With countries having only food to exchange for manufactures they are debarred from trading, for they are unable to effect the exchange that is essential to commerce. It is no answer to this objection to the Corn Laws that the whole exports of this country, with reference either to the character of the exports or to the countries to which they are sent, increase. It may satisfy the country that losing the markets of Europe has not yet been fatal to our commerce ; but it does not negative the fact that these markets are closed against us, and that the inconvenience arising from the terms on which alone we would allow trade to be conducted has induced those States to manufacture for themselves and to exclude the manufactures of this country.

And with respect to the Home Trade, it will not do to deny that it has been our policy to close and check the commerce between this country and other States. We have had a paper laid on the Table since the last discussion proving it to be the case. I will read the House an extract from the paper, consisting of the proposal of the Prussian Government to this country in 1826—before the Zollverein was formed —to enter into a Treaty of Commerce with us. The proposal runs thus :—

Assuming, then, that it will be agreeable to the British

Government to learn that Prussia is disposed to conclude a treaty of reciprocity, the Court of Berlin has directed the undersigned to propose to his Excellency, Mr. Canning, to enter into negotiation for that purpose. It would be ready to engage to make no change in its existing system for a certain number of years, and specifically not to increase the duties of import on English merchandise. But, on the other hand, it expects that the British Government will allow the importation of Prussian corn, subject to such duties as shall not exclude the possibility of carrying on that trade with a reasonable profit, and that it will grant greater facilities than it does at present to the importation of timber coming from the ports of Prussia. As the produce of English industry finds a very extensive market in the Prussian monarchy, whilst, on the other hand, Prussia can only import into England the produce of its soil, and principally corn and wood, it is evident that it is only by granting facilities to the importation of these two articles that it is possible to establish the relations between the two countries on a footing of reciprocity.

This was the distinct proposal submitted by the Prussian Government to our Minister. And what was the answer that Mr. Canning was compelled by the absurd policy of the Legislature of his country to make ? It was this :—

It becomes His Majesty's Government, in the judgment of this Committee, when a proposal for altering our Corn Laws is made to us by a foreign Government, as a condition of something to be done or omitted by that Government, at once to declare that we never can entertain such a proposal.

This was the answer that the British Minister was compelled to give to a foreign power proposing to enter into a beneficial Treaty of Commerce with this country, on whose manufacturing prosperity depends the livelihood of millions of our people ! This was the reception that the offers of the Prussian Government met with before the Zollverein was formed! And what do we hear since the formation of the Zollverein, at present including twenty-six millions of people who for commercial purposes are ready to act together ? From all our Ministers, from every Commissioner that we have sent to collect information on the subject, we hear that even now, before they again decide the amount of their tariffs as against this country, they are still ready to negotiate with us ; that it is the prevailing wish and desire among the people of those States to trade with us. But what can we do, if the Legislature pertinaciously refuses to allow us to place ourselves in a condition to negotiate with them ? For, as the French Minister wisely said, ' To get concessions from others we ought to be in a condition to grant them.'

If there be any doubt about the interest of the states in the Zollverein to trade with England, let the respective interests of the people on each side be examined. Admitting that there are twenty-six millions of people in these islands, and twenty-six millions in the Zollverein, what proportion, on the one hand and the other, is interested in agriculture and in manufactures ? I answer that in the Zollverein nearly eighteen millions in agriculture and the remainder only partially in manufactures ; whereas in England those who may be termed the agricultural interest are seldom put at more than one-fourth, and we know that this proportion has been gradually diminishing while the manufacturing interest has been increasing. It is clear, therefore, that the interests of the respective populations lie in an interchange of their mutual products; and consequently, as it is of great consequence to re-establish our commercial relations with these States, this is a most important moment. In 1842 the tariffs will have been fixed and, I believe, will not be altered again for twelve years. The same is the law with the United States. It is only an accident that their tariff has not been discussed this year : it will be next.

Now, I beg distinctly to call the attention of the House and of the country to these circumstances, in order to preclude all possibility of doubt as to the reason of our losing this advantage, if it is to be lost; and I make this statement deliberately in order that it may be referred to in future when the people are distressed and the manufactures are declining. The people will call to account for their condition those to whom they have intrusted their interests when they come to judge whether those interests have been protected or betrayed. It will be idle then to twaddle about what is called a 'System of Protection ; ' and the notion is absurd that the Corn Laws are only part of that system, when all other protected classes have repeatedly declared that the only Protection they desire is against the effects of the Corn Laws.

Even those who have been most tardy and timid in expressing their opinion on this subject (I mean those engaged in the silk trade) have rested their claim for Protection on the ground that there is yet maintained a Monopoly in all articles of necessary consumption. The weavers of Coventry have lately cried out against the Corn Laws, as one great cause of the diminishing demand for their labour and value of their wages. The people know and feel too well now—and they will have to feel it still more, though the rulers of this country may be ignorant of it—in what way Trade with other countries affects them; and what a fraudulent fallacy it is to assert that the repeal of the Corn Laws would reduce their wages. They know too well on what terms Foreign Trade is carried on now. They have the daily experience of orders coming over to them to be executed at certain low prices or not at all. And what a fearful struggle is constantly going on with men with large families, as to whether, working fourteen and sixteen hours a day at the expense of health and happiness for a miserable pittance, they shall execute the orders, or whether they shall refuse them and go at once to the workhouse. I know that this is a struggle that every year becomes more severe, and that the time will soon arrive when the prices offered to the operatives will be so low that they will be unable to work and sustain life upon them; and when they refuse them, the foreign merchant or, indeed, the English merchant will then get them executed in Belgium or Germany. What an insult it is then to their sense and to their poverty to tell them, when the money they receive is each year lower, that the price of food being high is an advantage to them! And it is by this difference between the condition of the manufacturing classes as compared with former years, it is by the result of these and other silly and suicidal restrictions on the freedom of commerce, that rivals are created, trade rendered languid, and industry cheated of its reward.

What excuse can any man of understanding pretend to find for such evils in the notion that the Corn Laws will avert a dependence on other countries for food ? This silly fear of dependence, which is an argument against commerce altogether if it be worth anything, has, after being ridiculed so as almost to preclude its repetition, been revived again this year on the authority of the President of the United States of America, and of Marshal Bugeaud in France. In short, the landed aristocracy of this country, having no argument of their own for the Corn Laws, eagerly seize upon what falls from a Republican President as applicable to his own country, to justify them in the maintenance of an anti-national Monopoly in this country. And what was the saying of this personage that has so delighted the landlords of England ? Mr. Van Buren declared that nothing could be more disastrous for a country than to depend upon another country for its food ; and Marshal Bugeaud, in the French Chamber, said that he would sooner see a Russian army march through France than see German beef consumed by French people. So that the people of England are to be half starved because such great characters have uttered these very wise sayings !

I could tell Mr. Van Buren, I think, what would be more disastrous than depending upon another country for food ; and that would be not to have another country to depend upon when you cannot supply yourself. And that must be the case with England, if our present policy is continued, whatever it may be with the United States. We cannot supply ourselves ; after twenty-five years' experience of the Corn Laws we have just experienced a greater deficiency than we have ever known before.

With respect to the French Marshal, he represented, I presume, the grazing interest of his country, and his doctrine has as much the good of the people to recommend it as the arguments of the land-owner in favour of the Corn Laws have to do with the general good of our country. But English people are not to be deceived by trash of this kind : they know that men do not grow grain to give it away ; and that it does not follow, as the case of Ireland pretty well proves, that a nation must be able to consume the corn that it produces. The people of this country must have the means of purchasing corn ; and the silly persons who are now injuring them by depriving them of custom for their manufactures are, in truth, only depriving themselves of their best market.

I have now exhausted the pretences of a public kind that are pleaded for the Corn Laws, and I contend that they are pretences that will not and cannot be much longer advanced. I think that there was some recognition of the truth of my contention during the last Debate. And, in proof of it, I would refer in the first place to what fell from the Member for Bassetlaw, who after beating about the bush a long while—at one time attempting to question my state-

ments about the wages of labourers and then disputing the accuracy of my reference to the Revenue,
finally said that he could not shut his eyes to the
great advantage that these Laws gave to the aristocracy ; that, in fact, by this means they tended much
to preserve the nice balance of power in the country
which had conduced so much to its greatness and
its glory ; and that on this account he would uphold
them.   A principle that certainly is intelligible,
whether or not it was discreet to avow it.   I know
no answer to it except that suggested by the question
of the people, whether the price they pay for this nice
balance of power is not rather too great.

The Member for Bassetlaw was, if I remember
rightly, followed by the Hon. Member for the North
Riding.   His defence of the Corn Laws was somewhat in contrast with that of his colleague on a
former occasion, who was in the habit of envelop-
ing the question with a cloud of statistics that left
us in doubt as to what we were discussing.   The
Hon. Member warned us on this side not to suppose
that the land-owners were so soft as to give up the
Corn Laws.   This was fair enough, for it at least
placed the question on intelligible grounds : between
him and the people it becomes simply a question as
to which will be soft enough to surrender their claims.
Thus we have it admitted that the Corn Laws give
extraordinary power to the aristocracy, and that the
aristocracy are not the people to surrender them.

And, indeed, this mode of arguing the question is not inconsistent with that pursued by the

Right Hon. Member for Tamworth, who also seems
to me to have abandoned the attempt to argue it
on its own merits ; and when the Noble Lord the
Member for Shropshire asks me why I do not reply
to the Right Hon. Baronet, I must tell the Noble
Lord that I have first to learn that the Right
Hon. Baronet differs from me. I suspect that he
agrees with me more than with the Noble Lord :
I argue against the Corn Laws, and the Right
Hon. Baronet does not argue for them, he only
fences with the friends of Repeal ; and the difference between him and his opponents is simply as
to the degree of mischief that they produce. The
sum of his arguments appears to be that the camel's
back is not yet broken ; on the contrary, he says
that the animal is very buoyant ; he seems almost
to doubt whether the burden does not conduce to
its buoyancy ; but if its back were broken, he contends, other backs have been broken also, and in
other places by other burdens. These are not his
words, but they are a fair illustration of what he
said. He proceeded with all that order and propriety
which distinguish his addresses, to dissect the statements and speeches of those who are in favour of
this Motion. He said that he would repeat to the
House the substance of what had been alleged against
the Corn Laws—namely, that they occasion a great
derangement of our monetary affairs ; that they cause
great fluctuations of price in corn ; and that they tend
to cripple the manufacturing interests. 'And then,'
he added, ' see how I will deal with these arguments.

In the first place you complain that they disturb the monetary system of the country. Now, I tell you that the Currency has been deranged before; and upon such occasions no person attributed that result to the operation of the Corn Laws. I say, further, that the Currency has been deranged in the United States, and that commercial embarrassment has occurred in France; and these results cannot have been owing to such a cause as you ascribe them to in this country. Again, with respect to the fluctuations in the price, this argument would imply that other articles are steady in price. Now, I can prove that coffee has fluctuated in price as well as corn; and that is my answer to your argument which would show that the Corn Laws have greatly aggravated the evils that are alleged to have occurred.' I could more fully illustrate the justice of my remark upon the Hon. Baronet's speech; but the fault in his argument was so obvious to everybody at the time, and it has been so commented upon in all the papers since, that I will not further take up your time by referring to it.

But the Right Hon. Baronet went on to show that there was error in supposing the country not to be in a prosperous state; and he showed this in a way that was certainly convenient: he assumed his own test of the fact. It was contended on this side that the people were badly off; that there was but scanty employment for their industry; that the difficulties cast in the way of trade by the restraints which the Corn Laws impose upon com-

merce prevent a steady or sufficient demand for
the labour of this country ; and we have shown
that internal consumption has declined during the
late year. Now, what says the Right Hon. Baronet?
He says : ' I cannot look at your proofs of declining
trade—they are unsatisfactory if they are just ; but
I have here that which is conclusive on the subject.
I have in my hand a Return of the exports to the
whole world from this country, and I find that
during the last year they have increased ; therefore
there can be no distress ; therefore the trade of this
country is extending to the different parts of the
world. [Lord DARLINGTON : ' Hear, hear !'] The
Noble Lord appears to assent by his cheer to the
conclusiveness of that reasoning. Would he then
at all times think an increased number of mortgages
and auctions conclusive of the prosperity of the
landed interest ? If he would not, does it not show
that the amount of property transferred or sold is
not conclusive as to the extent of the demand for it ;
and that unless a supply of any article is maintained
with a view to the steady and adequate demand for
it, it is rather a proof of loss or misfortune than of
prosperity ? And surely this is the reply to the
Right Hon. Baronet's reasoning from an unusual
amount of exports, in which he appeared to assume
that there cannot be consignments of goods arising
from necessity as well as to meet an increasing demand. The manufacturers allege that the articles
entered for home consumption have been less, while
the exports have increased ; and that the exports

have so increased because there has been less demand for them at home in consequence of a high price of food.

And here let me remind the Noble Lord who claims the Right Hon. Baronet as the champion of the landed interest, that if the Right Hon. Baronet fails in proving that the Corn Laws are compatible with the prosperity of manufactures, he is not so important an advocate of the landed interest as he assumes him to be; for the Right Hon. Baronet, if I understood him rightly, I will not exactly say threw overboard, but certainly set aside the favourite fancies of the country gentlemen on this question. It cannot but be remembered that after they had been for three consecutive nights showing us in their accustomed strain how it was that they had made the world go round, the Right Hon. Baronet rose and more than hinted to them how unadvisable it was to indulge in those notions of their consequence. He unhesitatingly avowed that it was not the idle and unproductive classes that had aggrandized this country, but that all her greatness and wealth were to be referred to her skill in manufacture and her enterprise in commerce; and then, after the admission of this truth, the Hon. Baronet showed the proper way to evade the real question; and he did this, not by disputing about the sources of our wealth and power, but by protesting that wealth and power had been attained, and that it would be dangerous to do anything to place them in jeopardy; that as we had become great with the Corn

Laws we should be unwise to attempt to become greater by repealing them : in short, by implying that we had become great in consequence of them, and not in spite of them.

If I am asked why I did not answer that argument in the best manner, I should say that it was because I had not had time to look into one of the Right Hon. Baronet's speeches in which he had been obliged to answer it himself because it had been brought against him. I knew that he had made such a speech ; for I remembered being in the House when he replied to an attack on this very ground upon Mr. Huskisson, when that statesman sought, much to his honour, to introduce more liberal principles into our commercial policy. Referring afterwards to the debates of that period, I found the following remark upon some senseless fear of change expressed on that occasion :—

Mr. Secretary Peel exhorted the House to firmness, reminding it that the eyes of Europe were upon it ; and he warned Parliament how greatly those sound and irrefragable principles of commercial policy, which they had heard so ably advocated, would be prejudiced, if it were to yield to the fears of the timid, or the representations of the interested.

This exhortation, I contend, might be applied with equal justice to the Right Hon. Baronet's argument in favour of the Corn Laws. What was his argument on this occasion ? He led us over half the globe inviting us to reflect on the vast possessions that we had acquired, on the grandeur and extent of our empire and the power that we possessed; and then, when we were lost in the contemplation of so much greatness and dominion, and hardly aware whether we were in England or Hindostan, he put it to us to consider whether it was not miraculous that we had achieved such glory, and whether it would not be presumptuous, and whether it would not be worse than folly, to place it in danger by any experimental theory like that of the repeal of the Corn Laws!

Now the Right Hon. Baronet knows well that this is precisely the sort of argument that has been used against himself whenever he has assumed the character of reformer, which as we know he does assume occasionally, and which we think suits his disposition far better than the character he is now assuming. He at one time employed himself very worthily in removing some of the black spots from our criminal code. We know since that he was then charged with disturbing what had been part of our system under which we had become great and glorious; and that he who was at the head of the Legislature deemed him a dangerous innovator in his own Cabinet.

Again, when the Right Hon. Baronet, highly to his credit, introduced a more perfect system of police, the old and inefficient system then existing was pointed to as being co-existent with all that we valued most in our institutions, and we had a sort of Saxon sentiment revived in favour of the old system of watch under which our habitations were unguarded and our streets in a state revolting to decency.

The Hon. Baronet knows that this is the hackneyed weapon with which every reformer is assailed whenever any abuse is attacked, and whenever any fallacy is worn out or exploded. And I take it to be the Right Hon. Baronet's predicament now that he has no other weapon to use. For what was the reason that the Hon. Baronet assigned for his vote, as he told it to us ? Why, that my Motion was one for a total repeal of the Corn Laws. In the first place that is not my Motion. I have, on the contrary, proposed only to test the House as to its determination of maintaining the Laws as they are : I move the preliminary form of a Committee of the whole House to consider the Corn Laws. The Right Hon. Baronet seems to dissent from my interpretation of my own Motion. Well, then, I will give him that of one of his own partisans. The Hon. Member for Lincolnshire [1] began his speech by saying that he considered this a very fair Motion, calculated to enlist all those who were not satisfied with the present Corn Laws ; that in fact it would test the opinion of the House as to the working of the present Laws ; and that he should oppose it because he was perfectly satisfied with the working of the present Laws. That was the view which the Hon. Member for Lincolnshire took of the matter on which he was about to vote ; and he, as we know, is among the most tenacious for the continuance of the Corn Laws.

But the Right Hon. Baronet said that he had

---

[1] Mr. Christopher.

no encouragement to go into a Committee of the whole House with me, for he observed that I treated one of my own friends with great asperity for not going my length in opinion, who nevertheless was willing to vote for the Committee. If I said a word in an unfriendly spirit to my Hon. Friend the Member for Cambridge, I owe him, and I offer him, every apology for it : to say anything in an unfriendly spirit, was far from my intention. Had I then heard his speech, which followed my own, I should have abstained from saying what I did. When I saw his particular plan I certainly did fear that he was going to give his great authority as an economist to a very trifling Amendment ; and I was not aware, till he announced it in his speech, that he was, as he said, bound up by connection and interest with the agricultural party ; and that he was returned for a borough in the centre of an agricultural district. I think that the Hon. Member did all that could have been expected of him in giving his sanction to some change in the Laws and delivering an excellent speech in favour of Free Trade.

But can such arguments as these have any weight in the country when gentlemen know that they can do just as they please on this question ? They may refuse all change ; they may grant ever so small a change ; and they have the power to retrace their steps whenever they please. Is it not idle, therefore, to pretend that they are afraid of the consequences of going into an inquiry into the operation of the Corn Laws ? Surely it is something like trifling with the question ; and certainly a question involving as this does the commerce of the country, the economy of the country, and the general condition of the people, ought not thus to be dealt with.

I can hardly suppose that the Right Hon. Baronet himself can be satisfied with the course that he is pursuing upon it. He must, I think, see that it is scarcely candid towards either side. If he cannot bring himself to utter the things that the common advocates of the Laws allow themselves to, it would be better for him to act upon his conviction and tell his friends that they are wrong. The Right Hon. Baronet appears to me by his arguments to confirm the advocates of Repeal in the justice of their opinions, and by his vote he encourages his friends in the injustice of their course.

It is not for me to warn him of the responsibility he is incurring on this question ; but I cannot help submitting to him that the question is one that differs materially from many others ; and chiefly in this respect : there are thousands who, refusing to inquire into it for themselves, depend entirely upon the Right Hon. Baronet's authority for maintaining the Corn Laws. And I have no doubt that there are numbers satisfied to uphold them upon the conviction that the Right Hon. Baronet, with all his experience, all his information, all the consideration that he has given to the varied interests of this country, would never persist in maintaining them and denying the evils that are charged upon them if he did not feel convinced of the policy and justice of his course. This is the way in which hundreds are now sparing themselves from all responsibility, and justifying themselves to their opponents.

But there is another peculiarity attending the maintenance of the Corn Laws that the Right Hon. Baronet has doubtless well considered : he cannot select the moment to retrace his steps on this matter should it prove that he has been in error. And, further, unlike some other questions, he cannot in this matter announce at pleasure the time to be arrived when he should change the law. No ! if the evidence is true that is now disregarded, the time will be past when the effects contemplated by the opponents of the Corn Laws have occurred : when rivalry abroad has been successful in supplanting us, when capital has been driven from the country, when our artisans have carried their skill to other countries, when our colonies are seen receiving manufactures from foreigners—then it will be too late to talk of removing impolitic restraints upon the employment of our capital and of extending the demand for the industry of our labouring classes. Distress will then have induced the working people to advance claims that Ministers will be unwilling to concede, but unable to resist. Can the Right Hon. Baronet really think that the experiment he is making is a safe one ? Does he see nothing in the social and political aspect of our affairs to deserve consideration ? Will he say that it would be unwise for us to turn our thoughts to that which is now giving constant anxiety to men who reflect upon the condition of this country—I mean the poverty, the sense of oppression, and the increasing intelligence that now prevail amongst that large mass of our fellow-beings who earn their living by their labour ? Would it be a useless application of our time to consider in what way we could diminish that distress and allay that irritation ? Surely we should face this question, however much the remedies that it involves may bear upon private interests ? A man may not be called upon to forego his own advantages for the public good ; but if he enters this House, he does, in my opinion, engage to do so ; and whatever the result may be it would be folly to neglect the inquiry I am suggesting.

And, after all, need we go very deep to discover the causes of this grave state of things ? How can people be contented who are suffering ; whose condition is deteriorating ; whose intelligence is increasing ; whose intercourse with each other is every hour extending, and disclosing to them their common interests and their common wrongs, disclosing to them the manner in which power is distributed and the manner in which it is used, disclosing the striking inequalities of many conditions—how in many cases the very idle are very rich, and the most industrious the most in want ; the whole resulting in a conviction on their minds that there is a connection between the Laws of this country and their misery ? Of this connection they are now persuaded ; and their impressions are confirmed by the avowed opinions of some of the most enlightened and estimable men in the country. They have not a doubt about the matter ; and all the sophistry and all the abuse that may be employed against them will not engender one. Their feelings are each day quickened by the distress which increases with their increasing numbers ; and though we may term any manifestation of their feelings Chartism, yet we may feel sure that we shall not rid ourselves of this social bugbear till we have removed its cause.

The people in this country do not want disturbance ; disturbance and agitation are opposed to their habits of industry and the feelings that have ever characterized them : they ask for better employment of their industry, better reward for their toil. They are ill-fed, over-worked, and under-paid : they seek the improvement of their condition ; and for this purpose they call upon you to inquire into their grievances. Is there anything that we have yet done or have it in contemplation to do that will render the country more safe or the people more satisfied ? Will anything be done to effect this by rudely refusing inquiry into the giant grievance that I bring before you ; or will such refusal be rendered more tolerable by the additional burdens that are now heaped upon those already borne ? Let it only be asked if this is wise ? How soon is it that circumstances may arise in the world that may make it most important for us to be found united at home ? What has always been the difficulty of those States where the institution of slavery exists in going to war ? Primarily and above everything the reasonable distrust that their Governments have of the great mass of the people.

They are conscious that they have earned their hate and they always dread their vengeance. It was so in the ancient States, it is so still.

I believe that in free communities want and necessity create a kind of social bondage under which feelings of a similar kind may be engendered. It is useless to deny that such indications have of late been apparent : I sincerely trust they may not prevail. What was the answer the other day, as we have seen it reported, of the poor peasant when he was asked whether the repeal of the Corn Laws would do him harm. 'Harm, Sir !' said he, 'how can I be worse off anyhow than I am ?' This was the man who was receiving for his labour the average pittance of 7s. or 9s. a week, and who had to forego what was essential to health, to strength, to decency in appearance, in order to provide for his wretched wife and children and preserve them from the confinement of the Workhouse. Feelings engendered by such circumstances cannot but work mischief. And yet such are the circumstances of very many of the working people in different parts of the country.

In the name, then, of those who love peace, who would have order, who dread confusion, I now entreat this House gravely and deliberately to take this question into their consideration : the question of the Laws that enhance the cost of food to a people hourly increasing and hourly becoming more distressed.

If you hesitate to do so, think for a moment whether you will be able to maintain these Laws— Laws revolting to justice and policy, felt to be so by ourselves and pointed at by all the States around us as a nuisance to them and a satire upon the pretended freedom of our Constitution.   Will you continue to make this experiment against the order of nature?—for this is what you are doing in attempting to confine the people of this island to the food grown within its limits when all experience of nature and the provision of nature shows that you need not, and that you cannot do so.   The opposite line of conduct is found in the history of the peopling of the world : it is when the population exceeds the means of support that man goes forth to find the means of life in a distant land ; it is as he advances in civilization that he finds that he can employ his labour in fabricating that which can be exchanged for food with a people differently circumstanced.

And this is the state in which we now find ourselves ; and it is this natural and traditional means of obtaining food that the Corn Laws attempt to prevent.   The necessary fruits of the experiment we have witnessed this year in the spread of destitution, disease, and death.   To render Laws with such results endurable, you must show them to be inevitable.   But can you believe this to be possible, in opposition to the deliberate judgment of those whose names are the most revered among us, who have denounced the principle of such Laws as impious, impolitic, and wrong?   Hear the words of Burke on the subject :—

God hath given the earth to the children of men ; and He, undoubtedly, in giving it to them, has given them what is abundantly sufficient for all their exigencies,—not a scanty, but a most liberal provision. The Author of our nature has written it strongly in that nature, and has promulgated the same thing in His word, that man shall eat his bread by his labour; and I am persuaded that no man, or combination of men, for their own profit, can, without great impiety, undertake to say that he shall not do so, and that they have any sort of right either to prevent the labour or to withhold the bread.

The authority of Dr. Johnson may be quoted on the same side. In a conversation with Sir Thomas Robinson upon a law that was proposed respecting the admission of Irish produce into England, when Sir Thomas Robinson observed that those laws might be prejudicial to the corn interest in England, Dr. Johnson said : 'Sir Thomas, you talk the language of a savage. What, Sir, would you prevent any people from feeding themselves, if by any honest means they could do it?' And Dr. Chalmers has declared that the Corn Laws infect the whole air of British society; and that there will be no peace until they are repealed.

I fear that I have occupied the House too long : I will now leave the question in your hands trusting that you will avail yourselves of the accident that has given you a second opportunity of considering it, and that you will consent to the Motion that I have now to make : That the House resolve itself into a Committee to take into consideration the Act 9 Geo. IV. c. 60, regulating the importation of foreign grain.

VII.

MANCHESTER, April 15, 1841.

On April 15, 1841, a public meeting attended by nearly 2,000 members
of the League, was held in the Corn Exchange, Manchester, to confirm the
resolutions passed at the meeting of delegates from the chief towns of
England, held earlier on the same day to consider what course should be
pursued by the League with regard to Mr. Villiers's Annual Motion. Mr.
Villiers made the speech of the evening. Mr. Cobden and Mr. Bright, not
then in Parliament, were present, together with many other leaders of the
movement, and both spoke. Mr. James Wilson's resolution, that deputies
from all the Anti-Corn-Law Associations in the kingdom should be invited
to assemble in London at the time when Mr. Villiers brought forward his
motion on the Corn Laws, having been carried, the Rev. S. Beardsall,
seconded by the Rev. W. Mountford, moved in accordance with Mr.
Villiers's speech, ' That the constantly increasing physical sufferings of the
labouring population, arising from want of employment and the scarcity
of food, are inimical to the progress of religion and morality, and this
meeting earnestly appeals to ministers of the Gospel, and to philanthro-
pists, and Christians of every denomination, to lend their aid in the effort
to abolish the unjust tax upon the importation of the first necessaries of
life—a tax which impiously thwarts the bounteous designs of Providence,
who has prepared abundantly upon the face of the earth for the wants of
all His creatures.'

I THANK you for your very cordial reception. It is
far more than my feeble efforts in the cause merit,
though it is consistent with the readiness that I have
always observed among the people to appreciate any
service honestly intended to them by their friends.

I view this meeting with great satisfaction as
offering further evidence of the interest that the people
are now taking in the subject of the Corn Laws.
And as the humble advocate of reason in Parliament,
I am specially alive to the importance of public mani-

festations of such interest; for experience has both taught me how little good can be done in that assembly without the influence of the people, and led me to expect success even in this case, with a manly-spirited and intelligent co-operation from without. This co-operation I think I have now secured. The country at last appears to be awakened to the true cause of the great evil that pervades it ; and people in every quarter are denouncing the error and injustice of a system that allows one class to rob another and the strongest to rob them all.

It is cheering to see the great principles of liberty invoked to redress the wrongs of industry and commerce, as they were in former times applied to relieve the mind and body of man from bondage. And, based as our cause is on truth, with justice and the common good for our end, I have no more doubt of the ultimate success of those principles in this case, than I have of the triumphs that we have achieved in the cause of civil and religious liberty.

Since I last had the honour of addressing an assembly in this great town, the cause of Repeal has made immense progress. Had it remained stationary, I should not have despaired ; but there are signs, and unmistakable ones, that we are advancing rapidly. The truth on this question is now penetrating the recesses of power, and the strongholds of Monopoly are beginning to be shaken. The appalling distress that for three years past has been bearing down the productive classes of the country has compelled public attention to the warnings and declarations of the opponents of the Corn Laws, and the Monopolists have at last been thrown on their defence.

Is there a candid man who can say that they have strengthened their case by the least pretence of justice in defending these odious Laws?   Or have they raised themselves one degree in public esteem by the weapons that they have had recourse to?. And, if you consider what a giant power the Monopolists constitute, deriving, as they do, their immense influence from social position, from political privilege, and pecuniary means, how could advocates of Repeal have advanced as they have but by the force of truth and the justice of their cause? Thanks to the zeal, untiring energy, and sacrifices of every kind of many whom I see around me, and of many more whom they represent, facts connected with the Corn Laws have been disclosed, circulated, and firmly impressed upon the public mind, that no subtlety, no selfish fears, no ignorant clamour, can ever hereafter efface or suppress.   And if those who have banded themselves together for the abolition of the Corn Laws are not appreciated by their contemporaries for their services in the great cause of Repeal, posterity will, I am quite sure, award them a full measure of justice and gratitude.

Narrowly and anxiously as I have watched this question for four years past, I can speak with confidence of the favourable change that the advocates of Repeal have already effected in public opinion.   By the diffusion of information on the subject, for example, I have seen some of the grossest and most favourite fallacies of the Monopolists completely exploded. I used to be asked, at first, how I could be really in earnest in wishing for the repeal of the Corn Laws, since I must know that but .for the landed interest, neither public loans could be raised nor the interest of the National Debt be paid ; that without the land-owners the manufacturers would have no customers ; and that the high price of corn was the means of giving employment and high wages to the labourer. I used to reply that all these and such like statements were false, that they were utterly fallacious from beginning to end. But they were readily and persistently swallowed in the House of Commons as soon as uttered until the supporters of Free Trade determined to have a Committee in the House to inquire how far such things were true or not ; and to learn whether the landlords were really subject to exceptional taxation because they were landlords or whether they were taxed only in the same proportion as other people. This Committee [1] made some noise. It was a Committee appointed to consider the duties that were imposed on articles

[1] The Committee on Import Duties here alluded to, was projected to refute Lord Melbourne's speech imputing insanity to any one who proposed the abolition of Protection. It owed its origin and success to Mr. Villiers, though the consent of the Government to it, after being refused to Mr. Villiers, was not gained till the veteran Joseph Hume, at Mr. Villiers's special request, moved for an Inquiry. Mr. Villiers presided at nearly every meeting of this Committee, and personally secured the attendance of all the witnesses except two. Sir Charles Douglas sat on it at the express wish of Sir Robert Peel, in order to see ' what these people [the Free Traders] are at, and what they mean by the Inquiry.' After the great change in his policy, Sir Robert Peel declared that the body of evidence adduced before the Committee would take the world by surprise, and disclose that a profound misapprehension 'on the subject of Import Duties had prevailed up to that time.

imported from other countries; and, perhaps, you will not think the worse of it because no other Committee has ever given greater offence than it gave to our friends the bread-taxers.

The first thing that the Committee did was to ascertain how much was collected on the imported articles; and we found from the officers of the Government that the sum amounted to upwards of twenty-two millions. We then inquired what these articles were; because it might still be that they were articles consumed solely by the landlords. Unfortunately for this view of the case, we found that upon ten of the articles in question more than twenty millions were collected, and that they were principally corn, tea, coffee, sugar, tobacco, spirits, wood, wool, fruit, &c.

Now I believe that occasionally these articles are consumed by other people than landlords; and you can therefore judge of the justice of a tax upon bread for the benefit of the landlords, because they have to pay the same taxes that other people have to pay. What would you think if all the bakers and butchers claimed an Act of Parliament to make bread and beef dear because there is a tax on tea and sugar, and they, like the rest of the community, have to pay it? Very convenient, doubtless, for the bakers and butchers if they got it, but a little unjust, I think, to other folks. And yet this is the whole question of the Corn and Provision Laws. The landlords produce bread and beef; and they have passed laws to make them dear, because they, like other people, have to pay taxes.

But they tell you that the manufacturers have no customers like themselves, and that without the Corn Laws they could not buy cotton goods. Well, this famous Committee inquired a little into that too, and we called your worthy Chairman to ask him about it. He soon settled the matter ; for he told us that four-fifths of the cotton manufactured here goes abroad, and that the rest is consumed at home by the community at large.

However, it was not enough to have only his evidence on the point. He, we knew, was an old offender ; he had been a friend of Free Trade too long to be generally believed, and, moreover, he was no longer in business. The Committee therefore called another witness whose business was entirely in the agricultural districts. He was examined for the special purpose of ascertaining whether the high price of provisions had not given him some rare customers in the country, as the Corn Laws were then in full operation effecting what they were intended to. He seemed quite startled at the very notion ; and declared that his trade had never been worse, for the very reason that it ought to have been good. He said that it was invariably the case—and he wondered how it could be thought otherwise—that when the labourer paid most for his food, he had least left to pay for his stockings ; and that it was proverbial with all their travellers who went through the country, that when bread was dear they could not get any orders in the agricultural districts.

This witness was a hosier from Leicester, and he was asked by the landlords to support the Corn Laws because they would ensure him good customers in the country districts.

But of all absurdities that are now circulated by the advocates of the Corn Laws, the drollest fancy is, that the labourers and artisans will be worse off if bread becomes cheaper. Of all the perversions of obvious truth that I have ever heard, this is certainly the most striking. How could bread become cheaper but by becoming more plentiful ? But this, notwithstanding our daily prayers for plenty, would, according to Monopolist logic, be an evil : the Monopolist argues that plenty would make wages low and that scarcity is the one thing needed to improve the working man's condition.

Sir W. Molesworth, the Member for Leeds, has agreed to move, as soon as Parliament meets, for another Committee to inquire into this one fact alone, and to ascertain what is the real connection between the rate of wages and the price of food. I am much mistaken if it will not be proved that as provisions rise, wages fall. And if there is any working man here present who has any doubt on the subject, I hope that he will come and give his evidence before the Committee. I will answer for it that he shall get a good hearing.

It is by persevering in this way that we shall succeed at last, and not leave the Monopolists a leg to stand upon. Every one can give us some assistance. There is no one too little, too insignificant to help in the cause. The fable tells us that when the lion got caught in a net, he did not get out by roaring, and he could not get out by himself. It was the smallest animal in the forest that released him. By constantly nibbling away at the net the little mouse at last made a hole big enough for the lion to get out. And it is on this principle that year after year I go on nibbling away—though the task is no pleasant one, I can assure you—hoping each time to make the hole in the horrid net of Monopoly a little bigger, until at last the British Lion shall be free.

I find nothing around me to induce despair. In fact I find in the utterances of various men which reach me from time to time, much to encourage me. The other day I heard a Cabinet Minister lamenting the injustice and folly of making a free people pay 40 per cent. more for their food than they need do in order to support a Monopoly. Nothing could be more just than what he said ; only, unfortunately, when he said it, he was talking of Jamaica and the negroes, and not of England and her people. But as I cannot of course suppose that this Minister cares more for an African than for an Englishman, I expect that when I bring on my Motion for the repeal of the Corn Laws he will express the same indignation at Englishmen's paying 40 per cent. more than they ought for their food, as he did at the injustice imposed on the negroes of Jamaica.

I was also, I confess, much pleased to hear the Noble Lord who leads the House of Commons denounce very distinctly, the night before Parliament broke up, the pernicious system of class legislation. All of us in this room, I believe, condemn that system. I, for one, will support any Minister, be he Whig, Tory, or Radical, who denounces it and who is ready to act against it. And the people, if they know their own interests, will give such a Minister full power to abolish it.

The Corn Laws are a great and flagrant deviation from the principle of legislating for the general good, and not for the particular interest. They are the corner-stone of Monopoly in this country. I am certain that if they were abolished a host of minor evils would speedily disappear. But whilst they remain, Monopoly and its attendant mischief can never be removed.

I think that the present moment is most opportune for the display of our determination to procure justice for the country, and alleviation of the distress in the manufacturing districts which has so long been shocking the feelings of every well-disposed man. I cannot but hope that many will now give their support to the cause who have hitherto held aloof from it. And here I would allude specially to the ministers of religion. For I cannot conceive anything more immediately within the province of the disciples of Him who said 'Feed my people;' and 'the labourer is worthy of his hire,' than to inculcate their Master's great lessons of charity by enabling the poor, through honest industry, to feed themselves.

Moreover, I think that it would be only wise in those who hold that no redress can be obtained till the suffrage is extended, to aid us in showing the community the frightful evils of the Corn Laws which were passed, and are maintained, under the present limited constituencies. For surely they must see that the chief reason they have for demanding the Charter is that there is no chance of obtaining the abolition of such Laws until the power of the people is increased. But if they sanction the notion that they approve of these Laws, what reason have they for urging the reform of Parliament?

Whatever other men may do, it becomes those who have leagued themselves together for the good and great purpose of procuring the repeal of the Corn Laws, to endeavour by every legitimate means in their power to convince the community of the truth that no more effectual means of promoting the well-being of the industrious masses, of adding to the wealth of the country and of preserving the peace of the world can exist, than a free and unrestricted commercial intercourse between nation and nation throughout the globe.

VIII.

HOUSE OF COMMONS, June 7, 1841.

The Budget of 1841 showed a deficiency of nearly two millions. To meet this the Government resolved on what was considered the bold stroke of attacking the Corn, Sugar, and Timber Monopolies. Accordingly on April 30, before the Chancellor of the Exchequer made his financial statement, Lord J. Russell, who before had vehemently resisted all proposals for repealing the Corn Laws as impracticable and mischievous, gave notice that on May 30 he should move for a Committee of the whole House to consider the Laws affecting the importation of foreign corn. This notice of a Motion, identical with that hitherto brought forward by Mr. Villiers in face of strenuous opposition, coming from Lord Melbourne's Ministry, took the House completely by surprise : the annual estimates and proposed alterations in the Sugar and Timber Duties were almost lost sight of in the all-absorbing topic of corn, and the debate on the Budget became simply a discussion of the Corn Laws. Agitation on the question throughout the country increased greatly. Lord J. Russell found it necessary not to delay the announcement of the terms of his Motion till the date originally fixed ; and on May 7 he stated his intention of proposing a fixed duty of eight shillings. Sir R. Peel declared strongly in favour of a Sliding Scale ; but Lord Palmerston, who only two years previously had voted against Mr. Villiers's Motion to hear the members of the Manchester Association at the Bar of the House, showed himself convinced of the soundness of Free Trade principles, and spoke admirably against Protection. The Government were beaten on the Sugar Duties ; and on June 4, before the corn question could be brought on, Sir R. Peel carried a vote of want of confidence by a majority of one. On June 7, Lord J. Russell announced the intention of the Government to dissolve Parliament, and to appeal to the country as soon as they had taken a Vote of Supply for the immediate requirements of the public service.

As the Noble Lord the Secretary of the Colonies and the Right Hon. Baronet have stated what they call their view of the position of parties, and the course they intend to take, and as Members seem to consider that all real business is over, I hope that I may make one or two observations upon the question that has caused this position of parties and upon which they are now about to disturb the peace of the country.

If I did not know what grave considerations this question involves, how closely connected it is with the misery of many of our fellow-creatures, I could really find matter for amusement in the predicament in which I see some around me placed by it.

It has been made matter of reproach that the demand for a total repeal of the Corn Laws is extravagant; and those who have leagued themselves together, out of the House, to instruct the people on the matter are told that they are too violent; that they should be more moderate; that they should leave it to the Government to bring it forward. Let the Government take it up, say some, and the landed interest will then consider it gravely; they will enter into it calmly; they will admit of some mitigation of the Laws, and settle the question.

Now I invite the attention of the country and of the House to the present position of the matter. The question was taken out of my hands by the Government; and I surrendered it with satisfaction, hoping that good might follow. They have proposed a measure; a moderate, a fair measure as some call it; a measure extravagantly in favour of the landed interest as I consider it. How are they treated? Why, worse than I have been! I have been allowed to have my say; I have been allowed to bring on my Motion; but the Noble Lord has not even been allowed to bring on his. He gave his Notice, announced the nature of his measure, and fulfilled every condition that I was told last year would secure serious attention to the subject, when down comes the Right Hon. Baronet opposite, and in the face of the Noble Lord's Notice carries by a majority of persons whose interests are supposed to be involved in it, a Resolution that has the effect of precluding the Noble Lord from bringing forward his measure, of preventing a deliberate consideration of the subject, and, in fine, of enabling themselves to escape from a division.

This, then, is the position of the question : the land-owners form the majority of the House ; they will not allow the Laws that give them a Monopoly to be altered ; and they will not allow them to be fairly discussed.

The question is now seriously engaging the attention of every State in Europe and the United States of America. Their interests are all involved in it. They see and understand the struggle. They know the parties engaged in the conflict : those who profit by a Monopoly of the subsistence of the people on the one side, and the advocates of unrestricted commerce with the rest of the world on the other. And this week presents them with a scene in the battle little creditable to the country, though doubtless a triumph for Monopoly : namely, a deliberate refusal on the part of the land-owners to allow the question to be fairly debated. This House represents only their interests, and they can do what they like with their own,

I referred the other night to the close analogy that exists between the Slave question in America and the Corn Laws of England ; that resemblance is now strengthened. In America they refuse to discuss the Slave question in Congress. Two years ago it was mooted and the Members all rushed from the House as they rushed from this House to-night. The subject of slavery is offensive to the interests of the majority in Congress as the Corn Laws are offensive to both Houses here, and all refuse to discuss it.

Does this discourage me? Far from it. Do I advise the country to be disheartened by it? Quite the contrary. No cause in the name of freedom has ever fared better at first. I am glad, indeed, that this course has been pursued. People in this country hate unfairness above everything, and this will rouse them. They will now see the relative strength of their friends and their enemies ; and they will see the necessity for acting with energy.

Moreover, I like the course taken by the opposite side on this account : it is bold and daring, and intelligible to all. I far prefer it to the trimming course pursued before. It is not a delusive course, which it might have been. It bids defiance to the people. It will compel the people to meet it.

I am satisfied that there is no ground whatever in justice for any tax on the people's food. Had the Government Measure been adopted, or spoiled by the landlords, the question of total Repeal would hardly have had fair play.

That question is now again fully before the
country, and I defy any man to show that the people
are not entitled to this full measure of justice.   They
bear the burdens of the country, and none I contend
are borne exclusively by the landlords.   I rejoice
that the question has been agitated in the country
upon this broad, intelligible basis, and that the people
have put the landlords to the proof of their claim to a
permanent tax upon the bread of the community.

As I have said before, I see nothing in what is
occurring at present that does not raise my most sanguine expectations of speedy success.   The question
must now exclusively engage the attention of the House
till it is settled in some way.   Constant reference will
be made to it in all the business of the next Parliament,
and I predict another speedy dissolution, upon the
same ground, of the Parliament about to be elected.
The question never can be smothered up again ; and
I firmly expect that in the end these iniquitous Laws
will be totally repealed.

I believe that the country would have supported
the Noble Lord had he on this occasion disregarded
the usual form and, in spite of the Resolution carried,
brought in his measure.   The country understands
the Noble Lord's position.   The Noble Lord had
given his Notice, had fixed his day ; his measure was
offensive to the majority in the House ; they inter-
posed a Resolution declaring that he had not their
confidence, which they carried, and threatened even
further interference.   I hoped that anything so unfair, so unusual, might have been disregarded by the

Government ; but I am told that in point of form the Noble Lord was precluded from bringing on his Motion, and that he could not have had a fair discussion if he had been opposed in doing so.

I think, however, that this matters little : the people understand the question now ; and the whole proceeding will mark clearly in what way they ought to act in justice to themselves and with regard to the interest of the country in its present deep distress.

IX.

HOUSE OF COMMONS, August 27, 1841.

The Government candidates went to the country in 1841 with Lord J. Russell's fixed duty as their election cry. Sir R. Peel admitted at Tamworth the prevailing deep distress, but declared his firm conviction that it was not in any way due to the Corn Laws, and was returned to maintain the existing Sliding Scale. Parliament met on August 19. The Queen's Speech dwelt on the suffering and poverty of the people, and explicitly stated that it was not only necessary for the Legislature to consider the Corn Laws, but also to determine whether they were not the direct cause of the distress of the great body of the community. Lord Ripon, in the House of Lords, carried a vote of want of confidence in the Ministry as an amendment to the Address. And in the House of Commons a similar Motion was carried on August 27, after four nights' debate. Mr. Cobden, who had just been returned to Parliament for the first time, spoke during the debate, and made a powerful impression on the House in his maiden speech, in which he acknowledged Mr. Villiers's 'great and incessant services' in the cause of the people.

HAVING often had occasion to address the House on the subject that has been recommended to its consideration in the Speech from the Throne, I have listened with great care during the present debate to the things that have been uttered on the other side in order to be saved, if possible, the trouble of repeating my former observations. For this reason I have given my best attention to those who have not observed the rule of silence prescribed to the party, and who undertook to explain the question to which as they said they were confined on this occasion.

I must confess, however, that they have failed to enlighten me. My Hon. Friend the Member for

Winchester wonders indeed how any one now dares to speak on this subject ; in short how any one can have the courage, in the face of the law and the Constitution, to discuss any other subject than that which he considers to be the subject before the House.

It seems to me that my Hon. Friend, whose skill in confusing juries I have often witnessed, was not less successful on this occasion in confusing himself and the subject of debate ; for with every wish to understand what he meant I failed to do so.

Another Hon. Member thinks that questions respecting the sufferings of the people are abstract questions and little in place at this time ; and so on with several other Members who all upon some ground or other seek to justify themselves in avoiding the questions really proposed to them ; but I own that I see as little in their reasons as in their silence to make the House think that this is not a fitting moment to discuss matters so deeply interesting to the people.

I do not mean to say anything offensive to Hon. Members on the other side, but I cannot help thinking that there is a way of accounting for their present silence considering the activity that they have lately displayed in giving circulation to every fallacy, in giving currency to every misrepresentation of the principles and objects of the Government measures.

I cannot but think that Hon. Members are somewhat ashamed of the means by which they obtained their seats, and that coming face to face with those whose policy and whose principles they have assailed so unscrupulously, they think it the most prudent course to maintain a perfect silence. There is doubtless some discretion shown in not committing themselves to opinions ; but the same discretion unfortunately was not observed elsewhere : allusion here, however, to the distresses of commerce or to the miseries of the people might check the ducal influence that arrogates to itself the power of making Ministers, as grandees of old in this country assumed the authority of making monarchs. On the other hand the repetition at this moment of reasons for keeping the people in their misery and preserving the tax on their subsistence, might have startled and disgusted the country in a manner not easily recovered ; and this perhaps has rendered silence a very prudent course.

Nevertheless in the performance of my duty, and of my promise to those who sent me here, I cannot forego the opportunity of discussing the vitally-interesting matters that the Crown has proposed for the consideration of the House. I will not be a party to wanton and marked disrespect shown to the Throne, in order to avoid the subject that above all others most nearly concerns the welfare of the people. Concurring fully in the principles on which the financial arrangements of this year are proposed, and believing that if those principles were carried further they would be attended with unqualified advantage to the country, I shall resist by every means in my power the opposite policy which I consider to be identified with the Amendment. For I cannot shut my eyes to the notorious opinions of the Hon. Member who moved the Amendment : opinions so earnestly expressed by him in the important district that he represents ; opinions by which he so largely profits ; and which cannot now be suppressed by any vague profession of attachment to the principles of Free Trade or any shabby reference to the opinions of the late Mr. Huskisson.

Considering the real opinions of the Hon. Member I cannot but think him well qualified to represent the party and the policy directly opposed to the policy recently professed by Her Majesty's Government. I consider that the Amendment places in issue the great questions that now divide this country, and for deciding which it is generally thought that Parliament has been called together.

The time is now come that I have much desired to see and that abler men have long expected : now, at last, when the principles by which the trade and taxation of the country should be regulated, absorb the consideration of the public mind. The case is now ripe for hearing. The parties concerned in it have been ascertained. On the one side is the community, on the other the aristocracy and protected interests. The plea is the general interest ; and the answer is vested interests and existing monopolies.

It becomes the House to elicit by every means all the evidence that can prepare it for a judgment. I am satisfied that the country at large will view with impatience the attempt that has been made to draw their attention away to the mere vulgar topics of party. This story of party is a short one here, and soon told. Hon. Gentlemen opposite represent the aristocracy and protected interests ; and they have achieved a victory over those who represent the general interests. How this great party fell from power is a question that might receive different answers. I certainly am disposed to think that the chief cause is to be found in the dissension existing in it. I believe that the Opposition obtained a majority because one section of the popular party made use of it for the purpose of chastising the other. The fruits of this strange confusion of parties has been seen. Supporters of the aristocracy and of Monopoly work their way into the House by appearing as the friends of the Chartist and the pauper, and they adopt against the Government the language of those who are discontented with its moderation. The reproaches of broken faith and unfulfilled pledges, indulged in by the Hon. Member for Yorkshire and others, are borrowed from the speeches of those whose hostility to the Government arises from its not going far enough. With such discordant allies the party opposite are coming into power not upon the principles that they themselves maintain but upon the errors of their opponents.

Hon. Gentlemen opposite listened with great attention to what the Hon. Member for Bath told them : he said that the grounds for condemning the Government are matter for Radical anger, and not for Conservative complaint. The Government has doubtless ceased to be popular. I myself am disposed to agree with much of what the Hon. Member for Bath said. I think that the Government has rather shrunk from the principles that placed them in power. They have been too much disposed to favour those who are more inclined to abandon than to advance their principles. But I must in common candour say that they have suffered as much for doing what would by many be thought right, as for doing what was wrong.

There are two points in their policy that have weakened their popularity. I mean their policy towards Ireland and their advocacy of the new Poor Law. I think that my Hon. and Learned Friend the Member for Cork [1] greatly exaggerates the prejudice that exists in this country against Ireland. I believe it to be less than my Hon. and Learned Friend represents, though it is impossible to deny that there does exist a great and unreasonable prejudice against Ireland. I do not know anything more unworthy or discreditable than this prejudice due I believe to that perverse principle of our nature which leads us to hate those whom we have injured. It exists in almost every class ; but I trust that it is diminishing every day. Many people in this country view with satisfaction the accession of the Noble Lord the Member for North Lancashire to power because they think he will put down the Irish. The impression is that the Noble Lord is very hostile to the Irish. ['No, no.'] I only say what the impression is, and I hope that the Noble Lord will falsify it when he comes into power ; but it does exist, and it is

---

[1] Mr. O'Connell.

undoubtedly a source of such popularity as attaches to his accession to office.

With regard to the new Poor Law, no one can deny that the Government have lost a great deal of popularity by their advocacy of that law. Their loss on account of it is proverbial ; and yet they have no possible interest or motive in the advocacy but the improvement to which in their belief it will lead. I firmly believe that it is a great improvement on the old law, and if it had not been misrepresented the people would see this themselves. In these matters it is quite clear that unpopularity has been acquired by the Government by the honesty of their policy.

I believe also that the Noble Lord the Secretary for the Colonies has suffered from incautious expressions made use of with respect to the Reform Bill. I always thought that a great deal more had been made of those expressions than there was any occasion for. The honest and candid construction of the Noble Lord's language is, in my opinion, that the Noble Lord, being somewhat timid after the confusion that he and his colleagues caused by passing the Reform Bill, was needlessly alarmed at the consequences of carrying out their principles. Having no reason to suspect the intelligence or integrity of the Noble Lord, I cannot believe that in announcing the principle that the people ought to be fully and fairly represented and that the system of nomination ought to cease, he could have considered that the Reform Bill was a complete and final development of that principle.

It is very well for those who object to all change, and who think that the old corrupt system ought not to have been disturbed, to oppose everything like further reform. But I cannot believe that a Government who have caused such turmoil in the country as Lord Grey's Government have done in proclaiming the principle that the people should be duly represented, could have intended no more complete fulfilment of their principles than is contained in the Reform Bill. Saying this, however, is a source of unpopularity. I am disposed to overlook much of what the popular party condemn in the Noble Lord, in consequence of the manner in which he has taken up the great principles of commercial reform.

I am bound to say that I believe that the Noble Lord has acted entirely from honest conviction in everything that he has said and done respecting the alteration of the Corn Laws. It is perfectly false that anything that happened in this House influenced the Noble Lord's determination to alter the Corn Laws. The determination was taken before the occurrence of those decisions that are said to have led to it. But probably there is no use in repeating this statement because appearances are against it. The presumption is that the decisions I refer to did influence the Government because their measures of commercial reform were not proposed beforehand.

However, I repeat, and I have no object but the truth in making the assertion, indeed there could be hardly any other reason for my saying anything in behalf of a Government about to go out, and I am certain that I am not under any obligation to any member of it—I repeat, however, knowing him to have been most unjustly accused, that the Noble Lord could have had no motive in bringing forward the measures that he submitted to the House, other than a conviction of the evil of the present Laws and a firm persuasion that no man ought to continue a Minister without proposing their amendment or repeal.

The Opposition are now coming into power ; and it is impossible to be blind to the fact that they are coming in on principles directly antagonistic to the principles of commercial freedom and unfettered industry. In the present alarming condition of the country—with commerce paralyzed, capital unemployed, millions of industrious poor in the lowest state of depression, the Opposition are coming into power with a distinct purpose of maintaining the destructive system of commercial legislation that at present prevails. I have lately had submitted to me detailed proofs that the existing distress is of the most frightful nature ; and in compliance with the request of those who represent the sufferers, I shall call the attention of the House to the nature of those proofs. I hold in my hand evidence not referring to isolated cases leading, as the Right Hon. Baronet opposite has said, to no general conclusions, but such as establish in the clearest manner the evils that result from the Corn Laws. I have evidence of distress from numerous and widely-separated districts, and referring to people engaged in every department of trade.

Hon. Members opposite are not disposed to receive very favourably anything that comes from those clergymen who lately assembled at Manchester.[1] But it should be recollected that they were delegated by their congregations, including many of our fellow-subjects who are now suffering and who requested those gentlemen to go in their behalf to a spot where they knew the subject of their condition would receive attention. On their authority this evidence was collected, and the names and addresses of the parties who gave and collected it are given in each case so that any one can test its correctness. And the evidence referring to all these different departments of trade comes from the following places :—

Hardware (Nos. 1, 2).—Walsall, West Bromwich, Darlaston, Willenhall, Wednesbury, Tipton, and Oldbury. *Hardware* (No. 3.)—Dudley. *Nail making.*—Belper and Forfar, N.B. *Herring Fishery.* — Caithness, N.B. *Silk.* — Coventry, Macclesfield, Middleton, Derby, West Houghton, Spitalfields, and Bethnal Green. *Woollens.*—Leeds, Huddersfield, Golcar, Lockwood, Rochdale, Bradford, Thornton with Denholme, Sowerby Bridge, Haworth, Wilsden, Allerton, North Owram, Middlesbro', Ossett, Martin Top near Gisborne, Radcliffe, Dursley, Stroud, Stonehouse, Wotton-under-Edge, Westbury, Bradford, Frome, Shepton Mallet, and Trowbridge. *Cutlery.*—Sheffield. *Carpet Weaving.* —Barnard Castle. *Hat Making.*—Denton. *Shoe Making.*—Daventry and Stone. *Hosiery and Lace.*—Nottingham, Mansfield, Sutton in Ashfield, New Basford, Beeston, Hyson Green, Leicester, Hinckley, Lutterworth, Loughborough, Earl Shelton, Arnsley, Ullathorpe, Oadby, Ilkeston, Belper, Melbourne, and

---

[1] The National Conference of the Ministers of all denominations on the Corn Laws, which was most violently assailed by the *Times,* assembled in the Town Hall, Manchester, on August 17. The Conference lasted three days, and was attended by over 700 Ministers of different denominations.

Tewkesbury. *Glove Making.* — Hexham (Northumberland), Worcester, and Yeovil, Somerset. *Agriculture.*—Beds: Leighton Buzzard. Bucks: Amersham, High Wycombe, Newport Pagnell, Olney, and Stoney Stratford. Berks: Reading and vicinity. Camb.: Bassingbourn. Cheshire: Knutsford. Devon: Exeter, Bideford, Witheridge, and Great Torrington. *Shipping.*—Liverpool, Bristol, Hull, Bridport, Whitehaven, and Falmouth. *Cotton.* — Manchester, Bolton, Preston, Carlisle, Kendal, Bury, Heywood, Wigram, Stockport, &c. *Mining.*— Forest of Dean, Pontypool, Talywaen, Rhymney, Sirhowy, Abersychan, Llanelly, and Mnyddyshoyn district.

I will not venture to weary the House at this time with the detailed contents of these documents, but I will read from one of them what I may term a specimen of the evidence they afford of the condition of the people ; it refers to the Preston Union, and is as follows :—

Population, 51,072. Inhabited houses, 8,974 ; uninhabited, 1,017. The Poor Rate has regularly increased from 1836 ; it was then 4,725*l.*, it is now 7,299*l.* It would have been much heavier but for the large voluntary subscriptions which have been raised. The reports of the dispensary show that in 1836, 1,911 persons were medically relieved ; in 1840, 3,072. Deaths in the Preston union : 1838, 1,269 ; 1839, 1,277 ; 1840, 1,739 - an increase in 1840 of 462 over the preceding year. This extraordinary increase in the number of deaths excited the attention of the Registrar-General, who wrote to the clerk of the union to inquire the cause. The following is an extract from the reply : ' The cause is, in a very great measure, insufficiency of food of a good quality, which·has tended to engender death among the labouring class, who have been exposed to high prices for provisions (and those of an inferior kind), whilst in the receipt of decreasing wages.— JOSEPH THACKERAY.' Many suffer their great privations with much patience ; others are discontented and sullen. Many give up all in despair, whilst not a few are confident that open rupture can alone relieve them. A very great indifference is felt towards constitutional efforts, such as petitions, &c., for the relief of their distress. Many of the hand-loom weavers live almost entirely on water-porridge, and are distressingly destitute of clothes and bedding.

Now the people firmly believe, and, in my opinion, justly too, that the frightful mass of misery exhibited in this evidence is entirely owing to the restrictions that Parliament imposes on their industry and on their commerce with other countries. A state of things has now arrived that has long been expected and that the ablest men who have studied the subject have always foreseen would arise when the population of this country exceeded its means of subsistence. We have become dependent on other countries differently circumstanced, for a supply of food. There is nothing unnatural in this when we have a population increasing at the rate of one thousand a day; and the time is at hand when this state of things will be universally acknowledged to have arrived.

I am not one who is anxious to bring before you distinct cases of suffering for the purpose of your legislating upon them; this I know would be useless. But it is generally alleged and believed that the distress is occasioned by the operation of the Corn Laws. These Laws you passed, and these Laws you can repeal. When such an opinion is well founded, and when such a general feeling prevails, you are called upon to repeal them. And therefore it is that I have heard with the greatest sorrow the opinions that the Right Hon. Baronet opposite and the Noble Lord have expressed upon this subject.

I am sorry to see the Right Hon. Baronet labouring in his public address to justify those who would maintain the Laws as they are rather than encouraging them to prepare for their immediate change. Certainly I expected, and my expectation was formed from what the Right Hon. Baronet said in this House, that when he came into power he would use the influence he possesses over the party to which he belongs to induce them to change the opinion they hold with respect to the Corn Laws ; but now that the Right Hon. Baronet is on the eve of coming into power I see by his speech at Tamworth that he has only exercised his ingenuity and talent in efforts to show that there are other causes than the Corn Laws for the prevailing distress. In thus acting the Right Hon. Baronet helps to confirm the hostility existing in the minds of the advocates of those Laws to any modification of them.

When the Right Hon. Baronet was speaking at Tamworth he was, it must be remembered, addressing the nation. Now, when he said that the Corn Laws are not chargeable with the present distress, that they are not the cause of it, I am sure that the Right Hon. Gentleman could not deny that those Laws have something to do with the derangement of the Currency ; he could not deny that they have produced a scarcity of money, which necessarily had to be exported ; he could not deny that there has been a scarcity of food during the last three years ; and surely every man's means must be diminished when he has to sacrifice more of those means for the purpose of procuring food : each one must inevitably suffer if he has to pay a higher price for food than he was previously in the habit of paying for it. What, then, does the Right Hon. Baronet mean by saying that the Corn Laws have nothing to do with the distress? Is it that high price for food is not an evil ; that it is no evil to see bullion going out of the country ; to find credit contracted, and the Bank distressed? And yet all these evils follow from them !

I do not mean to say that the Right Hon. Baronet made statements to this effect ; but these are the legitimate consequences of his position. When, therefore, he declared that the Corn Laws are not a cause of the present distress, he said what it is difficult to comprehend, and impossible to assent to. How any person of intelligence could come to such a conclusion I cannot understand.

Let us, for example, see how the Laws affect the Agricultural class. It is calculated there are about a million families employed in this country in Agriculture, and it has been further calculated that each family receives at least 30*l.* a year. If there are a million agricultural labourers, then there are 30,000,000*l.* to be expended in some way or other. Now it was found in the evidence before the Committee which has been already referred to in this debate, that when wheat was 57*s.* a quarter, the class of persons described had to pay 7*s.* 6*d.* out of their week's wages for bread and flour ; but when we know that, as in 1839 and 1840, the average price of wheat in this country is 70*s.* a quarter, what, I ask, do you think can be left to a man after paying for his bread out of his 10*s.* or 12*s.* a week when, with the quarter of wheat at not more than 56*s*., he paid 7*s*. 6*d*. a week? What is left to him to pay for clothing and household requirements after expending so much in provisions? Surely the manufacturing interest in this case must feel the loss of their share of the thirty millions. And what in fact do we hear from Leicester and other places—the people of Leicester produce coarse goods principally for the use of the agricultural labourers ? Is it not that they received no orders during those years for these articles because the people had to expend all their wages in food? The consequence is that in Leicester, where a large population is supported principally by manufacturing for the agricultural labourers, the people now have no demand for their labour, they are thrown out of work, and 14,000 are at present depending on the parish for support.

And yet with these facts before us we hear that the high price of food is of more advantage to the labourer than otherwise ; or that it is no evil ; or that it makes no difference to him whether or not we have Corn Laws !

I complain of the speech of the Right Hon. Baronet ; but I complain still more of the speech of the Noble Lord the Member for North Lancashire.[1] In the Right Hon. Baronet's speech it was not asserted that the Corn Laws are a positive good ; the Right Hon. Baronet confined himself to the assertion or argument that they do not produce

[1] The late Lord Derby, then Lord Stanley.

distress. But the Noble Lord the Member for Lancashire, in addressing the agricultural labourers, attempts to show that the high price of provisions is an advantage. I can scarcely believe that a man of common sense could honestly believe this to be the case—certainly no man of superior attainments could ; because of all the delusions that have ever been imposed upon human credulity this is the greatest. How could any man of intellect and common honesty attempt to persuade a poor creature that the less food there is in the country the better it is for him ; that in short the more scarce provisions are the more he will get? There is nothing in witchcraft, nothing in cajolery on a large scale, nothing that I have ever heard in the history of successful delusions practised upon the minds of ignorant men, equal to it. We know how those who say these things come to succeed. It is by using vague terms, by telling the poor that their wages will fall—the people believe that if wages fell their condition would be worse ; and then they clench their argument, if argument it can be called, by assuring the people of the cruelty of their employers.

The Noble Lord the Member for North Lancashire selected Lancashire as the proper place to set the men against their masters ; to tell them that it is cruelty that makes their masters Free Traders and anxious to promote the doctrines of Free Trade ; that Free Trade will ruin them and deprive them of their comforts ; and that these Free Trade masters

will take them from the occupations they like, and
transfer them to others for which they are unsuited.

But the Noble Lord went further and tried to persuade the people of that which I did not think it
possible for any one to revive now : he tried to persuade them of the stale and exploded fallacy that
was formerly used with regard to War taxation. He
used the same fallacy with respect to rents that had
formerly been employed with regard to the taxes ; he
said that the higher the rents were the more men were
employed.   That is the old doctrine that was started
by Mr. Vansittart when he said of the taxes, that
they come back to the country in 'refreshing showers,'
and that the more the people are taxed the more the
Government gives them employment.   The Noble
Lord stated of the landlords that it would be highly
dangerous to reduce their rents because if their rents
were reduced they could not keep so many grooms and
gardeners ; that now they employ the gardeners to
watch their pleasure-grounds ; but that if the Corn
Laws were repealed, then the landlords would be
obliged to reduce their expenditure, and to suit it to
their narrowed means.   This is the way in which he
attempted to prove that great evil would follow from
a change in the Corn Laws !   The grooms and
gardeners are to be well employed !   But, surely, the
weavers and the stocking-makers are human beings
also, and not less worthy of consideration !   I think
that it is just as essential for them to be supported as
the grooms and gardeners.   I should like to know
what the Noble Lord would have said if a weaver had

risen and asked him what he would do if a machine were invented for making clothes cheaper than they are at present; what he, who has such tenderness for grooms and gardeners, would do with respect to new inventions that injure the unfortunate artisan. Would he not scout the idea of taxing or suppressing machinery ? And yet I do not know why there should be more sympathy displayed for grooms and gardeners because the landlords might have lower rents, than for the weaver whose employment is superseded by the use of new machinery.

The Noble Lord said that land must be cultivated and high rents kept up, for the purpose of employing labour ; but the same argument might be used to keep up any existing trade or occupation. If the Noble Lord were to advocate a new line of railroad, and the people in business who occupied the houses on an old line of road, told him that they would be ruined by being deprived of their occupation and advantage, that would unquestionably be a stronger case than that of the grooms and gardeners ; and yet who would entertain it ?

But the Noble Lord spoke of the main principle of his policy being Protection. The Noble Lord ought distinctly to announce to the country what he means by Protection because he declared himself to be a disciple of Mr. Huskisson. It is said that he was the colleague of that gentleman, and he announced himself as clothed with his mantle. Now Mr. Huskisson, like other people in office, said a great deal to square his opinions with existing circumstances; but still throughout the course that he followed, it will be found that he never upheld the principle of Protection as opposed to the principle of Free Trade. It is not for Protectionists to state that Mr. Huskisson did so and so ; if they quote his authority, they ought to look to his recorded opinions in 1825 and 1826, or to look to the last speech that he made in 1830 : the one relating to the state of the nation, in which he gives his opinion as to the causes of distress and the proper remedies to be applied to them, when his opinions were unfettered by any connection with Government.

It may be remembered that a charge was made in this House against Mr. Huskisson, and made in a very unworthy spirit : very much, indeed, in the spirit in which the Noble Lord opposite now attacks the advocates of Free Trade. He was charged with cruelty and heartlessness, and with having no feeling for the rest of mankind. Then Mr. Huskisson explained his principles and vindicated his policy. On that occasion he read a petition from the merchants of London, from which I will now quote a passage :—

That of the numerous protective and prohibitory duties of our Commerical Codes, it may be proved that while all operate as a heavy tax on the community at large, very few are of any ultimate benefit to the classes in whose favour they were originally instituted ; and none to the extent of the loss occasioned by them to other classes.

That in thus declaring, as your Petitioners do, their conviction of the impolicy and injustice of the restrictive system, and in desiring every practicable relaxation of it, they have in view only such parts of it as are not connected, or are only subordinately so, with the public Revenue . . . . But it is against *every restrictive regulation of trade* not essential to the Revenue ; against all duties merely *protective* from foreign competition, and against the excess of such duties as are partly for the purpose of revenue, and partly for that of Protection, that the prayer of the present petition is respectfully submitted to the wisdom of Parliament. Your Petitioners therefore humbly pray that your Honourable House will be pleased to take the subject into consideration, and to adopt such measures as may be calculated to give greater freedom to foreign commerce, and thereby to increase the resources of the State.

What was Mr. Huskisson's object in reading that petition? In the first place, to show that what was ignorantly called a heartless theory of his own was anxiously maintained by all the great practical commercial men of the time ; and, in the second place, in order to declare his entire agreement with them. He spoke to this effect ; and these were his words :—

But I say now, as I always have said, that those who, either by their speeches in Parliament, or the exertion of their talents out of it, have contributed to bring the people in England to look with an eye of favour on the principles recommended in this petition, have done themselves the greatest honour, and the country an essential benefit.

It is plain, therefore, that Mr. Huskisson identified himself with the principles contained in the petition, and that his opinion was against all Protective Duties.

Persons like the Noble Lord say that they are against Prohibition, but in favour of Protection. They two are not opposed to each other : Prohibition is only a means of Protection. You may, to be sure, mitigate Protection ; but then it is opposed to the sound policy laid down in the petition for the abolition of all Protective Duties not essential to the Revenue.

And as long as the Right Hon. Baronet and the Noble Lord adhere to the restrictive system so injurious, as I am convinced it is, to this country, I for one will withhold all support from them.

I do not, however, despond : I see the progress that public opinion is making ; hardly a day passes in which we do not hear of fresh converts to Free Trade ; and I never heard of any who having been converted, ever honestly recanted.

I do not in the least regret the change of Government that is about to take place. I believe that it is highly useful, nay, actually necessary, that some such change should take place in order to secure the establishment of a Free Trade policy. We shall now have a large political party interested in converting the community on the subject. I am rejoiced that the dissolution has taken place, because it has produced discussion on the subject and invited the attention of the people to it ; and I am happy to see with what result. If I stood here as a partisan I should regret the result ; but the subject on which I am now speaking is the one that engrosses my attention. I am not here to promote any party whatever ; it is this question which so largely affects the welfare of the country, that chiefly excites my interest in politics, and I am watching its progress. The dissolution has, I am satisfied, contributed much to advance it. More persons have been returned favourable to Free Trade than ever before were returned ; and judging from the speeches of two or three, whom we have already heard, they will, I am sure, by their influence, render great service to the cause.

It must, for example, be greatly promoted by the facts and arguments so ably put forward by the Hon. Member for Stockport,[1] the effect produced by which was really creditable to the House. It is by constant discussion that we have hitherto advanced, and it is by the same means that we shall ultimately succeed. I, certainly, will follow out in practice the promise that has been made by the Hon. Member for Renfrewshire, and never cease, day or night, to elicit facts that will strengthen the case, and to bring into light every point that bears upon the subject.

I cannot now sit down without remarking upon the heavy responsibility that rests upon those who are coming into office. I suppose that the Right Hon. Baronet opposite will have to form the next Government ; and if so, he will have complete power to do what he thinks right. He has, I presume, moral influence sufficient to convert his friends to his own opinion if they differ from him, and he has strength enough to execute what he proposes ; and therefore it is that I shall attribute whatever disaster may follow from the present system, or whatever advantage may accrue from a change, to the circumstance of his coming into power.

If the sufferings of the people continue, if commerce languishes, if trade is checked, if the means of employment are diminished, the whole of the responsibility must rest with the Right Hon. Baronet opposite.

---

[1] Mr. Cobden.

I believe that he has the power to change our present commercial system so pregnant with evil ; and the determination that he manifests to support or to change it, will decide the opposition or the support that he will receive in the country.

X.

.HOUSE OF COMMONS, February 18, 1842.

Immediately on the formation of Sir R. Peel's Administration in September 1841, resolutions were passed at meetings held throughout the manufacturing districts, asserting the deep distress caused by the Corn Laws, and petitions to the Queen were adopted praying her not to prorogue Parliament until that portion of her Speech delivered at the opening of the Session, relating to the Corn Laws, had been fully deliberated upon and the distresses of her people taken into consideration. A cartload of these petitions was sent from Manchester on October 7. Sir R. Peel anxious, as he expressly stated, to gain time, had already resolved on the prorogation. The Queen, on the advice of her Ministers, expressed her willingness to receive the petitions through the Home Secretary; and thus Earl Radnor, Earl Ducie, Lord Kinnaird, and others, were frustrated in their intention of making a verbal statement of the existing distress when the petitions were presented. The Queen's answer to the petitioners was an acknowledgment on the part of the Ministry of the extreme distress prevalent, which, nevertheless, by the prorogation of Parliament on October 7 itself, they refused to take measures to relieve till Parliament should meet again, four months thence, in February. At that time there were 20,936 persons in Leeds alone whose average earnings were only $11\frac{3}{4}d$. a week. Parliament reassembled on February 3, 1842. The retirement from the Cabinet three days previously of the Duke of Buckingham, the zealous supporter of the existing Corn Laws, caused a panic amongst the Protectionists. The Speech from the Throne acknowledged with deep regret the continued distress in the manufacturing districts, graciously commended 'the exemplary patience and fortitude with which the sufferings and privations' resulting from it had been borne by the people, and recommended to both Houses the consideration of the 'Laws which affect the imports of Corn and other articles.' On February 9, Sir R. Peel, in a crowded House, deplored the distress, said that he could not attribute it in any degree to the operation of the Corn Laws—the wars in China and Syria, joint-stock banks, embarrassments in America, machinery, over-production, a succession of bad harvests, anything but the Corn Laws had caused it—and then introduced his new Sliding Scale, which would make the highest duty on Corn 20s. instead of 38s. 8d. Mr. Gladstone, not then a member of the Cabinet, spoke in favour of the Sliding Scale during the debate on Lord J. Russell's Amendment utterly rejecting the Ministerial measure, which was lost by a majority of 123. On the following Friday, February 18, Mr. Villiers brought forward his promised Motion for the total abolition of all duties on Corn:

the debate on it lasted five nights; and the numbers on the division were
90 for the Motion to 393 against. During this debate the Protectionists
distinguished themselves by their heartless merriment and violent abuse
of the advocates of Free Trade.

I AM anxious to read to the House a petition
addressed to them and signed by the Chairman of a
Conference consisting of delegates from all parts of
England, Scotland, and Wales, lately held in London.
The petition is as follows :—

To the Honourable the Commons of Great Britain and Ireland,
in Parliament assembled.

The Petition of the undersigned Peter Alfred Taylor, of the
City of London,

Humbly sheweth, that your petitioner was Chairman of a
Conference held at the Crown and Anchor Tavern, Strand, on
February 8, 9, 10, 11, and 12, 1842, of 720 delegates from all
parts of England, Scotland, and Wales, appointed by large numbers of their fellow-subjects, to consider of the total and immediate repeal of the Corn and Provision Laws.

That the delegates at that meeting were appointed from
large towns and extensive districts in which all the principal
staple manufactures of the country were carried on—viz. cotton,
linen, cloth, hosiery, hardware, cutlery, flax, &c.

That at that Conference the following resolution, expressing
a desire to forego all protection for their several manufactures,
was unanimously passed :—

'That the deputies present connected with the staple manufactures of the country, whilst they demand the removal of all
restrictions upon the importation of corn and provisions, declare
their willingness to aid in the abolition of all duties imposed for
their own protection.'

That this resolution was not passed without previous thought
and deep consideration, the same resolution having been passed
at large meetings held in the immediate towns and districts
where the several branches of manufacture are extensively in
operation, viz. at Manchester, at a meeting of those engaged
in the cotton trade of Lancashire; at Leeds, by those engaged in
the clothing trade of Yorkshire; at Bath, for the West of Eng-

land clothing trade ; at Derby, for the hosiery and other manufactures of the midland counties; at Birmingham, for the hardware of Staffordshire and Warwickshire; at Sheffield, for cutlery and plated ware ; at Dundee, for the flax and linen trade.

That as all the principal branches of manufacturing industrial employment and capital have thus expressed their desire to give up all legislative protection whatever, your petitioner prays your Honourable House that all classes of Her Majesty's subjects be placed upon the same footing, and that the trade in corn and provisions be left free and open, as well as in all the productions of manufacturing industry.

P. A. TAYLOR.

I trust that this petition will not be considered an inappropriate introduction to the Motion of which I have given notice—a Motion that, notwithstanding all that has been said with respect to the illogical order in which it is now submitted to the House, is brought forward at a moment that I can only consider as favourable to it ; for it follows a discussion in which the greatest ability and ingenuity have been displayed on each side of the House, in manifesting the evils and difficulties that belong both to the project proposed by the present Government, and that which was proposed by their predecessors ; which renders the Motion that I am about to submit so far opportune that whatever arguments may be urged against it, it is clear of those difficulties and those objections that have been urged against the two other measures.

I therefore now rise, in pursuance of my Notice, to ask the House to condemn *in toto*, and to abolish for ever the Laws that they were then in Committee to consider ; Laws the avowed purpose of which is to raise the price by limiting the amount of human subsistence ; Laws that, by the admission of a distinguished member of the Government, have the effect of raising the price of food and of raising the rate of rent, but not of raising the wages of labour ; Laws that, inasmuch as they have this purpose, this object in view, no matter under what impression they may originally have been passed—erroneous if you please, or gravely culpable as many think, I must consider can only exist now in gross and open violation of every principle that ought to regulate the economy and policy of any State. And I do not despair of yet persuading this House of the prudence and importance of abolishing, for ever, Laws of such a character.

I say that I do not despair, because I hail with hope, as I do with satisfaction, the admission that has been made this year : an admission hitherto refused on the ground that the Laws were good, that they had worked well—and therefore ought not to be changed. I now gladly avail myself of the concession made on all sides of the House, that these Laws ought to be changed, because they have worked ill, and because—to use the emphatic language of one of their sternest supporters, the Hon. Member for Lincolnshire—they are Laws that have worked well only for the purposes of dishonest men.

I stand then on this ground which our opponents have conceded, and I ask them to pause before they again attempt to regulate that which is beyond their reach ; and which, if they could attain it, would only be a success more fatal than failure.

I now implore the supporters of the Corn Laws to consult their consciences as to the motives and their experience as to the results of all such enactments; and then to say on what they found their hopes of being able to construct on the ruins of these Laws now discredited and about to be abandoned, any similar laws that would be more durable and less indefensible.

I ask their attention to the circumstance that for four centuries the proprietors of the soil have been attempting to legislate for the purpose of giving value to their properties ; and that the result of all such efforts has been to prejudice those properties, and greatly to lower their owners in the estimation of the country. I am not unwilling to admit that at an early period much error and ignorance prevailed amongst them on the subject, and that they might have believed that they were promoting the general interest by serving their own. But in more recent periods, and since the Crown has been subjected to Parliament and Parliament has been composed of the proprietors of land, they have been labouring with deliberate purpose to enhance the value of land at the expense of the community ; and in this century especially they have done so in defiance of the feelings and opinions of the community.

In 1815 the people of this country perfectly understood the principle of the Corn Laws, and ever since then down to the present day they have been suffering from their operation. And now you are about to attempt another experiment on the patience and

temper of the people by which, in the judgment of
every thinking man, you will jeopard your power far
more than the continued maintenance of these Laws
could.

This is not a time when, with full liberty of
thought and expression allowed, you can perpetrate
a wrong in open day with all men's eyes upon you.
Men who have knowledge may inflict much wrong
upon those who have it not ; but if this be your
principle of conduct, your folly in aiding to diffuse
knowledge and to promote education cannot be adequately described. The results of such folly are
already manifest ; for—and I say it without intend-
ing any offence to the House—this House does not
fairly represent the knowledge and intelligence outside
it. It is not a faithful picture of the information possessed by the middle and working classes. It is the
observation of every man who goes among these classes
that they now evince a knowledge of public affairs, a
shrewdness of perception, and an absence of prejudice
that was never remarked before.

I mention this simply to show how futile it is for
you to expect that any legislation bearing upon the
general interests can now escape the severest scrutiny ;
and above all is this applicable to the Corn Laws,
which specially engage their attention. The people
of this country, and I here refer to a sufficiently
large number of persons of all classes to justify me in
using this title, have determined that these Laws
shall not continue. I believe that the mind of the
great majority of the people is made up on the sub-

ject, and that they will use every means within their
power and within the law, to emancipate the industry
and commerce of the country from the Corn Laws.
They now distinctly demand us to relieve ourselves of
the discredit and the Statute Book of the disgrace of
continuing them ; and to cease to expose ourselves to
the charge of a mere vulgar breach of trust in abusing
for our own purposes the powers confided to us.

We have no reason to complain of the temper in
which the people now approach us in making this
demand. I know by the time and trouble that I have
given to the subject that nothing has been left undone
to insure a calm consideration of it. We have been
asked to consider it in times of comparative quietude,
in times of comparative prosperity ; we have been
asked to do little ; we have been asked to act slowly ;
but every change has been steadily and sternly refused : the smallest modification of the Measure has
been always refused.

Is it wonderful then that exhausted by distress
and perhaps excited by despair, they should now in
angry tones demand the total abolition of these Laws ?
We have heard much grumbling and complaint because the ministers of the Gospel, the pastors of the
people, have lately come forth to proclaim the sufferings of their flocks : I wish that the professed
friends of the people would think that they could
serve them better than by always pecking and carp-
ing at their proceedings. What are the people to
do ? They are not fully and fairly represented in this
House ! Where then can they with more propriety

seek for advocates to plead their wrongs than among intelligent men who live amidst them and are competent to treat of their sufferings? And where could they with more convenience or expediency have found such men than among their spiritual advisers ? It is because these men have assembled together to discuss the miseries of their people and to take counsel how they could relieve them, that we have heard such censure cast upon their conduct.

Knowing much myself and hearing much from others of the sufferings of the people, I can find only matter for admiration in their forbearance, and excuse in their violence.

I do not, however, stand here solely to vindicate the manner in which redress is sought by the people : I come here to justify the measure of relief itself that they seek. And I am prepared to contend that what they demand is reasonable ; that it would produce instant benefit ; that it would cause no national evil; that it is unjust to no one ; and that it ought to be conceded on every principle of justice and policy. And how can I better recommend the measure which is the subject of my Notice for this evening, than by pointing to the condition of the country and the operation of the Corn Laws?

What an anomaly England presents to the world at this moment! Abounding in natural resources, and possessing a power for their development more productive than that enjoyed in any other land, her industrious classes are nevertheless so reduced by want and distress that the Member who was appointed by the Government to answer the message of the Crown, stated upon the responsibility of the Government, that whatever might be said of the distress could not be an exaggeration. And far, far beyond the circle of Government we find it admitted that England—England rich in the gifts of nature, rich in knowledge, rich in the skill and the habits and disposition of her people, yet limited in extent and with her people hourly increasing—wants food : she has reached the point long foreseen when she must procure her food from other lands ; her food is now scarce and ever becoming scarcer ; and in pressing need of its ready and regular supply her people are daily sinking lower and lower in the scale of comfort and well-being. And yet is there a man who has been found so false and so foolish as to proclaim this as the necessary condition of our country? Is there any man so dull that opening his chart of the Globe and seeing this Island placed between the two great civilized continents of the world, he would not ask if it is possible that England so in want, cannot receive relief from neighbours so situated? Whether England has nothing of her own to offer in exchange for what she so wants? And if a man under such circumstances hears that these continents stand in great need of what England produces and yearly suffer from not finding vent for their surplus food, would he not in wonder ask for some solution of this mystery? And is there any that could be rendered save that the rulers of this country, who are also the owners of its soil, place a barrier to the commerce of the world in what they produce themselves in order to enhance the value of their own properties? The barrier of the Laws by which they notify that no man shall find a market in England for food necessary to the support of her people on which he can rely ; and which, thus impeding the trade in food, entails a dire distress which nothing but making the trade in food free can relieve?

This is my theory to account for the present anomalous condition of England ; if you dispute it, it is for you to prove that I am wrong. Try it by every test in your power and show if you can that I am wrong. But let me only be supposed to be right, and then I would ask whether there is a single feature in the present distress of the country that you would not expect to find? What would you look for under such circumstances? The high price of food now compels men to forego the comforts and refinements of life, and thereby it deprives of employment those who are dependent for their livelihood on the production of such comforts and refinements. Suffering from a deficient supply of food we are obliged, owing to the absence of all regular commerce in food with foreign countries, to send bullion that is needed at home out of the country to purchase at an enormous cost the food of other nations, thus, by contracting the basis of our credit, embarrassing and limiting still further the Home Trade. Other countries are forced by our refusal of their surplus food, to withhold their custom from us and become their own manufacturers ; and, in all probability, they will soon be our rivals. General discontent and disaffection among our industrious people are the inevitable result. Now all these evils exist in this country at the present moment, and are the constant and common subject of remark. Granted the truth of my theory, which of them would you expect to be absent? I call upon Hon. Gentlemen opposite who maintain the Corn Laws and who admit the condition of the country to be such as I have described it, to explain by what cause these effects have been produced if not by the cause that I have assigned.

The want of food and the want of regular trade I unhesitatingly affirm to be the chief cause of all the distress that is now admitted to exist; and I rejoice to observe that the good sense and sagacity of the people are at last prevailing on this subject as they have ever prevailed in former times when a great question has agitated the country.

In spite of every effort made to mislead and delude them, though the ground has been trailed in every direction by rubbish of every kind, the people have not been diverted from the right track which they are now pursuing. Most gratifying have been the indications of the influence of public opinion in this respect within one year. Two Governments have successively acknowledged the imperative necessity of dealing with the question. One Government indeed thought it of so much importance and attached so much weight to the opinion generally entertained about it that they were ready to sacrifice Office on it. And now we have another Government thinking proper to admit that which hitherto it has denied : that the existing Corn Laws must be changed. This is now to be done notwithstanding all that has been said in favour of them. Two projects for changing them and mitigating their evils are before the country at present : I object to both. I do not deny that the plan of the Noble Lord would mitigate the prominent evils of the existing Corn Laws, and I believe that much improvement would have followed had the plan been adopted. But I contend that his project and that of the Right Hon. Baronet are both unjust ; that there is no justice in the principle of either one or the other ; and that there is no ground whatever for the maintenance of any Corn Law.

The people are said to be unreasonable for condemning the measures alluded to ; but I am here to defend their claim upon the ground of justice ; and I do not know any teacher of morals, any writer on ethics, who justifies wrong in any form. The Corn Laws are right or wrong in principle. If they are wrong, why should they be maintained? This was what the people urged against the plan of the Noble Lord. The Corn Laws become more objectionable from the manner in which the plan before the House has been recommended to us. The present Laws are justified by the plan proposed by the Noble Lord. It is said that the plan of the Noble Lord is unjust, and that, therefore, he has no right to complain of the injustice of the measures others have proposed.

The Right Hon. Baronet the Member for Dorchester seems to take this view of the matter; and in addressing himself to the argument he said that he was cured of giving large measures of justice. His line of defence was this : 'If I am an unjust man you are another.' The Right Hon. Baronet, indeed, defended the injustice upon the ground of expediency, having as he said learnt by experience not to dole out too much justice at a time. When or where the Right Hon. Baronet acquired this experience I do not know; but I should like to know whether when the people remained discontented after having received a full measure of justice the Right Hon. Baronet may not have mistaken a large measure for a perfect one, and that the discontent he speaks of may not arise from its having been large in principle and promise yet defective and incomplete in execution.

The Right Hon. Baronet the Member for Tamworth seems to think that nothing more is required to vindicate his own plan than to expose the difficulties of that of the Noble Lord ; and he disposed of the claim that this Motion prefers by a sort of passing allusion to the party by whom it is represented in this House. He describes them as a small party that he believes to exist, holding extreme opinions and capable, probably, of violence in the expression of them. This is the way in which the Right Hon. Baronet treats the millions who in this country claim the repeal of the Corn Laws.

The small and violent party, however, have the consolation of knowing that in this respect they only receive the treatment that every party that has first advanced the remedy or reform of any abuse has ever received. It is in this way that the advocates of all the great measures of which England has most reason to be proud have been treated in this House. We have then simply to persevere in the course that we have hitherto pursued, notwithstanding the Right Hon. Baronet's charge of violence and unreasonableness. [Sir R. Peel denied this statement.] I am happy to hear the Right Hon. Baronet disavow this view of his Motion; it is one, however, expressed on both sides of the House. I do not confine it to the party opposite; and I do not doubt that it will be repeated again during the debate.

And here I should just like to ask those gentlemen who are so hostile to Repeal whether they consider ·that there is anything more unreasonable in asking for the repeal of the Corn Laws than after refusing for many years past to inquire into their operation admitting now that they have worked ill. Would there be anything more violent in their immediate repeal than there was in their precipitate enactment? Did we ever hear any of that cautious phraseology at the time of the passing of the Laws that we now hear in vindication of this minimum of concession? We have been invited to be careful in dealing with the vast interests at stake; we are told of the vast capital in question; of the social interests dependent upon the landed interests; but when these Laws were enacted, and since they have been in operation, when has a syllable been said or heeded by those who profit by them about the lives, the comforts, the well-being, the industry, and the capital of the millions of this country who are and who have been cruelly affected by them ?

The working people openly resisted their enactment and they have ever since complained of their operation ; but without the least regard to their manifold interests the Corn Laws have been maintained in force against them. To this day there has been nothing proposed in defence of the Corn Laws that might not with equal reason have been advanced in favour of any other abuse, any other Monopoly : the sum of it all—urged, indeed, with little grace to a people who have been for thirty years crying out for Repeal—is the alleged necessity of upholding the interest of a class by exceptional laws. Such arguments are, indeed, a mockery of the people. Thousands are now on the eve of starving. Is this the moment then to talk of the interests vested in the Corn Laws ? Is this the time to talk of proceeding with all deference for the rich when the poor through our unreasonable adhesion to these Laws have already been driven to the last extremity ? To give a pretence to such reasoning you ought long since to have begun your modifications. You have had ample warning and you have resisted all solicitation ; and now the people have neither time nor temper for delay : they are starving, and they must have food.

There is no wrong that might not be defended upon the grounds on which the wretched concession now offered to the people is justified. A short time since we read of a captain of a Turkish vessel who had inveigled a number of passengers to sail with him on the assurance that they would find a requisite supply of provisions and water on board ; but when they were out at sea he monopolized the water and would allow only those to drink who could pay the price he chose to extort.   There is not a Conservative phrase used by the Right Hon. Baronet in defence of the Corn Laws that might not with equal reason have been used by this captain in defence of his Monopoly : it would have been just as much in point in reply to the people whom he had engaged to supply and who were dying of thirst, that great interests were invested in the supply of water, that great expense had been incurred in fitting out the vessel, and that the navigation of those seas was attended with great hazard.   It would have been just as much in place, and quite as consistent with justice, as what we have heard in defence of the Corn Laws.

The question is whether you had any right at all to pass the Laws and whether they have not become altogether too disastrous to be endured any longer. My answer is that the Corn Laws are and always were atrociously unjust ; that the evils they are hourly producing are past endurance ; and that there is ample authority to show that the advantage to the nation that would follow from their instant repeal would not be attended by any injury to the landed interest.

There are, I know, honest and disinterested men who detest the Corn Laws, but who, nevertheless, have scruples about total Repeal, fearing the immediate consequence of such a step to the country. These persons are not, perhaps, very fully represented in this House ; but their opinions require deference and deserve to be considered.

They ask whether the total repeal of the Corn Laws might not be prejudicial to agriculture, and whether the landlords do not bear exclusively a large portion of the national burdens. These no doubt are points that call for attention, and those who claim total Repeal have not overlooked them ; but we have the highest authority for declaring that the plea they have furnished for the Corn Laws does not rest upon solid ground of any kind whatever.

Who is the first man that I can name in support of my view ? One of the most eminent statesmen of his day : I mean Lord Grenville, a man remarkable for his sagacity, his talent, and his character. How did he view the Corn Laws ? In the first place, he declared them to be a bounty to the grower of corn and thereby a tax on the consumer. And what did he say as to the policy of such a tax ? He said :—

The great practical rule of leaving all commerce unfettered applies more peculiarly, and on still stronger grounds of justice as well as policy, to the Corn Trade than to any other ; and irresistible indeed must be the necessity which could authorize the Legislature to tamper with the sustenance of the people, and to impede the free purchase of that article on which depends the existence of so large a portion of the community.

This was the opinion of the greatest statesman of his day when the first Corn Law was proposed.

Five years after that time what was the opinion of the commercial classes upon this and all similar laws as declared by the leading merchants of London, assembled in their Guildhall ? They denounced Protection in strong terms, and in the special interest of commerce and the general interest of the community called for the repeal of all Protective Duties whether for land or manufactures.

In 1821 we have the authority of this House itself against the system of Protection. The landlords deceived by the promise of their own Laws inquired themselves into the causes of agricultural depression, and the real sources from which they might expect the future prosperity of agriculture. And what do we find in the deliberate Report of a Committee of these land-owners ? Nothing less than a contrast in favour of Free Trade drawn between two periods : the one commencing at the beginning of the last century and continuing till 1773, during which legislation of every kind was attempted to raise the value of agricultural produce ; and the other during which the trade in grain was almost free, and which lasted till 1791.

Let the House hear the extract from this Report, and then say whether they can doubt that the opinion of this Committee was in favour of Free Trade :—

Your Committee cannot look at these contrasted circumstances coincident during the first period with a comparative stagnation of our agriculture, and during the second with its most rapid growth and improvement, without acknowledging that there was nothing in the system pursued up to 1773, which necessarily promoted this most essential branch of public industry and national wealth ; and also that there is nothing incompatible with the success of both these objects in the system which has practically prevailed since that date.

Again ; the Report says :—

That they may entertain a doubt whether the only solid foundation of the flourishing state of agriculture is not laid in abstaining as much as possible from interference, either by Protection or Prohibition, with the application of capital in any branch of industry. Whether all fears for the decline of agriculture, either from temporary vicissitudes, to which all speculations are liable, or from the extension of other pursuits of general industry, are not in a great degree imaginary. Whether commerce can expand, manufactures thrive, and great public works be undertaken, without furnishing to the skill and labour which the capital thus employed put in motion, increased means of paying for the productions of the land. Whether the principal part of those productions which contribute to the gratification of the wants and desires of the different classes of the community must not necessarily be drawn from our own soil, the demand increasing with the population, as the population must increase with the riches of the country. Whether a great part of the same capital which is employed in supporting the industry connected with manufactures and commerce, does not, passing by a very rapid course into the hands of the occupier of the soil, serve also as capital for the encouragement of agriculture. Whether in our own country, in former times, agriculture has not languished from the want of such a stimulus ; and whether, in those countries, the proprietors of the land are not themselves poor, and the people wretched in proportion, as, from want of capital, their labour is more exclusively confined to raising from their own soil the means of their own scanty subsistence.

This Committee was composed of shrewd landowners carefully considering their own interests.

But at the present day also we have some of the largest proprietors of land in the country—men of great intelligence and experience who have devoted much attention to agriculture, in favour of the abolition of all Protective Duties : they do not need Protection, and see no danger in its abolition. I may mention among them such men as Lord Spencer,

Lord Fitzwilliam, Lord Radnor, and Lord Leicester, who repudiate absolutely the justice or necessity of Protection as an advantage to their properties.

Where is it that skill and economy in husbandry are most displayed? Surely in Scotland! And in Scotland there is not a public meeting, not a demonstration against the Corn Laws, in which some occupier of land is not ready to declare that his interests are directly opposed to them. For the last ten years this has been the case. And the Scotchmen always support their speeches by facts.

The same opinions were expressed in 1836 by farmers before a Committee of the House of Commons.

In consequence of the part that I have taken on this question I have received many letters dealing with it; and from none have I received letters expressed in greater bitterness of language against the Corn Laws than from farmers themselves.

I have here also some works on the subject by country gentlemen, who when they commit their thoughts to paper are well worth consulting. Quite lately I read a pamphlet published by one who is not unknown to the Right Hon. Baronet the Member for Dorchester—a person of great experience in agriculture who describes himself as 'A Cumberland Landowner.' I believe that the Right Hon. Baronet is acquainted with the author, who invites the attention of the landed interest to his opinions. [Sir J. Graham was understood to say it was not his work.] I do not mean to say that the Right Hon. Baronet is the author but that he knows him, and

knows him to be what he represents himself to be in
the following passage (p. 69) :—

> One of their own body; one who has no ambition to gratify,
> no purpose of the day to serve; but attached to the interest of
> that yeomanry, which he knows to be the pride and the strength
> of this great nation, he feels the love of truth predominant in his
> heart; and well satisfied of the grounds of the assertion herein
> developed, he boldly affirms that a free trade in foreign corn is
> the real interest of the land-owner, and the only safe policy of the
> State.

Again; after detailing the mischiefs to be expected from restrictions on trade, he says :—

> On the other hand, what have we to fear from the open com-
> petition of Free Trade? Nature and art have fitted up our native
> land with the means for carrying on production and barter
> beyond any other nation in the world; while its civil institutions,
> and the spirit of its people, are every way qualified to bear out
> these great advantages. Look at our roads, our canals, our docks,
> and our public works; arms of the sea traversed by bridges;
> hills, and even rivers, undermined by tunnels; our steamboats
> covering every navigable water. Then consider our natural
> advantages—our sea-girt islands, intersected by mighty rivers
> worthy of a continent; our meadows fertilized by living streams;
> our verdant pastures; our climate favourable to the growth of
> corn; our sheep and cattle on a thousand hills. Look at our
> smiling land, where nature has been prodigal, and where art has
> supplied what nature has refused; then say whether we need fear
> competition with any foreign State; whether we have not the
> start of a century in the career of commercial rivalry; and
> whether, with open ports and trade unfettered, the half cultivated
> sands of Poland, or even the vine-clad hills of France, need
> excite the envy or the fears of Great Britain—of Britain, the
> seat of wealth, of freedom, and of arts.

Again (p. 63) :—

> The prosperity of the home trade, and the advancement of
> British agriculture, has always been soundest and most rapid
> when our foreign trade has been most prosperous and free. Give

the industry of Britain only a fair and open field, and it has
nothing whatever to dread from foreign rivalship.

And at page 61 :—

What have the landed interests of England to fear, either politically as a body, or in reference to the retention of their incomes,
from the utmost prosperity of commerce that can possibly arise ?
The whole soil is theirs ; and the more prosperous our towns are,
the more must the rent-rolls of the land-owners increase.

And again (p. 62) :—

We hear a great deal about emigration, the increase of the
commission of crime, &c., &c., and the inability of our shipping
and manufacturing interests to enter into free competition with
foreigners. Give to the people profitable employment, and a
price of provisions at home more equalized with prices abroad,
and all these complaints will at once vanish like a mist before
the morning sun. No wonder that we have an overstock of
manufactured goods, when the operatives, to gain the most
limited livelihood, are compelled to work from fourteen to sixteen
hours in each working day. Equalize the prices between corn
and wages, and these men would immediately cease to labour so
excessively ; the overstock of the market would disappear, a
greater ability to purchase would ensue, and a rapid rise of prices
would at once show how destructive the influence of Corn Laws
has been.

I will now turn to another publication[1] by an
intelligent land-owner in Surrey, known to many
Members in this House : —

I am the owner of a tract of land, which probably contains a
larger portion of poor land, as compared with the good, than
most other land-owners in this county ; yet I am confident that
not an acre would be rendered useless by the opening of the ports
for the introduction of foreign corn : and it has been repeatedly
shown that every acre of land which it was possible to cultivate with profit last year (when wheat was at 55s. 6d., rye 31s.,

[1] *Cheap Corn best for Farmers, proved in a letter to George Holme Sum-
ner, Esq., late M.P. for the County of Surrey*, by one of his Constituents.

barley 33s., oats 22s.), might continue to be so cultivated, were every restriction and prohibition abolished, and the public allowed to purchase their corn in the cheapest markets. But such a reduction of price, as would not be sufficient to cause even the very poorest lands now under corn to be laid down to pasture, would so increase the comfort of the labourer, and give such an immense stimulus to industry in general, that the progress of the country in wealth would be accelerated in a degree that can hardly be conceived. The more the landlords contend that corn would be cheap if the ports were open, the more they prove what a nuisance the present Corn Laws are.

Referring to the interests of the farmer he says (p. 36) :—

I again repeat that until the ports are open no farmer who knows his own interest will bind himself by a lease : if he does, he ought to take it at a corn rent, that is, with a lease fluctuating with the price of corn : if he does not do this, he puts his fortune, and the independence of himself and children, at the mercy of his landlord, or of the Bank Directors, or of the Government.

And he concludes his able and argumentative work by the following summary which he declares he has proved (p. 37) :—

1. That the land-owners' monopoly of corn is the heaviest tax which the people have to pay.

2. That the land-owners and their families are the only persons who gain by this tax.

3. That all other classes, including farmers, are injured by this tax.

4. That of all taxes, it is the one which presses hardest upon the labourers.

5. That the gain to the landlord from this tax is not so great as the loss to the people.

It follows that the immediate abolition of the monopoly of corn which the landlords now enjoy under the present Corn Laws is a measure of bare justice and absolute necessity.

And now I will ask the House to hear the latest

opinion of a land-owner who formerly represented the district for which I sit, whose whole income is de· rived from land, and whose estate is not dependent on a manufacturing neighbourhood : I mean Mr. Whitmore. Mr. Whitmore in his 'Letter to the Agriculturists of the County of Salop' says :—

The present law, without conferring any real benefit on our own agriculturists, does infinite mischief to the rest of the community ; so the change, without any injury to the former, would do infinite good to the latter. (p. 11.)

I am inclined to believe that a free trade in corn would not admit of any considerable quantity of wheat being sold in our markets under from 45s. to 48s. (p. 7.)

Taking these circumstances into consideration, I cannot entertain any apprehension of the slightest ill-effect to our own agriculture by the change. I believe we shall consume easily all the corn we can grow, and all we can import ; but I believe also we should want more of meat, and of beer too – matters of immense moment to the graziers, the breeders of stock, and the barley growers of this country ; and who, amongst the agriculturists, will not come under one or other of these descriptions. (p. 7.)

A larger consumption, and consequently a greater demand, for every species of grass produce, in a fresh or uncured state, such as milk, butter, meat, &c., is the necessary consequence of a population at once increasing and well employed. The large proportion which grass land bears to arable, in every densely peopled district, cannot fail to have struck every observant agriculturist. (p. 10.)

I can, from my own experience, assert that, even now, the laying down land of every quality, including the very best, to permanent pasture is a profitable application of it. (p. 10.)

I could quote many other authorities among agriculturists who have most considered the subject, to the same effect, and still more from writers who are not connected with the interest in question ; but I know that these are not popular authorities, more especially

if they deserve the title of political economists. I will
therefore content myself with quoting two only of the
latter class, and these I choose because they are men
whom the Right Hon. Baronet looks upon as authorities for some of his positions, and because he is in
the habit of quoting them in the House. I mean
Mr. M'Culloch and Mr. Tooke. I will not quote
Mr. M'Culloch for all his opinions, but I will quote
him for the reasons that the Right Hon. Baronet
assigned when he last quoted him : namely, as
' One of the most intelligent and able advocates of
Free Trade ; one who takes a dispassionate and able
view of the case, looks at it calmly, reasons upon
it closely, a clever and able man ; ' and because I
am told that my Motion is unreasonable, and the
' calm and clever man ' has given his opinion upon
the subject of it. Mr. M'Culloch says :—

> The truth is, that the agriculturists have nothing to fear even
> from the total and unconditional repeal of the Corn Laws. It
> admits of demonstration that it could then do no real injury.
> It would not throw an acre of land out of cultivation, nor sensibly
> affect rent. The prosperity of the agriculturist does not depend
> upon the miserable resource of custom-house regulations. Though
> these were swept away, the excellence of our soil, the skill of our
> husbandmen, the wealth of our commercial and manufacturing
> classes will ensure the continued prosperity of agriculture. Those
> who investigate the matter will find that the existing regulations
> respecting the corn trade are little less injurious to the agricul-
> turists than to the other classes.

This is what Mr. M'Culloch says ; and he, I am
informed, is a land-owner as well as an author.

I will now refer to Mr. Tooke, the able and experienced writer on this subject, and one whom the

Right Hon. Baronet delights to cite.   I quote from
his work published in 1840, in which alluding (pp.
43, 44) to total Repeal he says:—

Although, however, there is every reason, founded on the
experience of that period (1834–5), and on other grounds which
it is not here the place to enter upon, that at a range of prices
of about 45s. for wheat there would be no just cause for appre-
hending any diminution of the breadth of arable land, unless the
land were to become, as I believe it will with the growth of
population become, applicable to more valuable productions than
corn; it would form no valid reason for perpetuating on the
country the infliction of the Corn Laws.   At the same time, if
it could be fairly shown that the growing lands of this country,
constituting any considerable proportion of those destined for the
supply of food for the community, could not be continued under
cultivation, except at prices much higher than those of the foreign
grower, such difference might be a ground for rendering the
transition more gradual; and the degree or extent of difference
should serve as a guide for determining the gradations by which
that difference should be reduced.   But from all the information
which I have been able to collect, not omitting that which the
Agricultural Reports of 1833 and 1836 by the Committees on
Agricultural Distress of the House of Commons, and of 1836 by
the Committee of the House of Lords, are calculated to afford, I
am firmly persuaded that the difference is very inconsiderable, so
inconsiderable as not to form a valid objection to a very early
resort to the only system which can hold out the prospect of
security, to farmers in their leases, to landlords in their incomes,
and to the public in having their supply of food divested of an
impost which is felt grievously by the consumer (not to mention
the other grievances attending it), while it adds little, if at all, to
the permanent income of the producer.

And now, having Mr. Tooke's book in my hand,
I will just finish the passage that the Right Hon.
Baronet partially quoted the other night in order
to show the danger of depending upon foreign
countries; and one that the House will see was

written not exactly for that purpose, but rather to show the policy of Free Trade. Mr. Tooke says :—

> No one can be more alive than I am to the circumstance that within certain degrees of longitude and latitude, extending over the central parts of the continent of Europe, there is, in the majority of seasons, a prevalence of weather of the same general character, of propitiousness or unpropitiousness, to the growth and gathering of the corn crops, as prevails in this country. But this circumstance, instead of being an argument, as by some persons it has been set up to be, against a free trade in corn, is the strongest ground in favour of it. An extension of the radius of our habitual supply to the north and south-east of Europe, to parts of Asia bordering on the Black Sea and the Mediterranean, to Egypt, and, above all, to the United States of America, would greatly mitigate the effects of visitations of peculiar inclemency of weather prevailing simultaneously in this country, and within a certain range on the continent of Europe.

So much, then, for the opinion of theoretical writers. But do they differ from the practical men whose opinions are deemed of most weight in this House, when they give it as their opinion that little land would go out of cultivation, and none out of use if the trade in food were free ? And in estimating that the price of wheat would be between 40s. and 48s. per quarter if restrictions were removed ? What was the evidence given before Committees in 1836 ? I will read the opinions expressed before them by one or two witnesses. Mr. Bennett, a land agent and farmer, was interrogated on the subject :—

> Do you think, with reduction of rent and the reduction of prices, the farmer can cultivate his land at a profit ?—Looking to the seven years back, and having taken those farms under very low prices, I have not a question that some may do it profitably, and I have no doubt some will.
>
> At what price do you estimate wheat for the next seven

years ?—If I was going to take a farm myself, I should not expect, nor would I calculate for the next seven years, to have wheat above 5s. to 6s. a bushel.

Will the Duke of Bedford's tenants, who have re-taken those farms, be able to pay the rent for which they have just agreed, with wheat at 5s. a bushel ?—I think they will. I think the majority do not expect to see it at much more.

I adduce evidence of this sort to show that there is nothing violent or dangerous in the propositions of those who advocate the total repeal of the Corn Laws. And I will trouble the House with one more extract from the same Report for this purpose :—

Supposing that mutton had borne the same proportionate price when wheat fell to 40s., do you think the Scotch farmer would then have been enabled to make a good living ?—The Scotch farmer would have tried something else than wheat ; he would have extended his grass cultivation.

And if the price of barley had been also reduced ?—Those are all regulated by the demand of the manufacturing and commercial classes.

Thus, then, we have the evidence of statesmen, of landed proprietors, of theoretical writers, and of farmers, to prove that there is no real danger to be apprehended to the country from the repeal of the Corn Laws. This is the case that I had in the first place to make out in support of my Motion for Free Trade.

We next have to consider the other ground on which the Corn Laws are rested : namely, that the land-owners bear exclusive burdens, and that the Corn Laws are maintained as compensation to them. The first evidence that I shall adduce on this point is that which cannot be disputed : the admission of the land-owners themselves. And here I would remind the House of what the Right Hon. Baronet the Member for Dorchester said on this point ; for I now look upon him as the personification of Protection ; and as a stanch Protectionist he is more trusted, perhaps, by country gentlemen than any one else.

I heard the Right Hon. Baronet make a speech on the Malt Tax in which he referred to the Corn Laws ; and in that speech he said that the Malt Tax is the only *locus standi* that the landed interest have for the Corn Laws. I have just referred to the debate, and I find that he was correctly reported. After asserting this connection between the Malt Tax and the Corn Laws he went on to state that he for one should consider .that if the Malt Tax were repealed, the Tithes commuted, the Poor Law reformed, and a portion of the County Rates thrown upon the Consolidated Fund, that then the total repeal of the Corn Laws would be irresistibly forced upon the House.

I will not go into the question of the Malt Tax upon this occasion further than to call attention to the enormous injustice to the community of imposing the Corn Tax to indemnify the landlords for the Malt Tax, the removal of which they think might enable some of their lands to be more profitably employed. Does anybody dispute for a moment that the community pays more for beer on account of the Malt Tax ? And could greater injustice be imagined than to compel them to pay more for bread in order to indemnify the land-owners for what they

suffer through the Malt Tax ?   What is to indemnify
the community for the two taxes : the tax on their
bread as well as the tax on their beer ?

But now what has actually occurred with respect
to those other changes the accomplishment of which
the Right Hon. Baronet thinks would irresistibly
force the question of total Repeal upon the House ?
The Poor Law has been reformed in the manner
most beneficial to the land-owner; a great portion
of the County Rate has been cast on the Consolidated Fund, and Tithes have been commuted for
Rent Charge.   Therefore, according to the Right Hon.
Baronet's own doctrine, there remains but the Malt
Tax between him and his obligation to vote for the
total repeal of the Corn Laws.

And does any man suppose that the community
would not gladly submit to the charge of four and
a half millions a year—the amount of the Malt Tax—
to get rid of the incubus of the Corn Laws acting as
they are with a tenfold pressure upon all their means
and energies ?

And was there ever such a pretext for a great
national burden as the local charges that are named :
the County Rate, the Highway Rate, and so on ?
These are for local purposes ; and they are locally
beneficial to the proprietors and occupiers themselves.   What would be the value of land without highways, how could they bring their produce
into market, and take back manure to restore the
land without them ?   The Right Hon. Baronet the
Member for Tamworth said that the bread of the

whole nation ought to be taxed to relieve land-
owners from the Highway Rate ! Surely the words
escaped him unawares ! Suppose a parallel case:
what would be thought of a tax upon land-owners to
indemnify people who live in towns from the payment of Borough Rates, and Poor Rates, and Police
Rates ? And yet why are they to have these to pay
for as belonging to themselves and the bread tax
besides in order to indemnify the land-owners for
paying what equally belongs to them ?

Moreover the County Rate is not an exclusive
burden. I have been told that the town for which I
sit pays 1,200l. a year towards that Rate. What is
to indemnify them for this charge as well as for the
tax on their food ?

Again, the Tithe is now nearly all commuted
for Rent Charge, so that it is little or no grievance
to the cultivator as it was formerly when he had a
tenth of his gross produce taken, and was consequently often prevented from making improvements.

But what can be more rude than such an indemnity for such a charge when we have no certain
account rendered of the amount of the land that is
Tithe free, or of the proportion of the Tithes belonging to the land-owners themselves ? I am informed
that one-half of the land of the United Kingdom is
Tithe free, and one-fourth at least of the Tithes is in
lay hands. However, the better way of testing the
point as it rests upon a ground of justice, is whether
any landed proprietor can show any claim to compensation in any Court of Justice ; whether he can

say that the repeal of the Corn Laws would injure him by means of Rent Charge for which the Tithe is commuted and which varies with the prices of produce ; and whether he can say that he did not take or buy his land subject to the charge, or whether his land is not Tithe free.

Once more, if the Corn Laws are a compensation for their local charges why do we not hear whether they are justly proportioned ? Why is not the amount of these charges and the advantage of the Corn Laws placed side by side in a regular account so that the public may be satisfied that they are not paying more than they need ? We know that it is because the Corn Laws are a burden to the public out of all proportion to the burden alleged on the ground of these local charges ; and we also know that during the last twelve years though great reductions have taken place in the local charges none have been made in the Corn Laws, but that on the contrary they have become more oppressive than ever. Show me then the justice of what is called Protection.

Is it claimed on any other ground ? We ought to hear it if it is. I trust that this question of Protection will be well sifted. What does it mean ? Is it to support an interest by law when it cannot support itself? And if so can it be universally done ? If it cannot how can it be just ? Is it fair or right to protect land and not to protect labour ? But who ever thinks of protecting the artisan or mechanic against the improvements of machinery ?

And yet there is not really any difference between preventing the public from having access to fertile soil for cheap and abundant food in order to uphold the fortunes of landlords, and preventing the community from deriving the advantage of the steam-engine in order to keep and to rear a class of mechanics whose labour would be superseded by the adoption of this power.

A short time since, in opening the ' Travels of Humboldt,' I found a circumstance mentioned that well illustrates the absurdity of this claim to Protection. Humboldt refers to a class of men who had earned their living for nearly two centuries by carrying passengers in baskets on their backs over the Andes but whose occupation ceased when the Government made regular roads passing through the country. Immediately the Government made the roads these men were up in arms against them for thus encroaching upon their interests, and prayed for Protection against good roads and in favour of their baskets. Is there anything more absurd or monstrous in the claim to protect the bad clay soil of this country against the wants and well-being of the whole people who could be provided by free access to the produce of good land, than there is in the claim recorded by Humboldt on behalf of bad roads and baskets ?

But perhaps there is some other ground on which this claim can be rested ! We may well be prepared for anything after what fell from the Right Hon. Baronet the Member for Kent the other night.

Perhaps we shall hear that land-owners pay more towards the general taxation than other people ; and that on this account the tax on food is just. Anticipating this possibility I cannot do better than read from a petition to this House the case of a labouring man who complained of the proportion of his scanty pay that was taken for the Revenue. And then let it be judged whether the land-owners pay a greater proportion of their income to the State than the poor man pays.

The case is that of William Blaxland, of Birmingham ; and the petition shows that he uses weekly two ounces of tea, two ounces of coffee, eight ounces of sugar, three pounds eight ounces of meat, seven pounds of flour, seven pints of ale, a quarter of a pint of brandy, and one ounce of tobacco ; the cost of which, freed from Tithe, Corn Customs, and Excise Duties, would be 2s. 4⅜d. But with these taxes these articles cost him 7s. 7½d., being a weekly tax of 5s. 3⅜d., amounting in the year to 13l. 13s. 6d. The average rate of wages in this county be it remembered is under 11s. a week.

I mention this case in order that people, after connecting it with the known fact that the Customs and Excise yield more than 75 per cent. to the Revenue, may judge with what justice land-owners allege as an excuse for Corn Laws the undue weight upon themselves of the general taxation. Clearly the Corn Laws are nothing less than a purely arbitrary act, resting solely upon the particular interests of those who profit by them at the expense of the community. They are said to be simply a question between land-owners and manufacturers ; but in truth they are a question between the owner of the soil and every other consumer in the community ; a question, in fact, between the interest of about 30,000 persons in raising the value of about fourteen million of acres of arable land and every other interest almost that could be named.

This is anything but a mere manufacturing question. What the interest of the manufacturers in the question is it is easy to state : the manufacturer loses a good customer at home on account of his customer's means being exhausted in paying too much for food, and he loses a profitable customer abroad by not being allowed to exchange his goods for grain ; but the manufacturer has no interest in lowering the price of food in order to reduce wages. If this were his interest in order to get labour cheap, he could not be better off than at present, for wages were never before so low : low wages are but too often the consequence of food being dear, because of the numbers who must on this account lose their employment.

With respect to its being a farmer's question, I do not believe that there is a single one of the land-owners whom I am now addressing who honestly believes that his tenants have any real interest in the Corn Laws. And I say that he cannot believe it if only for this reason: he knows that if ever he has a farm to let there are twenty farmers offering to take it. Now how can the farmers with such competition among themselves avoid offering the highest rent, or

be able to get more than the average rate of profit
for their own capital, and how can it be an advantage to them to pay more instead of less for the use
of the land ?   High prices can be no object to them
for high prices require a greater outlay ; and if they
have to pay more for seed, more for servants, more
for horses, more for Poor Rates, they will require
larger capital to engage in farming, which, though it
may tempt men with insufficient capital into this
business or exclude men of small capital from it,
can never be the means of procuring a higher rate
of profit.

The Right Hon. Baronet the Member for Tamworth once said that the Corn Laws are a labourer's
question, and doubtless they are.   I have always
thought them peculiarly so ; more so than that of
any other class ; and fortunate indeed it is for those
who maintain them that the labourers do not see it
as clearly as others see it for them.

In this country, where capital is abundant and
the demand for labour naturally great, the general
condition of the labourer must depend upon the sacrifice he has to make to obtain food.   Why is a labourer
in the United States so much better off than he is in
England ?   Because in the first place he has no difficulty to get food ; and capital being abundant and
a wide field existing for its employment, his labour
is in demand.   But why is food plentiful in America ?
Because it can be produced with but little labour
owing to easy access to good land ; but it is not
because of the extent of territory or the mere un-

occupied soil that plenty prevails ; it is because by little labour a man can procure food ; and this is precisely what would be the case in England if Free Trade were allowed with grain-growing countries.

A man by devoting his labour to manufactures to exchange for food might obtain food as easily as by occupying new land and tilling it himself.   Let any one test this by the supposed case of an island that we could appropriate, rising up in the Channel : is there any doubt that if our labourers could occupy it, or if it were inhabited by men wanting clothes who had an excess of food, our population would be much under the same circumstances as the people of the United States would be if we could exchange freely with them ?   And would not the man whose labour was in request and who paid little for his food be in a condition either to toil moderately or to possess himself of the comforts or luxuries of life ?   But once let the labouring man have to make great sacrifices for food, or be unable to exchange freely what he produces for food, and I would ask whether any condition could be found lower than his?

It is said, however, that the repeal of the Corn Laws, by throwing land out of cultivation, would deprive labourers of employment ; and in order to exaggerate the evils of such a result it is stated as if every quarter imported from abroad would displace a quarter grown at home : some indeed go so far as to suppose that so much would be imported that vast tracts of land would be thrown out of cultivation.   But what is the utmost that the most sanguine

Repealer expects to come in under a system of Free
Trade ? Barely more than four million quarters.
And there is no reason why this should displace as
much grown at home.   In the first place, the deficiency of the supply for the existing wheat-consuming
population is nearly two millions ; but the calculation is that one-third of our population do not eat
wheaten bread owing to the price, which if lowered,
or if the people's condition improved, would greatly
increase the consumption.

How, then, is the land to be deteriorated in value
in this country, seeing that our arable soil does not
amount to more than 14,000,000 acres, and grows
about 20,000,000 quarters of wheat ? How can
the addition of 4,000,000 quarters of wheat from
abroad, giving a greater stimulus to manufactures
and commerce and thus improving the consuming
power of the population, increasing income and the
demand for land, cause such deterioration in the
value of land ? Why, is not the bare contemplation of the land losing its value in this small
island with a dense and industrious population full
of resource and adding to its numbers every hour,
positively ludicrous ?   I should like to hear the plan
that the most ingenious man could devise for keep
ing down rent if commerce and industry continued
productive ! I really believe that the only way in
which it could be effected would be by some such
means as the Right Hon. Baronet's Scale : in its
anti-social and anti-commercial operation this may
have the effect of driving capital and skill out of

the country, which, as they are the source whence
land derives its value, may by their withdrawal
effect a serious depreciation in land that will be
aggravated by the burdens consequent on maintaining an unoccupied people. But allowing the energy
and enterprise of the nation to have full scope, what
people could be more fortunately circumstanced than
those who own the soil of this country ? For what,
then, are our land-owners jeoparding all this ? For
what are they imperilling all the institutions so
favourable to themselves ; losing the esteem of their
fellow-countrymen ; making all men politicians ; and
driving the middle and working classes to think that
they are misrepresented and defrauded, and that the
present system is maintained simply for the benefit
of a class ? It all seems to be for the vain hope of
giving to their estates by artificial means a value that
natural circumstances would give them in a tenfold
degree.

The only ground on which they can rest for
keeping their bad land in cultivation—the ground that
it gives employment to the poor, is no argument
for the Corn Laws : it is only a reason why some
provision should be made for the existing generation
of poor who are so dependent. For to keep these
bad lands for ever in cultivation is to rear for ever
a class of men with interests adverse to the community. And this applies equally to the occupiers
of the land, a generation of whom may have come
into existence since the last Corn Laws were passed
who would otherwise have occupied themselves, or

who would have employed their land differently but for the continuance of these Laws.

The continuance of the monastic institutions might have been, and probably was urged upon the same ground as the Corn Laws : namely, that they provided for the poor ; but if so, the plea was unheeded except so far as it led to our public provision for the poor.

However, even if greater consideration for an interest affected by an improvement is required in one case more than in another, this is no ground for the continuance of a bad land system ; though it may, possibly, be for compensation or for some special provision which the transition might require. But I contend that there is no such case here with respect to the poor ; for the Corn Laws do not provide the poor with employment in the agricultural districts.   It has been shown in the analysis of the last Census that but for the town and the manufacturing districts 350,000 people would have been left in the Agricultural Market who could not have been supported and who would have dragged down the rest to the lowest level.

I will no longer try the patience of Hon. Members ; but I will leave to my many friends on this question to supply what I have omitted in developing the case to the House.

I have attempted to show that under the present circumstances of this country there cannot be any advantage in the Corn Laws and that there is not any pretext for them ; that there is now a deficient supply of food for the people ; that but for these Laws the people have the means of procuring an ample supply, and that obstructed by them they are suffering the severest privations ; that commerce is impeded ; that employment is withheld ; and that, identified as it is with the ability to consume, our Revenue is yearly declining. On these grounds I beg to move, That the duties on corn do now cease and determine.

When I say 'now,' I mean to mark the coincidence of my opinions with those of the petitioners to this House who pray to be instantly relieved from the operation of the Corn Laws ; though, of course, if it can be shown that the public would suffer in any way from the immediate removal of restrictive duties, we are neither so foolish nor so bigoted as still to insist upon this taking place ; nor if it can be shown that greater good could be derived from their gradual than from their immediate abolition should we reject the benefit. But at this time, and considering the unreasonable attitude assumed by those who profit by the Corn Laws, I think the people quite right to call for their entire and immediate abolition ; and unless any clear, certain, and definite evil can be pointed out as likely to result from it, I hope that those who are for total Repeal will not shrink from supporting my Motion.

XI.

HOUSE OF COMMONS, April 18, 1842.

When the Budget for 1842 was brought forward the Revenue fell short of the expenditure for the current year by two millions and a half, and showed a deficiency of upwards of ten millions for the previous six years. Sir Robert Peel's financial scheme to meet this state of affairs was a new departure. The distress in the country and the depression in trade were no longer due to foreign wars, joint-stock banks, and such like. The Ministerial policy openly admitted them to have been caused by restrictive laws operating on our Foreign Trade : commercial reform alone could effect their removal; and the price to be paid for the remedy was an Income Tax of 7*d.* in the pound. The Budget of 1842, at a first glance, might almost have been taken for a Free Trade Budget ; but though the reform it inaugurated comprised the reduction of import duties and the removal of restrictions upon no less than seven hundred and fifty articles, embracing almost the whole range of the tariff, there were two fatal exceptions—corn and sugar : the great scheme of financial reform commenced with the egregious omission of the duties on corn, the real root of all the misery and suffering of the people, and the ever increasing depression of trade. Lord J. Russell moved an Amendment condemnatory of the Income Tax, which after a debate of four days was rejected on April 13 by a vote of 308 to 202. The debate on the Amendment, proposing that the Bill should be read on that day six months, during which Mr. Villiers made the following speech, took place on April 18. The Motion was lost by 285 to 188.

THE Right Hon. Baronet's speech is, I think, in one respect the most important speech that he has made since he announced his financial scheme; for it has done what his former speeches have left undone : it has given the public some insight into what his general views and intentions are with regard to the peculiar tax that he is about to impose on the country.

His scheme has been so ingeniously contrived and his speeches have been so cleverly composed that up to this moment he has succeeded in leaving many, and particularly those who are opposed to him, in doubt as to the course they should pursue.

There are many, and I am among the number, who are far from satisfied with the justice of our present system of taxation, who think that it is oppressive to the poor and partial to the rich and who are strongly in favour of transferring from poverty to property the burdens of the State. There are many who see nothing to approve in the particular purpose of this tax and the occasion selected for its imposition, but who yet think that it is the recognition of a sound principle as regards taxation, and that it will be wise to endure its inconvenience with the view to its general application ultimately—always assuming, however, that this is the view taken by the Right Hon. Baronet, and that he is alive to the evils of which we complain, and is not wanting in will to apply the remedy.

The speech that we have just heard will dissipate this illusion at once and enlighten the country as to the Right Hon. Baronet's views of the object of a property tax. Called upon to-night to vindicate his consistency in opposing a property tax in 1833, the Right Hon. Baronet candidly tells us that the ground of his opposition then was one that he would maintain now ; that a property tax, in lieu of the indirect taxes that exist now and of which the people complain, is one that the Right

Hon. Baronet would join any party in opposing. No man would be found more firm in opposing any substitute for the duties on malt, on soap, or any of the indirect taxes now existing ; and the Right Hon. Baronet has distinctly said that all that he proposes the Income Tax for now is as one means of maintaining the public credit and of getting more revenue, without the least intention of ever proposing it as a substitute for any other tax, much less for any indirect tax now pressing upon the people.

This is candid and intelligible, though calculated a little, I should say, to influence the impression to which the Right Hon. Baronet has alluded as prevailing in the country in favour of his plan, but which, I think, has been produced by the vague, uncertain, and inconsistent things that hitherto have been said on the subject of taxing property, and that pervade every speech the House has heard from the Right Hon. Baronet, in which he seems to mark out the rich as the proper objects of taxation and expresses sympathy with the necessities of the poor.

It will, however, be clear hereafter that this is a tax imposed not in lieu of any other tax, not in any spirit of benefiting the poor, but in aggravation of every other tax and because other means are not relied upon for getting the money required. It ought certainly to settle the doubts now floating about on this side of the House as to whether evil should not be supported that good may come. The Right Hon. Baronet unquestionably has at last confirmed the view that I have entertained from the beginning :

that the financial difficulty which it is intended to
remove results from the financial and commercial
system maintained so long and opposed so long in
this country, and that this tax is really to meet its
necessary consequences.

It is the peculiar system which places the people
of this country under the two-fold contribution of
paying taxes to the State and taxes to particular
classes that has caused our present condition ; and,
as one of those who have long since deprecated the
principle and predicted the effects of this system I
can only consent to relieve the difficulty by removing
its cause.

The fact is, this peculiar system of finance which
makes the Revenue dependent upon the general condition of the people is now breaking down.   Its failure
is caused by Monopoly in food and restraints upon
trade : the former by exhausting men's means in
enhancing the cost of subsistence, and the latter by
narrowing the field for employing their labour.
The Revenue now begins to feel its effects, and the
struggle is really between the means of maintaining
public credit and maintaining Monopoly.

The actual question that the House has to examine
is whether public credit is to be upheld by abolishing
Monopoly or by imposing fresh taxes ; and I am
glad to think that this year at least those who take
my view of the influence of Monopoly upon the
Revenue are spared the trouble of proving what they
have so often said ; for, as a fact, it may this year be
numbered with those many admissions on which the

Noble Lord the Member for North Lancashire has declared that there has been perfect unanimity.

Last year I was tauntingly asked what the Corn Laws had to do with the Budget ; and when I replied that they were not only a heavy tax imposed upon the community for a class, but that inasmuch as the article corn was essential to life it was also the first tax people had to pay, and that upon the amount of this class tax depended what was left for the State, my assertion was treated as a vision of the Free Trade party—one of course to be neglected. This year, however, we hear of the influence of the cost of living upon the value of an income, and the connection between harvests, which govern the cheapness and dearness of food, and the Revenue derived from Customs and Excise ; and notwithstanding all the vulgar tirades that have been uttered against commerce and manufactures, solicitude is now expressed at the languor of commerce while the importance of easing the springs of industry with a view to revenue is freely admitted.

It is well that it should be so. It is high time for the old note to be changed ; but the thing that the House has now to feel is that these admitted truths ought to be acted on and applied. I, for one, have yet to learn that they are very earnestly entertained : if they were we should not, I think, have seen such a Corn Bill as that which has been passed ; nor have had such an Income Tax proposed ; nor would so small an instalment of what is due to the people have been offered as the proposed tariff.

Indeed, I think it incumbent upon those who have proposed this Income Tax to declare explicitly to what they attribute the declining tendency of our Revenue, what they think of its cause and its character; for upon this turns our prospect of the duration of the new tax, and also of the proportion of the burden not being increased.

It is not because it is a direct tax that I oppose it: this is not the objection that I or my constituents have to it. Many of my constituents indeed think, and, in my opinion, think justly, that property is a good test or evidence of a man's ability to contribute to the support of the State; and I have received a memorial from those politically opposed to me approving of the principle of the tax *quâ* property tax; though greatly objecting to the rude and reckless manner in which it is proposed to be applied: assessing all income without reference to its origin or its liability.

It is not enough to say in the present state of our finances that the deficiency occurred under the late Government and that the supporters of the late Government cannot therefore object to supply the deficiency in any way proposed. This view does not satisfy those who stand aloof from both parties. They believe all the harm that Whigs say of Tories or that Tories say of Whigs when the charges have reference to matters of which they have no other cognizance. But the people are pretty well satisfied as to those who have so long had the management of their affairs; they have ascertained clearly enough by whom the

Government has been administered that has brought them to their present state. And, if I mistake not, the Royal Commissioners appointed to consider the state of the hand-loom weavers a short time since, decided that point in their Report upon the condition of the unfortunate section of our fellow-subjects whose state they were led to connect with the operation of our commercial laws. They seem to have been led into a reflection upon the character of the Legislature in consequence : they reminded those who rule this country that the Government resides in a small minority of the community, who occupy entirely one branch of the Legislature and greatly preponderate in the other, and whose interests are entirely identified with one description of property ; and they cautioned them on the importance of their acts being above the suspicion of partiality, as such a Government could only rest upon public opinion, which would not sanction legislation observed and known to produce the misery and sufferings of the masses of the people.

This was announced on authority to be the real Government of this country ; and the people being neither Whig nor Tory, were disposed to think that the Monopolies springing out of what they termed class legislation had so far exhausted their means and restricted their energies as to be answerable for the decline of this great industrial nation.

The people, too, will soon learn that the tax now proposed to be imposed on income is only a mode of escaping one of the temporary, but necessary, consequences of the system. The people are not so dull and not so easily deluded as Hon. Members opposite think when they assume that the labouring classes believe the Income Tax to be favourable to them because it apparently falls on those above them. I have heard the opinions of many of them upon the subject ; they say : ' We shall take no part in the matter. We are not deceived by the fallacy that because the Income Tax is imposed upon those above us we are not affected by it. If the capital of those above us is taxed or diminished we must feel it, so far as we are dependent upon the capital, in the diminished demand for our labour ; but then, on the other hand, we are not blind to the effects of making the middle classes discontented as a means of extending our political power.' They believe thoroughly that the resources of this country have been wasted by Monopoly ; and the arguments that are used in favour of part of this scheme, when the importance of reducing the cost of living is dwelt upon, leave them no doubt of what has hitherto been lost to this country by that means.

This being the case, if permanent improvement is intended, why has the root of the evil not been avowed and struck at ? What hope is there of ever discontinuing this tax or of making any other productive without its being done ? Why has a tax been resorted to that above all others must necessarily aggravate the evil, if the deficiency springs from the poverty of the people ? And why have you not looked round to see if those who profit by Monopoly con-

tribute their due and fair proportion to the State?
That source at least should have been exhausted before resorting to a tax that all must admit is oppressive to men in trade, and unfair to professional men.

And is there not yet a fund untouched by these
unequal taxes? It is but a few weeks since I myself
enumerated nearly one million that has been taken off
the landed classes, and out of pure favour to them.
Has anybody denied that they were exemptions favourable to that interest, and that if the House were to
reimpose them under the present increased value of
real property they would probably yield more than
that million now? Has any satisfactory reason been
assigned why the duty imposed upon the descent of
personal property is not attached to the succession of
freehold property? Some subtlety was, I know, employed the other night to make it appear that some
landed property is assessed for this purpose; but can
any man doubt that a very large sum might be
annually derived from this source; and that it is
foregone merely to favour the landed proprietors?

But the Right Hon. Baronet says to-night that
in spite of all that has been said we have a deficiency
to make up, and that there is no certain way to
do so within his knowledge but that of taxing the
income of the people. The Right Hon. Baronet,
however, had already precluded himself from making
such a statement by an admission which he made the
other night—though not called upon to make it: the
Right Hon. Baronet said that a very considerable
Revenue might be collected immediately on foreign

sugar (now almost prohibited) by lowering the duty
upon it; which of course is true and well known ;
but it is a truth that hitherto has been met with the
taunt that it is one of the theories of the political
economists for getting revenue by reducing duty.

And the Right Hon. Baronet knows, and now
admits, that it is the fact, and that to-morrow, if
he choose, the coffers of the Treasury might be re-
plenished by allowing the people to consume foreign
sugar.

I should like to place the necessity and the policy
of an Income Tax as explained this evening before
the country, and to let sensible and humane people
judge fairly upon this issue : whether the expectation of preventing slavery in a foreign country by not
consuming their produce is sufficiently well grounded
to warrant the policy of precluding the people of this
country from the advantage of a cheap necessary,
and for imposing a fresh and heavy burden upon
them. I have seen a comment upon this policy in a
foreign paper that I cannot but hold just. They call
it the laughable hypocrisy of the English. Under
all circumstances I think the description is really just ;
for few people believe that it will succeed, and most
people believe that it is insincere. If there is any sin-
cerity in all this talk about slavery the real sacrifice
to make is, to refuse to send goods to a slave-pro-
ducing country; for it is to buy goods that sugar is produced; it is to get these goods that men are retained
in slavery ; and it is notorious that the slave-holding
communities are now becoming some of our best

markets, and that if they were to reject our goods or to raise the duties unfairly against us we should be more disposed to go to war with them on that account than to commend them for adopting this means for preventing slavery.

I, however, am not indifferent to the opinion of many benevolent men who think that dealing with slave countries is a means of encouraging slavery; but I know many who no less benevolent, no less zealous or serviceable in opposing slavery, are of opinion that this partial restraint on the trader with such countries is calculated to do harm rather than good. Let us see, for instance, how this policy may work for the continuance of slavery. What do you practically tell the West Indian proprietary? Why, that as long as slavery continues in other countries their Monopoly is safe. Thus they have a strong interest in maintaining slavery; and they have something else: they have very great influence over the British Government—they always have had and they continue to have it. How then can any Government better secure the adherence of these partisans than by not making an effective remonstrance with the Slave States which they now profess it to be their intention to make? The West India influence may and probably will depend upon their not doing it.

Again, it is urged with great justice that if those countries saw that sugar would be produced more cheaply by free labour than by slave labour and that our markets might be supplied by countries in which there are no slaves (which they might be), this would be more likely to influence the slave-owning countries, now said to be wavering on the question of slavery, than any impotent threat or feeble remonstrance on our part to withdraw our custom—more important to ourselves than to them.

Is it not notorious that the sugar grown in those parts of the world where labour is free, is brought to the European markets as cheaply and as good as that from Brazil? There is the sugar from Manilla, from Java, from Siam, from Cochin-China, all produced by free labour, all supplied to different countries at one-half, or less than one-half the price of our plantation sugar. You say that we are bound by treaties with Brazil not to let in the sugar from those countries on better terms than it is introduced from Brazil. But this is precisely the reason for opening our ports to all. The only country where there is a chance of getting any terms for slaves is Brazil. I know that in that country there are districts or provinces where the proprietors doubt the importance to themselves of maintaining slavery, attended as it is with expense and insecurity. But they are a minority in the Legislature of the country; and if you succeed in making them abolish slavery you cannot let in their sugar unless you get the people of Cuba to do the same; of which, as you know, there is not the remotest chance : they profit too much by it from the manner in which the slave trade is carried on. And I believe that by treaty you are bound not to show more favour to trade with Brazil than you do to that with Cuba.

What a fancy, then, it is, if it be an honest speculation at all, that by refusing to allow their produce
to come out of the warehouses of this country you
can abolish slavery in those countries! For it is a fact
that you allow it to come here and that you export
it refined, and that, moreover, you receive payments
for other manufactures by means of other slave
produce sent here or to other countries on your
account. And what vast sacrifices you are making
for this purpose at all times, and particularly at this
moment, when you are about to visit the trading
classes with an odious assessment, sooner than get
revenue not by the addition but by the remission of
duty on this article! I should really like the question
to be rested on this issue as the remission of the duty
would obviously be an easy, advantageous manner of
supplying the Revenue.

To maintain the immediate credit of the country
there are, I believe, ready means in the equalization
of the Stamp Duties and other duties now imposed
with a view to favour the landed class, and by the
reduction of differential duties on tropical produce.
For what I say of sugar applies to all differential
duties. Differential duties imply that the same
article is brought to this country at different prices
from the different countries where it is produced;
and their object is to preclude the community from
consuming the article at its lowest marketable price;
though if the community were not subject to such
restrictions the article would be more generally consumed, and, the duty being collected upon the whole

amount consumed, the Revenue would be increased
and the cost to the consumer diminished.

Looking, then, at the Right Hon. Baronet's whole
scheme I object to the Income Tax. Part of it I
consider as mischievous and uncalled for, and imposed
without any admission of the real cause of the deficiency, and without a view to its removal; and,
therefore, likely to be continued beyond the time now
intended.

I do not, however, underrate the importance of
those changes in our wretched commercial system
that are proposed by the Right Hon. Baronet. I
like the disturbance of the system, and expect that it
will lead to a wider and far more beneficial change
than any yet proposed.

I should like to see more changes made in the
spirit in which the Timber Duties were handled.
The change effected in those Duties was, I am satisfied,
very beneficial and one, I think, that at present is
underrated in the country. I do not speak altogether
in ignorance on the subject, for I once called the attention of the House to it, and at the time I made a
very full inquiry into the whole case. I was really
surprised to find the extent of the evil produced by
the Timber Duties ; and the vast importance to an
old, cleared, densely-peopled, manufacturing country
like this, of a cheap and abundant supply of wood.
Excepting food, there is not, I believe, anything for
the supply of which the circumstances of this country
render us dependent on other countries, of such
importance to us as timber. I may be wrong, but

I doubt if there will be so great a sacrifice of revenue as people imagine from the change ; for the same quantity of timber that used to come from Canada, and that came, though bad on account of the differential duty, will now come from the Baltic and pay 25s. instead of 10s.: there will be, then, an increase of duty of 150 per cent. upon that portion of the timber.

I can mention another circumstance that will probably secure to the consumer the full advantage of the remission of the duty which some say we shall not have in consequence of the price rising in the Baltic countries. I think that this rise will not occur if those countries again have to apprehend competition with Canada, which they will with the duty entirely remitted ; and therefore there will be an increased supply from the Baltic without increase in price.

In saying this, however, with regard to the advantage of the remission of the duties on timber, I say nothing in favour of an Income Tax proposed under the present circumstances. I am speaking of the change in a commercial point of view. And speaking generally, I should say that if a temporary deficiency of revenue were occasioned by making some beneficial change in our commercial dealings with other countries with the prospect of ultimately recovering the loss both by improved commerce and in revenue—I should say that in this case a loan by issue of Exchequer Bills or otherwise to meet the deficiency would be justifiable, provision being made for the repayment of such loan upon the success of

the experiment. I do not think that loans are justifiable in time of war; for in this case the money is
certain never to be recovered and the debt is consequently rendered permanent. But when changes
are made in the spirit and with the purpose of the
reduction now proposed in the Timber Duties, the
country would justify and approve a loan.

This, however, is positively the only instance that
I know of in which any great sacrifice of revenue for
a commercial purpose or with the view to benefit the
consumer is expected in the new tariff The tariff is
said to be the boon in return for the tax, yet most of
the alterations in the tariff are, as the Right Hon.
Baronet has told the House to-night, changes from
prohibitive duties to those that can be collected. In
fact, so far from making a sacrifice, the tariff is really
an application of the principle that recognizes the
Revenue to be dependent on the easy access of the
consumer to the articles that are taxed; the only
sound principle to apply as long as we continue the
present system of indirect taxation, and while taxes
fall on the articles that the general consumer demands.
And the fault that I have to find with the scheme of
the Right Hon. Baronet is that he does not carry this
principle out, and that by his Income Tax he will
even diminish the ability of the people to consume
those articles on which the Revenue depends. If the
Revenue sinks because the people are poor, the object
should be to increase their means, not to add to
their burdens. The Government will now no longer
deny the connection between the cost of living and the

ability to consume.   It certainly has not been recognized in the Corn Bill; but it is their argument in support of the tariff that makes more striking the anomaly of a scheme that purports to relieve the consumer and to add to the Revenue, yet does nothing to reduce the price of that which he must pay for and consume before he can touch any other article : and a scheme in which the connection between the price of corn and the amount of revenue is established beyond a doubt; but in which while it is sought to supply a deficiency nothing is done to cheapen that article, the cheapness of which determines the state of the Revenue! I believe that I can demonstrate this by Official Returns.   I will read to the House a comparison between the price of wheat and the produce of revenue in 1835, 1836, and 1837, contrasted with 1838, 1839, and 1840 :—

I. Wheat Average.

	s.	d.
In 1835–7 the average of the 3 years was .	47	10
„ 1838–40 „ „ „ .	67	2

The price of wheat therefore rose 40 per cent. during the last three years.

II. Total Revenue.

The gross Revenue of the United Kingdom amounted in the aggregate to—

	£
In 1835–7	159,851,000
„ 1838–40	159,240,000
Decrease	611,000

The population increased at least 4 per cent. between these three-year periods. Had the Revenue increased in like ratio, it would have been in the last three years, 166,205,000*l*., or 6,965,000*l*. more than it was, being at the rate of 2,321,000*l*. per annum virtually lower than in the former period.

III. CUSTOMS AND EXCISE.

The revenue for Customs and Excise in the United Kingdom was :—

	£
In 1835-7	117,833,000
„ 1838-40	116,996,000
Decrease	837,000

The total Excise duties decreased, in the same period, from 47,117,000*l*. to 46,610,000*l*. ·

Had the Excise and Customs Revenue increased with the population it would have produced 122,025,000*l*., or 4,692,000*l*. more, by which amount it virtually fell in the latter period.

IV. MALT, BRITISH SPIRITS, TEA, AND SUGAR DUTIES.

These are the four duties that produce the largest revenue. They produced—

	£
In 1835-7	51,830,000
„ 1838-40	49,289,000
Decrease	2,541,000

This shows a decrease of nearly 5 per cent.! Had these duties increased with the population they would have produced 53,903,000*l*., or 4,614,000*l*. more than they did; which shows a virtual falling off of 1,538,000*l*. per annum.

From this I deduce the fact that concurrently with the rise in the price of wheat there has been a virtual falling off in the Revenue to the amount of 2,321,000*l*.; nearly the same amount as that of the actual deficiency that has occasioned the Income Tax.

This falling off of revenue has taken place notwithstanding an increase of duty paid on the importation of foreign corn to the amount of 1,477,000*l.* during the last three years, over the former three years ; and above one-half of the falling off has taken place on articles most used by the industrious classes.

I will show this by another table :—

I. GROSS REVENUE OF THE UNITED KINGDOM.

Years.	£	Years.	£
1835	. . 52,589,000	1838	. . 52,979,000
1836	. . 54,973,000	1839	. . 53,345,000
1837	. . 52,287,000	1840	. . 52,916,000

II. GROSS EXCISE AND CUSTOMS REVENUE.

Years.	Excise. £	Customs and Excise. £
1835	. . . 15,229,351	38,378,000
1836	. . . 16,587,992	40,747,000
1837	. . . 15,300,406	38,208,000
1838	. . . 15,493,810	38,714,000
1839	. . . 15,488,248	38,996,000
1840	. . . 15,628,818	39,286,000 ·

III. MALT, BRITISH SPIRITS, TEA, AND SUGAR.

Years.	£	Years.	£
1835	. . 16,844,000	1838	. . 16,658,000
1836	. . 18,366,000	1839	. . 17,341,000
1837	. . 16,620,000	1840	. . 16,290,000

Here, then, it is established that the Revenue of this country is necessarily connected with the cheapness and abundance of corn. And what is the remedy for the ever-increasing deficiency of the Revenue? Clearly to secure a constant, regular, abundant supply of corn, thereby ensuring cheapness and improving the ability of the consumer to consume the articles on which you expect your tax.

But do the Ministers come forward with a full and ample admission that the Laws that have made food dear and scarce and given Monopoly in other articles of general use, are at the bottom of our commercial embarrassment and financial difficulties ; that preparation must be made for the total change of a system so fraught with evil ; and that though some inconvenience may be expected at first, a permanent advantage being in view, reason and good sense call for an endurance of the evil for a while ? No such thing ! They bring forward a Corn Bill. And not professing to relieve distress, not admitting the evil that the Corn Laws have produced but asserting the advantage of such Laws, denying the injustice of our present system of indirect taxation and pledging themselves to its continuance, they further propose to diminish every man's means of expenditure by taking a certain proportion from his income. With the view, as they say, of maintaining public credit they call upon people to support their Measure *because* it is a tax upon property which is a just tax. The Income Tax does not raise any question of a property tax such as many men would wish to see and many here to-night would support : a property tax *in lieu* of taxes pressing upon the poor, upon industry, and upon the productive capital of the country, and one that would fairly place the burdens of the State on those best able to bear them.

The present Bill is a plan to provide for one of the consequences of a system that is a constant cause of evil, and to relieve those who profit by the system of their only drawback in its continuance ; and therefore so long as the system continues it will necessitate the retention, if not the augmentation, of the tax now sought to be imposed in addition to every other.

The people of this country are increasing rapidly ; no provision is made for the increase of the food that is their first necessary of life ; each year their difficulty to consume other articles will increase ; and by the imposition of an income tax the other taxes will become less productive. The people want more food, more trade, and fewer taxes. And what has been done for them? You have retained a Corn Law which makes food scarce ; and you have done nothing to extend trade with the two best customers that England now possesses—the United States and Brazil : you refuse to take the slave produce of one, and you will take only the slave produce of the other. Thus with her people unemployed you leave this country seeking fresh markets for her industry ; and without any improvement of her Foreign Trade you impose a tax on income that must embarrass the trade at home.

I say this to show that there is no reason for people to expect any immediate advantage from a change that, at present, I look at as little more than a fanciful disturbance of the old system and a very capricious application of a better principle. If any advantage is to be expected from the change, it must

arise from the future action of the Right Hon.
Baronet who will see the importance of going forward, and next year will introduce the reforms that
he refuses this year, as now he accepts principles that
he repudiated in the past.

XII.

MANCHESTER, January 3, 1843.

Sir Robert Peel's omission of the Corn Laws from his financial scheme of 1842 gave a fresh impetus to the Anti-Corn-Law League movement. A fund of 50,000*l*. was set on foot to carry on the agitation for Repeal, to which subscriptions in thousands poured in from all the great manufacturing towns like Leeds, Manchester, Huddersfield, Bradford, Rochdale, &c., and in multitudinous small sums flowed in from insignificant boroughs, villages, and out-of-the-way hamlets, all alike driven at last to action by the deadly pressure of the Corn Laws. This roused the fears and fury of the Monopolists and Protectionists. The 'Quarterly Review' took the lead with a long article of abuse in which it denounced the League as the most dangerous conspiracy of recent times, and was vigorously supported by most of the leading journals of the day. On January 3, 1843, by which time the failure of the Government's attempts to revive the industry of the country, and to put an end to the distress, were made apparent by an appalling deficiency in the quarter's Revenue—the Excise alone showing a falling off at the rate of three millions per annum—Mr. Villiers went down to Manchester and vindicated the constitution of the League at the weekly meeting of the Association. The chief leaders of the movement were present at the meeting, which was a very large one, and Mr. Cobden, in seconding Mr. Mark Philips's vote of thanks to Mr. Villiers for his untiring exertions in the cause of Free Trade, reminded all present how almost alone in Parliament and without support in the country Mr. Villiers had, in the face of determined opposition and an apathy if anything worse to contend with, ceaselessly looked after their interests before they knew how to look after them themselves.

I FEEL extremely flattered at the consideration that you show me. I wish that I had done, I wish that I were able to do enough to deserve such notice. Had my services corresponded with my zeal in this cause, I might have been more worthy of your attention; but my single title to your regard is that since I have been a Member of the Legislature I have striven to do everything that according to my judgment it was in my power to do to further and promote the cause for which your great and spirited combination here is formed. And I now come before you with no other claim than that of being ranked as the humble and disinterested advocate of the repeal of the destructive Laws of which you complain, as the friend of perfect freedom for this country in her commerce with every other, and as the undeviating and consistent opponent of Monopoly of every kind.

It is from a conscientious conviction that this course is right that I have hitherto acted ; and it is because I believe that the system that you assail is impolitic, dangerous, and wrong, that I intend to persevere. So long as my services can still be made available in co-operation with your great and spirited efforts in this cause, I can only say that they shall be most cordially rendered.

The friends of this cause must, I believe, still co-operate heartily wherever they are to be found : we must not separate, for we must not disguise from ourselves that the task that is imposed upon us is not yet achieved—there are still great difficulties before us. We must not repudiate assistance whencesoever it is offered; and we must conciliate hostility wherever we find it, as far as we can do so consistently with honour to ourselves, and with the truth of the principles that we have espoused and are pledged to uphold.

You have done great things for the cause in this neighbourhood, in fact you have done wonders : you have contributed largely for the furtherance of the principles you avow ; and you have produced distinguished men who, both in Parliament and out of Parliament, have advocated perfect freedom of commerce. You have Mr. Cobden in the Senate, and you have Mr. Bright in the field. And truly it does rejoice me when I read and when I hear of the honours with which they are covered and of the enthusiasm with which they are received wherever they go. For it shows that there are no personal rivalries, no local jealousies, no political prejudices, intervening to mar the course and progress of the cause that we are pursuing. This cause is really far above the ordinary level of party strife ; it is the cause of humanity, it is the cause of the nation in future ; and every man who cares for his country or wishes well to mankind should accord to it his best ability and support.

I was grieved to be obliged to refuse an earlier requisition to attend these gatherings ; but I am glad that circumstances have allowed me to appear at this moment, for it enables me to congratulate you upon your progress, and to inform you of the impression that your proceedings are producing at a distance. I do not hesitate to say that you are daily and hourly winning upon the public esteem ; that your usefulness is becoming more generally acknowledged ; and that people are seeing and saying that it is by some such instrumentality as a National League that this interested and selfish legislation can alone be changed.

People generally think that you have wisely

occupied this vacant moment in the public mind by
bringing before them the facts and arguments of your
case. You have found men in a right mood for
learning the causes of their past embarrassments. And
I must say that the tone of tolerance and carefulness
as well as earnestness and decision that has pervaded
the language and proceedings of these meetings has
done much to conciliate opponents and bring over
honest and cautious men to your side.

For though I have not had the pleasure of being
among you, I have not been altogether idle, where
I reside, in seeking to learn the obstacles to the
progress of our cause with a view to remove them.
And I already have had occasion to see the success
of your labours : I find in the metropolis that from
frequent discussion people who had not before considered the subject are now familiar with the arguments that expose the fallacies of our opponents ;
and if you will only persevere in the course that you
have hitherto pursued, you will fortify their minds
against those further fallacies that, I doubt not, are
now being prepared for the ensuing Session.

With respect to the object that the Members of
the League have in view in soliciting the aid and
pecuniary contributions of their friends, I have
never heard any right-minded man say aught of it
but praise, or wish it other than complete success.
You are not addressing men's passions, you are not
trafficking with their ignorance, you are not proceeding secretly, or acting with violence ; you are deli-
liberately proceeding to address their understandings

in a way to bring knowledge and information home to
the humblest persons in the country. You have seen
your opponents appeal to the lowest classes in the
country upon this subject and skilfully confuse their
minds ; and now you are about to bring the truth
within reach of all, and to give your opponents a
fair opportunity of establishing their case if they can.
Persevere in this course, and there will be no question
of your success—your victory will be certain.

I myself have already witnessed instances of the
result of your publications : I allude specially to
the tracts that are now circulated by the League. I
have seen their influence upon men's minds. I have
heard men who have read those prize essays that have
recently been disseminated, express their astonishment
at the truths they contain. They had no notion previously that the persons who are said to be protected
by the Corn Laws could have such reason for opposing
them ; and that the tenants of the land for whose
benefit these Laws are said to exist could have put
their pens to paper to denounce them as a delusion
under which they had been suffering. I have known
men receive tracts from the League, read them, be
convinced by them, and at once tend a subscription
to forward the cause.

This, in my opinion, proves the judgment with
which you are now acting, and justifies the course that
you are pursuing in defiance and regardless of the
opinions expressed by your opponents. Yes ! you may
venture to proceed in your course in spite of the Dorsetshire squires. Lately they have done you the favour

of expressing their opinion of your conduct and character. This I think is all to your advantage : it is
likely to raise you in the people's esteem, for I know
not on what superiority of their own they presume to
cast aspersions on the character of the League.

To-day, as I was coming to this place, a person
who was travelling with me showed me some speeches
that had been made. at a recent meeting in Dorsetshire where they seem to have been chiefly occupied
with the proceedings of the League. Their first
charge against you is, if I remember rightly, that you
are warring against the spirit of the Constitution.
And in this I am not sure that they are not right ; for
I believe that the spirit of the Constitution as now administered is manifested at the dinner-meetings of Dorsetshire squires rather than in the redress of grievances
from which millions are suffering. I have no doubt
that whatever so great a person as a Member for the
county of Dorset says to his fellow-squires passes for
proof as soon as it is uttered, and circulates as gospel
truth wherever he has influence. And he says that
he has never known a society so un-English in its
character, so odious in its object, and so contemptible
in its means as the Anti-Corn-Law League. It
struck me when I read this that even during my
Parliamentary career I had heard of societies far
more deserving of this character than the Anti-Corn-
Law League. And I think that there was one such
society to which some of the Dorsetshire squires
themselves, or some of their friends and connections,
might have belonged. I heard in Parliament only

about five years ago of societies that administered secret oaths, tampered with the army, held views upon the succession to the Throne, and entrapped humble men into their designs for the purpose of upsetting the Government. And so captivating were the doctrines of this attempted league that many of the nobility and clergy, together with one or two bishops, were found to belong to it. These were not corn associations certainly : they were Orange lodges. And it struck me that the gentlemen who ride so high a horse when they talk of the Anti-Corn-Law League, might have remembered that many of their political connections and friends were thought to be members of these societies at the time I refer to.

And now I will tell the squires why I do not think that the Anti-Corn-Law League ought to be considered un-English. In the first place, everything the members of it do is open and above-board. They complain of a great grievance ; they go forth into the highways and say what the grievance is, and why they complain of it. They arraign the rulers of the country to their face, throw them upon their defence before the world, and ask the country to judge of the character of the cause by the nature of the defence.

I think that I could also tell these Dorsetshire squires why this Anti-Corn-Law League is a Conservative institution. It is because the English are not slavish or spiritless : they do not belong to a race that ever was so ; and when they are conscious of being wronged, when they have a strong sense of injustice, they must be heard or they will be felt. And it seems to me that even if the squires were to succeed in stopping this national vent for the expression of public opinion they would not convince the people that the food Monopoly is a righteous arrangement : they would simply induce them to find some other mode of expressing their opinions ; and one perhaps more inconvenient to the squires than the Anti-Corn-Law League.

I think, moreover, that I could show these gentlemen that the League is a justifiable institution, and for this reason : it was formed only after everything had been attempted in what might be called a constitutional way to induce Parliament and the public authorities to attend to the grievance, and had failed. The people petitioned ; they asked to be heard at the Bar of the House; they asked for a Commission of Inquiry ; they asked for a slight change of the Laws ; they asked for a gradual change of the Laws ; and everything was refused, and with exactly the same stubbornness as the claim they now advance is refused. And though the Legislature tells the people when they agitate that they will not yield to clamour, they have shown too plainly that they will not yield to anything else.

At present they say that the object of the League is odious ; odious to them, no doubt. But are the members of the League the only persons who consider the Corn Laws odious? I want to know who there is except the landlords, those distinctly interested in the Laws, who do not consider them odious. There are many who do not belong to the League—who do not think the League genteel and therefore of course do not belong to it—but who yet think the Corn Laws very odious. Only a few years ago I read in that great organ of the present Government, the 'Times' newspaper—the leading journal of Europe —that the Corn Laws which we must not call odious, are a combination of madness and inhumanity ; and that, so long as they continue, they are a sort of rebellion against Providence for which the people at large may be in daily expectation of some visitation. These are the squires' Corn Laws. Latterly, within a very few years, the same paper, the organ of the same party, has declared that there is nothing out of the despotism of the East that can be at all compared to them ; so outrageous are they in character, so arbitrary in operation, and so prejudicial to the people at large, that they are only worthy of Mehemet Ali, and governments of the like order.

But the Dorsetshire squires alluded to this subject as if it was something just started by the League ; as if they had never heard of it before. Why, one of the most philosophical divines of Scotland,[1] one of the most intellectual men that I can name, and a Conservative too, has come to the conclusion that the Corn Laws literally foul the air of British society ; he says that they are so monstrous in their character and consequences that he can describe them only in that way.

In fact I do not believe that any intelligent and disinterested man can be named who is an advocate of the Corn Laws. You may find people who are

---

[1] Dr. Chalmers.

under the influence of self-interest who will advocate them ; but I doubt whether a single disinterested and intelligent speaker or author can be produced who will say one word for the Corn Laws. Even landlords who have brains in their heads and their title deeds at home have given them up.

But then the Dorsetshire squires say your means are so contemptible ! If so why do they talk about them ? Why are they always cackling about this League ? If it is such a contemptible thing why do they not let it die of its own insignificance ? Their organs never cease filling their columns about it ; never a day passes but this Anti-Corn-Law League is brought before them ; and yet it is so contemptible and insignificant that it cannot live many days ! Their discussions seem to have reached a point that we sometimes see attained in personal disputes when one man having nothing more to urge resorts to abuse of the winning side. And in our case this is really a very cheering sign. It looks as if our discussions were coming to a close, and we had the best of it.

In a recent publication upon this subject no less than seventy pages are, I believe, devoted to your abuse by an old opponent. That looks well. It puts me in mind of a story that Lord Brougham, I think, used to tell of a case that he had on the Northern Circuit. His client, who was the defendant in a cause, had no case ; but this he did not like to acknowledge, so he retained the most eminent counsel and delivered him a brief which when looked into was found to contain these instructions : 'No merits ; but please to abuse the plaintiff's attorney.' Now, this is something like the answer that the old 'Quarterly' got when he tapped at the door of Monopoly to ask what he was to say next October after the shock that Monopoly had experienced at headquarters in the early part of the year. His instructions were : ' No merits ; but please to abuse the Anti-Corn-Law League.' And it is impossible to deny that he has earned his fee: so long a yarn about nothing at all was, I should say, never produced by any lawyer. There is, however, perhaps this difference between the two cases, that in the former the Court itself, when the advocate came in, might not have been prepared for the issue being changed, and might have given a verdict for the defendant, thinking that the character of the plaintiff's attorney was the only thing in question ;. but, fortunately for us, the public is fully apprised of what will be the tactics of our opponents ; and I have not the least doubt that when we meet in Parliament we shall not hear a word said about the Corn Laws : the merits will all be put in the background, but the people's attorney—the Anti-Corn-Law League, will be brought very prominently forward. And I consider this, as I said before, a very favourable point to have brought the discussion to. They have sunk the question altogether and have begun to abuse the advocates on the other side ; and they have only one other thing to do, and that they do not dare to do : to put down discussion altogether. It has been suggested, I dare say, in the Cabinet ; but it would be inconvenient generally.

The fact is, if we had an Act of Parliament to suppress discussion, it might include other societies that
are very laudable : the Royal Agricultural Society,
for example. The Royal Agricultural Society is very
much like the Anti-Corn Law League so far as detail
and arrangement go, but there is this difference between them : the Royal Agricultural Society is to improve the breed of cattle ; the Anti-Corn-Law League
is to improve the condition of the people.

Certainly, some unworthy practices have been
attempted lately in the metropolis. I believe that
they were attempted in the provinces formerly, but
they are not now : I mean sending persons to create
confusion at public meetings, which is only another
way of preventing discussion. It is quite clear that
there is no honesty in an interference of this kind ;
and the purpose of it is defeated, as far as I can
observe, by the effect it produces ; for it only makes
all the persons who are disturbed by such a proceeding warmer partisans in the cause for which we
are now met. Discussion will therefore go on ; and
with discussion we need not fear for the result.

Indeed, as far as I have been able to observe, we
have not much difficulty now with our regular opponents ; they do not seem to me to show much fight
this year. But there are some persons, nominally our
friends, who are generally very dangerous characters :
they complain that the Anti-Corn-Law League and
those who uphold it are very extravagant in their
claims. They say : ' You want complete justice,
but you ought only to ask for an instalment of

it.' Now, I fancy that I have been considering this question as much as any one ; and I think that the reproach is just as unreasonable as they allege our claims to be. Because there is not any immediate prospect of our getting a little justice, I do not see what we could gain by only asking for a little ; and it is really of consequence for us to show that we are in earnest upon this question. And as we do attach to it the greatest importance, believing that the welfare of the people at large depends upon it, it is worthy of consideration whether the part that we take is judicious and the best calculated to realize the object we have in view. It is after the most mature deliberation that I fail to come to any other conclusion than that it is not at all unreasonable that we should demand the total repeal of the Corn Laws, and that the people should have complete justice rendered to them without delay.

Now, observe what is the state of the question. There are persons who say : 'If you will be more moderate in your demands, if instead of a total repeal of these Laws you would just ask for a fixed duty, you would improve your position very much, and there would not be so much agitation in the country.' But what say the rulers of the country, whom I take to be the landlords? Do they entertain the notion of a little justice, of a fixed duty? No ; they say : 'Of all the fallacious, of all the roguish, of all the deceitful things ever proposed, a fixed duty is the worst.' They say : 'Sooner let us have a total repealer ; we would have him a hundred times sooner than a fixed duty man ; the project is Whiggish from beginning to end ; we will not concede it.' And they bring forward a scheme that all mankind, except themselves, are opposed to—the Scale. The present Government say : ' We will not have a fixed duty ; we will only have the Scale.' But we will have neither—neither the fixed duty nor the Sliding Scale ; we demand total Repeal. And surely we have with us, against the Scale, the largest party that is to be found in the country ! So that when we defeat the Government upon the Scale, as they will not take a fixed duty, they must take total Repeal : there is nothing else left for them.

And we have the farmers joining our ranks ; for, in that sturdy, manly sort of way that one would expect from them and that belongs to their character they say: ' We thought that we had a right to be preferred to the rest of the community ; we thought that we were to be put upon rather a better footing than anybody else ; but we find that we were deceived. We do not want to injure the rest of the community ; and unless we get some benefit from it, away with all Protection—fixed duty and all.' Farmers have come to say : ' We find that this Scale does not give us the promised Protection ; therefore we have no objection to Free Trade.'

Just now, in fact, we have attained a point at which everybody seems to be divided between the relative merits of the systems of Protection and Free Trade. Protection now means the Scale that everybody is decidedly against ; and Free Trade is the alternative. Why, then, should we not stick to a principle that is intelligible to everybody ; that we have professed hitherto ; and that there is no reasonable ground for abandoning?

I really cannot understand any ground for advocating a fixed duty except that which appears to be passing in the mind of the present Liberal leader of the House of Commons, Lord John Russell. He seems disposed—and as a politician and a leader he no doubt occasionally must be—to hold the candle to a certain gentleman. I should have no objection to hold that light myself if it were likely to be of any use, if we were likely to obtain justice by doing so ; but then this gentleman will not accept what we offer. He says : ' I repudiate a fixed duty ; I won't have your light upon any terms.' I then say : ' Why concede a great principle ? Why concede in the abstract what the whole community want, without prospect of any practical result whatever being thereby obtained?' And until I can see some better ground for abandoning the principle upon which we started, and upon which we have united a greater number of people than any other principle was capable of uniting, I shall adhere to it : namely, the abolition of all Protection, and, above everything, a perfectly open trade in the necessaries of life.

But independently of this consideration, I am quite convinced that there are many here connected with the Foreign Trade of this country who know how great is the importance, the necessity now indeed, of removing every obstruction to that trade. With respect to the rivalry that is growing up against us in every foreign country I should like to hear whether any person who has experience of what is going on abroad or who knows what sort of competition it is to which the productive power of this country is exposed in foreign countries—I should like to hear whether such a person thinks that anything less than entire freedom of trade can enable us to meet that competition? It is my firm belief, from what has been disclosed to us by persons on the Continent, that nothing short of this will do. If I wanted any further testimony than what my own senses afford in favour of Free Trade, it would be furnished by what our manufacturing rivals on the Continent themselves say. There is nothing that they view with such horror and apprehension as Free Trade in this country. I assure you that the Anti-Corn-Law League is just as unpopular with the manufacturers on the Continent as with the agriculturists at home. From morning to night they are blessing English landlords and English Corn Laws. They say: 'Our continued salvation is in these Laws; they have enabled us to start up here as a great protected interest; and so long as they last we shall flourish; but we none of us know what will become of the capital that we have invested in this interest, so soon as there is Free Trade in England.'

I saw an intelligent manufacturer in Russia this year, and I asked him what he thought would be the effect of such a change. He said: 'The instant that there is Free Trade in corn in England, there will be an increase of the cost of living on the Continent ; and that will be a great disadvantage to us : it will make our home market worse, as the people will have to be fed at a greater expense than they are now ; and the instant you open your ports to the produce of Russia and the north of Europe you will find them objecting to their own tariffs, at present designed to exclude your manufactures.'

I speak from high authority with respect to the Russian tariff—almost a prohibitory one—when I say that were our ports open and trade free, a very large proportion, at least, of the aristocracy in Russia who desire to send their produce to England, would be opposed to their own tariff, to which they are at present reconciled by the concurrent existence of our tariff here. And they would then be exactly in the same state that we are in ; they would see that they could export more of their commodities if they took English manufactures in return. Now, though we consider the Russian Government a very arbitrary one, it is far from insensible to the interests of those who rely upon it. And it is the authoritative opinion of all those with whom I have conversed on the subject, that if our ports were open and the trade in grain free the Russian tariff would hardly last a year.

In considering the sort of opposition that we may expect in a continued advocacy of a Free Trade policy, I would just refer to a form of obstruction that lately has been frequently advanced in the organs of our opponents : I mean the assertion that we ought not to utter a word on the subject of the Corn Laws this year. We are told that an experiment is going on ; that we must not interfere with it but allow it to work ; that it would be very unreasonable to breathe a syllable about Repeal because a change was made in the Corn Laws last year.

The other night I was looking into the ' Standard,' the paper that represents the Government, and there I found how long the trial is to last : they allege from ten to twelve years. And they add that it would be especially unreasonable to say anything about the Corn Laws next year. Now, I want to know why the Anti-Corn-Law League is not to say anything. Did they call for the change enacted in the Corn Laws ? Did they approve of it when proposed ? I remember that when it was first announced my friend here [1] rose up and pronounced it what many felt, what all here feel it to be—a perfect mockery. He denounced it in plain language to the House, though, of course, it was thought very bad taste. Members were very much shocked at what he said : that was not the way to speak in the House of Commons. But my Hon. Friend had the courage (and it really does require great moral courage to rise up and do justice to the people, and thereby offend the taste of the House of Commons) to condemn the Government measure ; which, indeed, I also thought a perfect mockery, and I have never changed my opinion. He voted against it, and I acted with him in every stage of the Bill because I thought that if

[1] Mr. Cobden.

A A 2

it passed we should be called upon to abide by an experiment, and be told that there was something at work that we must not disturb.

But what do the very organs of the party who proposed the new Laws say ? They say now, I know not with what object or authority, that there is not a single advantage derivable from them that would not have happened under the others ; and I believe that not a single intelligent man could be found who would not tell us, that not one evil had occurred under the old Laws that might not occur under the new. We shall be told next Session, I dare say, that the price of wheat has very much fallen ; and as the Corn Laws have been changed, the coincidence of two things will be sought to be connected as cause and effect.

However, we must bear well in mind what these party organs say : they want to conciliate their agricultural friends, and they say that nothing has been done. This is true ; nothing has been done. Not one particle of grain has come into the country that would not have entered under the old Laws, and entered at a duty of 1s. while now it has paid 8s. This is the only difference that I know of. And I never met with any man, be he Tory or Leaguer, who does not maintain that everything that has happened under the present Laws would have happened under the old. Why then are we to try any experiment ? What are we to expect ?

There was some sense in keeping the old Laws when the people had been got to believe that restricted trade increased the quantity of food ; that when food was scarce the reward of labour was greater ; and that the public credit depended on the Protection of the agricultural interest : this was something like argument, or ground to stand upon. But the first Minister of the country abandoned all that ground when he declared it to be true that the people increase in such numbers that they cannot be adequately supplied with home produce.

He said also that the proprietors of the soil of this country have no right to be protected as a class ; he said it last year. And he said something else, which is very important and which we shall not lose sight of : he said that by reducing the price of food the burden of the general taxation would be much less. He told the people that by his arrangement with the tariff and the Corn Laws he would lower the price of food so much that they would not feel the Income Tax. Well then, I say, this admission is no ground for a new Corn Law, in fact it does away with the ground for any such Law at all ; because if the people are not sufficiently supplied at home they ought to be able to get what they want from abroad at the very lowest rate and at the very best advantage. If the proprietors of the soil have no right to be protected they can have no reason to complain when we propose the abolition of Protection Laws ; and if the taxation of this country is felt more or less according as the price of food is high or low, upon what conceivable pretext do you prevent it from being as low as possible ?

Sir Robert Peel says upon this matter that the less people have to pay for food the more they will have to pay for other things, and therefore they will feel the taxes less. But just see how this applies. What are the other things upon which the people spend their surplus income ? They are the things that are taxed, such as tea, coffee, soap, sugar, wine, malt, and spirits ; and the more they buy of these things the more the Revenue gains. Now the Revenue has been sinking of late years, and why ? Because the price of food has been high and the people have not been able to invest in these other taxed articles. Just look at the consequences : the price of food having been high of late years on account of the Corn Laws people could not consume other articles ; the Revenue dependent on the price of food has fallen off ; and we supply the deficiency by an Income Tax. You see then the close connection that there is between the Income Tax which you are all so fond of and the high price of food caused by the Corn Laws.

And remember, I am not using my own argument but that of Sir Robert Peel. It is Sir Robert Peel who says that if food is low you will not feel the Income Tax. If, then, food were always low and you were without an Income Tax you would not feel other taxes. And in speaking upon this matter I ventured to lay before the House a statement which I believed unanswerable, showing that the deficiencies of the Revenue did occur during the three years in which food was so enormously high. And I say that under these circumstances the Income

Tax ought not to have been imposed, and the Corn Laws ought to have been repealed. I say that the Revenue suffered because the condition of the people was bad ; and that therefore the condition of the people ought to have been improved.

I do not know where any man can have learnt that an Income Tax will improve the condition of the people : if men are too poor to travel, it is not by raising the toll that you will get their money. You get the Revenue of this country by the people's consumption, by what they expend ; if they are too poor to expend, it is not by taking their income that you will make them expend more. And in my opinion the Government have committed a great mistake in putting on an Income Tax at this moment.

It is dangerous to prophesy ; but last quarter fulfilled the prediction that some gentleman ventured to make that though the returns might show the profits of a direct tax on income they would show also a loss from other sources ; and in the October quarter there was upwards of half a million lost from other sources. To-morrow we shall see what the present quarter gives ; I believe that it will be little better. I believe that the instant the Income Tax was announced every man studied how he should save it. Some turned off a servant, others laid aside a carriage, or did something to save the new tax, and consequently diminished their expenditure. The only remedy was to have improved the condition of the people.

The Minister should have endeavoured to discover

where the people could have got more trade ; but precisely in those quarters where there was an opening he has done nothing. In the United States and Brazil, the two quarters where our trade might be most extended, nothing has been done. It seemed as if everything was to be touched except the restrictions on sugar and corn. And the trade with the United States and the Brazils having been left as it was, the condition of the people remains unchanged.

The condition of the people is not improved nor, apparently, is there any likelihood that it will be ; and hence I venture to express a doubt whether the Government will be able to supply the deficiency in the Revenue as they anticipate. What did I see the day before I left town ? I saw printed in the largest letters in the chief organ of the Government, the announcement that the Corn Laws passed last year are to be considered a final settlement of the question and that no further changes are to be made—the new Laws under which, as their own organs say, everything that occurred under the old will occur again ; and your experience tells you what has been suffered during the last five years from Laws that are it seems now finally settled.

I ask any person who considers the thing impartially, whether, after this, we can adopt the recommendation of the Dorsetshire squires to show ourselves no more and to give up our agitation ? I myself cannot come to that conclusion. I can only see that exertions are rendered more necessary. The Legislature does not I fear pay such attention to the general interests of the community as will justify them in taking no care for themselves. People who have anything to do in this country are not fond of agitation : it is only when imperious necessity forces them from their business and their homes, to which they would gladly return, that they come forward and take a share in public affairs ; but with the prospect they have before them of no real change being effected in the Corn Laws, and of being required to wait until an experiment of what is no improvement has been made, no true friend can say : ' Cease to agitate.' I am much more disposed to say : ' Continue to agitate ; keep up your movement ; for you will get nothing by remaining still.'

The cause of Free Trade is one of a peculiar nature : it is not merely the cause of the moment or the place, but of the future and of mankind at large. When you consider it in all its bearings, in its ultimate consequences, above all when you consider the friendly relations that it tends to promote between men in different climes and countries, you will see that nothing that you can undertake is more likely to spread the spirit of Christianity and to diffuse the blessings of the earth among the nations of the world. In short, I believe that the establishment of Free Trade is the next great step in the progress of civilization in this country ; and, therefore, I cordially recommend the cause for your adoption, trusting that you will never abandon it until you have achieved the victory.

XIII.

DRURY LANE THEATRE, March 22, 1843.

In March 1843 the League made London its headquarters; and as no other building of sufficient size was available, Drury Lane Theatre was engaged for the weekly meetings of the Association. The first meeting was held on March 15. At the next, on the Wednesday after, Mr. Villiers made the following speech. Boxes, pit, and gallery were literally crammed. It was, in fact, the greatest assembly that could be brought together in the metropolis under one roof. The audience showed by their well-timed cheers and comments their thorough appreciation of the bearings of the question, and the firm hold that the cause of Repeal had taken of the popular mind.

THE moments assigned to the purposes for which we are assembled here are so precious that I must not waste them upon points of mere formality or upon matters that might be deemed personal to myself. Otherwise, I should have desired to explain the circumstances under which I now present myself to you, and detain you, perhaps, from those whose eloquence is far more worthy of the attention of the vast assembly before me than anything that I can say. I may, however, just tell you, who have consented to countenance these spirited efforts of our friends of the League in their endeavours to bring before the country and the world the question which has united them, that I should have been ashamed of myself if, at the summons of our excellent friend who determines the movement of this union, I had shrunk from contributing my feeble aid by bearing testimony in favour of the cause.

The first thing that I feel prompted to notice and to assert on the present occasion is the immense service that you are rendering the cause, and those who are toiling for it, in marking your interest in these proceedings by attending here with so much spirit and in such great numbers.

Speaking from the knowledge of the progress and position of Repeal in another place I venture to say that if you feel certain of the justice of our cause when you go hence, you may also feel satisfied that you have greatly promoted its success by your presence here to-night. For this meeting is not a meeting of an ordinary kind. It has not been assembled under common circumstances, and it will produce no common effect. It has been assembled in spite of influence used to prevent it. Aye, in spite of threats to the courageous man who owns this building. In spite of all the abuse, and ridicule, and calumny that have been poured forth by the organs of fashion and Monopoly to prevent the public discussion of the Corn Laws.

This is the second time that this house has been filled to overflowing; filled, not by persons who have come for mere recreation, or idle amusement, but by those who wish to manifest their interest in the condition of the country and their sympathy with the distress of their fellow-men. And, indeed, so great has been the demand for places that as many have been disappointed of gaining admission as have been able to be admitted.

It will be a cheering sign to the country that the people of London are at length roused on the subject of the Corn Laws, that they will no longer endure the reproach of being either ignorant of the real interests of the country, or indifferent to the sufferings of their fellow-subjects. It will be a sign to the Monopolists that the citizens of London will no longer be deluded by the silly things that have been told them ; that they will now judge for themselves ; that they are determined to inquire for what purpose or to serve what interest the whole economy of this great country has been disturbed, and discontent, misery, and ruin have been spread on every side, leaving nothing more cheering in prospect for the future.

Hence you have done quite right, in my judgment, in joining heartily with those who from the first have warned the Legislature of the mad course they were pursuing in resisting the claims of Nature, and quarrelling with the designs of Providence ; with those who from the first have denounced the principle of legislation that has caused so much evil, and who have called incessantly for the total abandonment of such a principle.

And now I will tell you why, in my judgment, you render such essential service in manifesting publicly your interest in this matter. It is because we have arrived at that point in another place from which we can advance no further without your assistance. I

believe that fresh argument or new facts would be of
little avail now in that place. They have reached
the point in the House of Commons with regard to
this question that the priests and augurs of ancient
Rome were said to have reached with regard to their
religion : they no longer imposed upon themselves ;
and a great man of the time wondered how any two
of them could meet in the street without a smile.
It is the same with respect to the Corn Laws in
the House : they have almost ceased to be discussed
with gravity ; and few take the trouble to deny
that the Sliding Scale of which we have heard so
much is anything but a mischievous contrivance to
retain Monopoly at the expense of the commerce,
industry, and revenue of the country. Few now
doubt that any permanent duty or impediment to the
import of the necessaries of life must needs diminish
the amount of them consumed in the country, and
raise the price of all that are grown at home. This,
I believe, is a matter on which there is, in private,
perfect unanimity. Indeed, the young and intelligent
Monopolists laugh in their sleeves at the subtleties
of their artful leader, and the older ones maintain the
silent system, thinking, probably, that the least said the
soonest mended.

I conclude that you too have collected such to be
the case from the manner in which recent discussions
on the distress of the country and on those questions
that have reference to the Corn Laws have been
treated. You have seen the eagerness that prevailed to shift the question from the principle to the

person. You remember when our friend the Member for Stockport charged those who have the power to alter these Laws with the responsibility of their maintenance. You observed in what a spirit and with what justice that well-merited reproach was treated. Why even a principal organ of the party was compelled, after denouncing our friend and charging him with all the offences under the sun, to admit that his speech had been left unanswered. They did not doubt that he was in connivance with the criminal of whom we have heard so much ; they did not hesitate to join in the cry raised against him ; but still not satisfied with their friends they said : 'He has made a striking speech on the subject of Monopoly, but we cannot find that any of you have offered any answer to it.'

Again, but a few nights since, my Hon. Friend the Member for Sheffield [1] tested the Monopolist party on the ground that they have always assumed with the greatest confidence whenever I have submitted a Motion on the Corn Laws to the House of Commons : namely, the ground of special burdens. Their constant plea has been that they regret the existence of the Corn Laws ; that they would repeal them if they possibly could ; but that they are groaning under special and exclusive burdens which for the benefit of the community at large they took on themselves, and that therefore they could not now consult the interests of those who complain, in the way they desire. The Hon. Member for Sheffield

[1] Mr. H. G. Ward.

was curious to know what the charges could be, so he brought forward his Motion; and asked for a Select Committee—a Committee upstairs—before which the Monopolists might state their extraordinary and exclusive burdens.

How was the Motion met? We heard nothing more of peculiar burdens on land. Monopolists would not go into anything specific on the subject; but they drew the House away from it by raising discussion on the conduct and character of the labourers in Dorsetshire. The Hon. Member for that county, who rose immediately after my Hon. Friend, led us away into that rural paradise of the peasant, the county for which he sits; and there the discussion was carried on for the rest of the evening. The question turned upon the enjoyments of the labourers of that district, and whether the wages which a man had the happiness to earn, and enjoy with his wife and five children, were 8s. or 8s. 6d. per week.

But what does this prove? It proves that these Laws can no longer be defended with any show of policy or justice; and that their repeal is resisted solely because it is thought that there is no immediate occasion for it. We, however, who have been in the habit of watching politics in Parliament know what an 'immediate occasion' for changing a law means. We know that there is a sort of Sliding Scale there for justice and humanity as well as for corn: pressure from without is like the price of grain; if it is sufficiently high the ports are open, but the instant it is withdrawn—as with the fall of prices—down goes the bar, and justice and humanity are shut out.

We are as earnest and sincere as anybody in the wish to see an end put to all the turmoil and agitation now prevailing, and evidenced by the assembly of vast numbers such as this ; but we are also earnest and sincere in the wish to see the Corn Laws repealed, and—I speak from long experience of the progress of the question in Parliament—without this high pressure we have no chance of success.

Looking at their character and consequences, I have come to the deliberate conviction that there is nothing more prejudicial than the Corn Laws, not even excepting personal slavery itself. I believe that through the want they occasion they make men slaves in their physical condition, and thus tend to debase their moral state.

When laws produce such effects, when the wisest among us have come to the conclusion that these are their characteristics, then legislators, at least, are bound to acquaint themselves with the subject, and to form a deliberate judgment on it. And how can any man remain in doubt about the Corn Laws when all doubt can be solved by putting to himself a few plain questions? He has only to ask what is the result of these Laws? Are they just in principle? Are they beneficial? If they have done no good, have they done no harm? Have they not aggravated the embarrassments of the community? Have they not subjected the working man to privations the bare allusion to which makes the blood recoil? If these things are alleged—and they are—I say that no man has any excuse for not informing himself upon them ; and, in this instance, no man has any right to complain that he cannot learn the truth, because the very object of the League, and of these meetings in connection with it, is to afford to every one who is honestly desirous of learning the truth the means of doing so. The League does not ask you to come here to adopt its views ; it does not uphold any crotchets or nostrums of its own ; but it brings under your consideration the views and doctrines of the strongest and wisest minds amongst us ; it collects the facts which our best experience has possessed us of, and then it asks you to draw your own conclusions.

You are well aware of all the miseries that now surround you. Think of the multitudes of the working classes suffering from an inadequate recompense of their labour ! Think of the property being wasted in the accumulation of goods, the produce of the industry of the country ! Think of the men reduced and worn down by unequal competition ! Now, the question that we ask you to consider is, whether the people shall have the means and the power afforded them of working for their food. Will any one say that if the food comes in it can be paid for otherwise than by labour ? If the food does not come in, where is the advantage of the existing Laws to the working man ? These Laws exist solely for the purpose of excluding that food. If they did not exist, food would not come in, and could not come in, without

labour being employed to pay for it. Those who
have returned me to Parliament are chiefly engaged
in working for other countries that have no means
of paying them for what they do except by their
own special produce ; and over and over again they
have begged that the food from those countries
should be released from the warehouses in order to
enable them to gain their living by their labour.
What, then, has really prevented them from gaining
their living but these Laws, this restriction upon the
importation of food? What becomes of them thus
hindered from earning their living ? They are compelled to have recourse to the parish, to receive
relief from public charity. And when I am asked to
go to Parliament and to demand the repeal of the
Laws that prevent them from obtaining an honest
livelihood, I am told by those who oppose me that
Parliament has imposed peculiar burdens on land,
and that they cannot change the system.

But how stood this question when the Corn Laws
were passed? Lord Liverpool did not scruple to avow
that they were passed for no other purpose than to
maintain the rents at their existing rate. The rents
were enormously high at that time, and fear was entertained that they would fall. Lord Liverpool said
that the rents must be maintained, that they must be
prevented from falling, and that the only effect of the
Corn Laws would be to require tenants to make fresh
bargains with their landlords ; and hence things
would adjust themselves. This was the opinion of
Lord Liverpool when the Corn Laws were passed ; and

he never altered it. He never alluded to any peculiar burdens on land, because it was fresh in his recollection that land claimed peculiar exemptions. He was a colleague of Mr. Pitt; and Mr. Pitt had proposed that a certain measure of taxation which he brought forward should embrace all sorts of property—land included. I refer to the Probate and Legacy Duties. The landlords resisted the proposed tax on land, and ultimately it was rejected. Lord Liverpool therefore never talked the nonsense that we now hear talked. And he never argued that we could not have Free Trade in this country because we should then be dependent on other countries: he remembered that even during the French war we received food from France and the French soldiers were clothed with the produce of British labour. But this is an argument that is now used, though it cannot have any weight with the country. It is an argument that applies equally to every description of commerce, and therefore it cannot be confined to the single article of food. In matters of commercial intercourse we must be dependent on those with whom we trade, and the argument does not apply more strongly to those who supply us with food than to those who supply us with the other wants of life.

And Lord Liverpool never spoke of Poor Rates as being a peculiar burden on land. Nor did he entertain the notion that high prices were likely to secure good wages; for he remembered that when the price of food rose to an enormous height at the end of the last century, the sufferings of the working classes had never before been so great, and every contrivance was resorted to in order to prevent wages rising higher than the point at which they then stood.

Neither did we hear of hostile tariffs at that time, because the system of hostility that the Corn Laws have provoked had not commenced. There was no tariff on our manufactures, because all countries depended on us for them ; and if we had adopted the same line of policy that was then pursued, I have little doubt that for a century, at least, we should have maintained our supremacy.

Such, then, was the origin of the Corn Laws. Many people would no doubt like to bolster up their interests and to increase their incomes at the expense of other classes. But if a man had houses to let what would you say to a law that confined people to their locality ? Where, therefore, is the justice of endeavouring to give to one class an advantage by law over other classes?

And what do you think of the justice of those Laws that raise the rent of land by a monopoly and allow the labourer to be exposed to competition to settle his wages? Such, however, is the nature of the Laws that are intended exclusively for the benefit of the landlords.

They say, indeed, being careful of the general interest, that the Corn Laws are for the advantage of the farmer : they secure him steady prices. Now if the Laws benefit him, he surely must know it after twenty-eight years' experience of them. But what is the case ? Look at the state of the rural districts.

The farmers are badly off; there is no class in a worse condition; no class more distressed; and no class more clamorous for relief, or more full of complaint at their condition. What is the reason of this? They are not able to fulfil their engagements; they agreed to pay a higher rent to the landlord than they find they are able to pay; and they entered into the contract because the landlord persuaded them that the Corn Laws would secure them high prices.

But this part of the subject was so ably treated by the Hon. Member for Stockport last Wednesday, that it is not necessary for me to go further into it. He showed you by five or six distinct examples how it is that the landlords are enabled by their political contrivances to obtain increased rents from the farmers; which rents the farmers in most cases can pay only by expending their capitals.

We have been told, indeed, that the present condition of the farmers has been caused by the partial application of Free Trade principles. There is already unquestionably a panic amongst the farmers; but it has not been induced by any application of the principles of Free Trade. I believe that the panic was produced by the doubts that have arisen in their minds as to the opinion of their friends on the subject of Free Trade. It simply indicates their feeling that they have been grossly deceived by their own friends. They were very much encouraged at the last general election to vote for those Members who were staunch adherents of the Corn Laws.

They made great exertions, and great promises were
made to them in return ; but their expectations have
not been realized.   They find that their friends
have taken the opportunity to alter the Laws ; and
the very persons they trusted at the time of the election have, they now complain, adopted the views of
their opponents.   The farmers are frightened.   There
is a panic, most certainly ; but the panic is because
the farmers, still liable to all their engagements, know
not whom to trust.   Farmers are not different from
other men ; they are open to argument and reason, and
if they saw good ground for making a change in the
law they would readily submit to a change being made.

We know what occurred last autumn when persons were engaged at different places and meetings
to prepare the farmers for a change.   I saw them
going about from place to place telling the farmers
to be ready to resign their peculiar protection, and
to trust to their industry, intelligence, and skill,
like other men.   After the election the farmers'
friends altered their views and changed their tactics;
but the farmers did not know why.   The gentlemen who addressed them at dinners and public
meetings had certainly commenced to exhibit a
wavering in their opinions which the farmers could
not understand.   They gave out, at first, that the
Government were preparing to alter the Corn Laws
as soon as Parliament met ; but afterwards they went
back to their old policy; they remembered, probably,
the threat of a Noble Duke[1] that if ever they proposed

---

[1] The Duke of Richmond.

in Parliament to abolish the Corn Laws, he would bring in a Bill to change all existing leases; and they were afraid of the threat.

One important consideration connected with this question in relation to the condition of the farmers is that the farmers appear to have no chance of getting rid of their distress. They complain that they cannot sell their produce. What is the cause of this? It has no other cause than the impoverished condition of the people. The people are too poor to pay for the farmers' produce, and therefore they do not consume it. The condition of the labourers is everywhere so bad that the guardians of union-workhouses have passed resolutions to deteriorate the food of the paupers; otherwise, it is said, it would be better than the food of the independent labourers. For the same reason they have resolved to reduce the quantity, as well as the quality, of the paupers' diet.

But the distress is not confined to the working classes. It begins to affect the middle classes. I have only to-day received a letter from Devonshire, which states that the distress there is making rapid progress amongst the middle classes. [Mr. Villiers here read the letter, which was from Totnes, and stated that the distress was rapidly extending from the labouring classes to the classes above them, and that many families had given up eating bread, and had taken to live solely on potatoes. The reading of this letter was accompanied with loud cries of ' Shame! Shame!' and ' Shocking!'] There is much more evidence of the same kind ; and it can no longer be doubted that the depression in the price of agricultural produce is caused by the distress of the middle classes.

Now such being the condition of the middle classes, what must be the condition of those below them when no less than 1,300,000 of them are dependent upon public charity? And what must be the condition of that other 1,000,000 who are struggling to keep themselves out of the workhouse and independent? One of the consequences of this state of things is a great increase in the rate of mortality. I have seen a letter sent to the Registrar-General of births, deaths, and marriages from a large town in Lancashire, showing a very marked increase in mortality there; and without the least doubt it is owing to the impossibility of getting the food requisite for their subsistence. These circumstances have induced the members of the National League to solicit the attention of their countrymen to the subject, in order that together they may take steps to put an end to such alarming evils; for not only is the condition of the people reduced, but their impoverishment is seriously affecting the condition of the producers.

Another consequence of the diminished consumption of the people is its effect in weakening the sources of the Revenue taxation. If the middle and working classes do not consume sugar and tea, and coffee and malt, what is to become of the Revenue of twenty million pounds levied by the Excise and Customs on these articles? The deficiency of the Revenue at present is not less than 5,000,000l. a year. Do you expect that this state of things will be improved by more taxation? The Income Tax was imposed to make up the deficiency of the Revenue; and, let me ask you, is that likely to improve the condition of the people? Is it sound policy to increase the poverty of the people which diminishes the Revenue, instead of promoting their prosperity which increases it?

There can be no doubt whatever that the Revenue depends very much upon the condition of the people. And it is admitted by all Chancellors of the Exchequer that the returns from the Excise and Customs inevitably vary with the varying price of food, and vicissitudes of the harvest. In 1835, for example, the price of food was very low, lower than it had been for many years; and in that year the surplus Revenue was not less than 1,600,000l. In 1841, after the price of food had been very high for two or three years, the deficiency of the Revenue was not less than 2,500,000l.

And what is the object of the League, which we invite you to support, but the repeal of the Laws that make food scarce, and the establishment of a system under which food would be permanently abundant? That this justly describes the purpose of our exertions I would refer to the arguments of our opponents, the very foremost of which is that the attainment of our object would tend to inundate the country with food, and would greatly lower its price throughout the kingdom. Then, I ask, if that would be the case, and if the Revenue is always flourishing when food is abundant, what better prospect have you of lowering

taxation, or of being relieved of that tax so specially
odious which you have now to bear, than by first
abolishing the tax upon food. If food has been rendered high before by means of the Corn Laws, it will
be again. But can the condition of the people be
improved by such means? And if the condition of
the people is not improved how can they consume
other articles that are taxed for the increase of the
Revenue? And if the deficit of the Revenue is aug-
mented will you not expect additional taxation rather
than to be relieved of any that professes to be only
temporary? Satisfy yourselves, therefore, whether
you have not an interest in repealing Laws that make
food artificially scarce, besides doing mischief to trade
and manufacture.

I will not weary you further. I have ventured to
speak at such length because I am sure that you came
here not to be amused or excited by declamation, but
to join in the deliberate consideration of a most serious
matter with all the gravity that belongs to it.

I have now only to add that on you and on your
manifestation of opinion on this question depends our
influence in Parliament. Within this week you have
been represented in both Houses as caring nothing,
as utterly indifferent about a matter vital to your
interests. And this will be repeated if you allow it.
The whole case is before you. You have had a full
trial of the system, and with you rests its fate. You
are told that the Corn Laws were altered last year, and
must remain as they are for an experiment to be made.
The experiment has been made. The principle of

the Corn Laws has been proved to be faulty and iniquitous, and its practical results you are suffering from at this hour. If you have a doubt of the policy of demanding Repeal now, when do you think that you would have a better chance of obtaining it? And what experiment do you think would ever satisfy our opponents? If prices do not rise, as they expect, do you think that they will repeal the Laws that they believe prevent them from falling lower than they are? And if prices rise, do you think that they will sacrifice that which gives them such an advantage? But if you will have no better chance in the future than you have at present, act now. Act now upon your knowledge of all the evil, of all the misery and ruin that the Corn Laws are calculated to produce—that they have produced; and, as you would pray to be rid of a plague or pestilence scattering death and destruction throughout the country, call in a tone there shall be no misunderstanding for their immediate and total repeal.

XIV.

HOUSE OF COMMONS, April 25, 1843.

On April 25, 1843, Mr. Ricardo moved, 'That an humble address be presented to her Majesty, respectfully expressing the opinion of this House
that it is not expedient that any contemplated remission of import duties
be postponed, with the view of making such remission a basis of commercial negotiations with foreign countries.' Mr. Villiers, Mr. Cobden, Lord
Howick, and Lord Russell supported the Motion, and Sir R. Peel and Mr.
Gladstone spoke against it. It was negatived by a majority of 74 votes.

I RISE to meet the only two objections that can be
said to have been fairly opposed to the proposition of
my Hon. Friend. One of these was made by the Hon.
Baronet who has just sat down,[1] and the other by
the Hon. Member for Shrewsbury. I notice them
because I know that they pass current in some quarters,
and that there are persons influenced by them.

The Hon. Member for Liverpool considers that
the system of freedom proposed by my Hon. Friend
will lead to further restrictions by other nations, because, he says, the relaxation of our system of late
has already been met by hostile tariffs in six different
States. I do not consider this objection to be in
point; but, on the contrary, a confirmation of the view
taken on this side of the House, that the example
of this country greatly influences the policy of other
States. For though we have talked much of the re-

---

[1] Sir H. Douglas.

laxation of our system, the fact is that we have steadily and avowedly adhered to the principle of it, which is Protection. And this is what foreign States look to. They observe that though we shift the duties a little, we boast with as much firmness as before of sticking to the principle of Protection ; and observing our example they follow it and raise their tariffs to secure Protection for themselves.

If we had honestly denounced the system and declared it to be proved wrong by experience, and if we had reduced our duties whilst other States still persevered in the same system, the remark might have been just ; but as it is foreign States are imitating this country.

The objection urged by the Hon. Member for Shrewsbury is that if we regard only our imports the precious metals will leave this country and we shall experience great derangement of the Currency : as we did in 1839 upon the occasion of a great import of grain. And he expects that this can only be prevented by a Reciprocal Treaty by which the nation from which we import stipulates to receive our manufactures.

Now, let me inform the Hon. Member, for his consolation, that though our relations with the grain-growing States remain as they were in 1839, that though we have imported grain for four or five years successively, we have nevertheless ceased to export bullion ; and that the trade with those countries having become more regular, payment has been made in manufactures : which shows that it is under the present system, when the trade is not suffered to be regular, that upon a sudden demand we are obliged to send out bullion ; but that when the trade continues the exchange with manufactures is regular. In fact, the grain that we have imported during the last four years has been paid for in this way.

But there are instances in which the tariffs of other countries are almost prohibitory as regards our manufactures ; and yet we contrive to take their goods without sending bullion. Russia is an instance. The value of the exports of that country to England is about 5,000,000*l.*; and we take the pitch, flax, tallow, and hides of Russia without paying for them directly in goods. There are other instances that I could name, and enough to show the Hon. Gentleman that no direct trade is carried on, and that direct interchange of goods between this and any other particular country need not occur. The merchants discover the liabilities existing between different countries, and may be safely relied upon to adjust the account resulting from trade between them.

So much for the objections urged against my Hon. Friend's Motion, which are without foundation. Whatever else has been said against it is either a misrepresentation of its objects or something uttered with a view to confuse it.

I will now just recall the attention of the House to the simple point that is raised in question by the proposition, which really is no other than the purpose of our trade, and the principle that ought to guide any regulation of it.

My Hon. Friend proceeds upon the principle that the great object of trade in any country is imports, which he has expressed with epigrammatic brevity : 'Take care of your imports, the exports will take care of themselves.' This raises the whole question of our commercial policy, and decides it ; and if it is sound, the Minister-statesman who occupies himself with our commerce will know how to promote its interest. I entirely assent to the doctrine, and have often asserted it. The great object of all our traffic with other countries is to get into this country as many of the objects of human desire as possible, in order that the largest share possible may fall to each person. This cannot be done, unfortunately, without producing equivalents at home to purchase them with ; but certain it is, that these imports cannot take place without so much capital and labour being employed to produce the equivalent. In short, imports appear in this country as customers, they are the means by which our productions are bought, and every duty imposed on them is like restricting or destroying a customer. An import duty and an export duty has in this respect precisely the same effect ; each prevents or hinders some customer for our labour ; and whenever we want to encourage the demand for labour, the reduction or removal of an import duty is the mode of securing it.

If we lived in a more simple or in a savage state, nobody would doubt that the great object of trade, or going forth to toil, is not to take out what we have, but to bring home what we want ; and had we our own way, we should probably take what we want without giving an equivalent ; in our present condition, however, we are doomed to be honest, and we are compelled to work for what we want. Still, the end is to multiply a deficiency of what we have and wish to possess in abundance. This, then, is a distinct view of the object of all our trade, and once admitted a great point will have been gained.

We have seen this evening that there are some who, like the Noble Lord the Member for Liverpool, think that we import goods without exporting anything in return. We are lucky if we do, that is all I can say. But the Noble Lord should show us how we do this or we must doubt what he says. There are others, however, who are ever talking of trade and employment as the great objects to be gained and as if everything is accomplished if that is got. Now the difference between these gentlemen and myself is this : I regard trade and labour as merely the *means*, the things that are gained by them as the *end*. But simple as this seems, it is not yet conceded ; if it were, all this haggling and delay whilst Reciprocal Treaties are negotiated, would never occur and deprive us of great advantages.

The truth is, if we took the common views of the interests of this country, and rejoiced in the errors and disadvantages of our neighbours, so far from waiting till other countries have reduced their duties, we ought to be satisfied that such countries as France and Belgium exclude many products of this country that are essential to their prosperity and would facilitate their rivalry with us. Can anybody doubt, for instance, that France would gain an immense advantage were she to import coal and iron free of duty ; and that she injures herself and retards her progress by her wretched Protective system?

I am glad to see that we are going to have the opinion of the Right Hon. Baronet at the head of the Government on the matter, and I hope that he will give us his views distinctly.

I sincerely wish that the principle involved in my Hon. Friend's proposition could be decided upon ; for I am sure that nothing would sooner remove the difficulties that seem to involve all our commercial relations, or tend more to simplify the regulations that we are eternally framing for what is called the good of trade.

END OF THE FIRST VOLUME.